kan
BOO

kamerabooks.com

OTHER BOOKS BY DOUGLAS KEESEY

Neo-Noir
Contemporary Erotic Cinema

Douglas Keesey

TWENTY FIRST CENTURY CENTURY HORROR FILMS

kamera
BOOKS

First published in 2017 by Kamera Books
an imprint of Oldcastle Books,
PO Box 394, Harpenden, Herts, AL5 1XJ
www.kamerabooks.com

ISBN
978-1-84344-905-8 (print)
978-1-84344-906-5 (epub)

2 4 6 8 10 9 7 5 3 1

Typeset by Elsa Mathern in Univers 9 pt
Printed and bound by CPI Group (UK) Ltd, Croydon, CR0 4YY

To my mother, for taking me to the drive-in so that I could see House of Dark Shadows *when I was ten;*

To my father, for accompanying me so that I could see Carrie *when I was fifteen; and*

To my brother, for loving The Legend of Bigfoot *and* The Giant Spider Invasion *as much as I did.*

A NOTE TO THE READER

This book gives explanations of what these movies mean. Because a film's ending is often essential to its meaning, there are spoilers ahead. Readers who wish to avoid them are advised to see the films before reading this book.

CONTENTS

INTRODUCTION

Horror has, as one of its primary aims, the goal of frightening us. This fear might be a matter of jump scares or creeping dread. It could be provoked by shocking gore or shuddery ghosts. But whatever the particular cause or impact, fear is horror's defining element.

Of all the film genres, horror makes the least sense. We can see why audiences would be attracted to comedy, action-adventure, or romance, for people like to laugh; they enjoy excitement; they want to fall in love. Even a disreputable genre like pornography has an obvious appeal in that its images incite and satisfy lust. But horror is, by definition, frightening and thus repellent. To be 'attracted to horror' seems logically impossible – and psychologically perverse.

For what kind of viewers would voluntarily expose themselves to terrifying images and even seek them out to experience a strange sort of enjoyment? Are horror fans sadists who find pleasure in watching on-screen victims subjected to fear and suffering? As Roger Ebert wrote about Australia's most notorious example of torture porn, 'There is a line and this movie crosses it. I don't know where the line is, but it's way north of *Wolf Creek*. There is a role for violence in film, but what the hell is the purpose of this sadistic celebration of pain and cruelty?'[1] Eli Roth, director of *Hostel* and *The Green Inferno*, may seem to confirm Ebert's worst suspicions about horror filmmakers and viewers by saying, 'I wanna see gore and bile. I love playing with the blood – everyone says I'm like a kid on Christmas morning, it's so much fun!'[2]

Or are horror fans masochists who derive pleasure from unpleasant or dreadful experiences? Roth's goal, he says, is to provide a 'scene where people go "I shouldn't have gotten a ticket for this movie; it's going to be too much; I don't know if I'm going to make it to the end; this is way more than I thought it was going to be" … everyone's been waiting for that big scene and … the gore, the scares, and the kills [must] really deliver'.[3] According to Roth, 'If you've made an effective horror movie, at the end people should feel like shit.'[4]

Is it any surprise that horror is the most polarising of film genres, with its passionate defenders and equally vehement detractors, with its avid fans and others who wouldn't be caught dead attending films of this kind? There are those who believe that horror films are a force for evil in the world. 'Evil resided within the very celluloid of the film – that's what Billy Graham said about *The Exorcist*', director Scott Derrickson reminds us, noting that in his own techno-horror movie, *Sinister*, 'evil resides within the very celluloid of these Super 8 films, and I think that it is an attitude that a lot of people have about the horror genre – that it's not good, that it's not healthy … to subject yourself to watching such awful things – which I obviously disagree with'.[5]

If we, too, disagree with the idea that such films spread sickness or evil, then we must ask, how can horror be healthy? The brilliant film critic Robin Wood once wrote that 'the true subject of the horror genre is the struggle for recognition of all that our civilisation *re*presses [psychologically] or *op*presses [socially]'.[6] Novelist Clive Barker, who knows a thing or two about the genre, said that 'horror is a leap of faith and imagination in a world where the subconscious holds dominion; a call to enter a territory where no image or act is so damnable it cannot be explored, kissed, and courted; finally – why whisper it? – embraced'.[7]

Like Wood and Barker, I see horror as a way of exploring our fears, a place for confronting them and figuring out what – if anything – we should really be afraid of. A question I often ask when approaching a film is whether its horror is regressive, progressive, or (as in most cases) some combination of both. I define a progressive horror film as one that leads us towards overcoming our fear of difference, enlarging our understanding of and sympathy for 'othered' persons and experiences too often considered inimical to ourselves. By contrast, regressive horror solidifies old fears and refortifies traditional boundaries between us and 'them', confirming and even exacerbating phobic responses. The most intriguing horror films, it seems to me, are the ones in which the characters (and the filmmakers) are trying to work out how they feel about 'others', questioning received notions – and genre conventions – regarding what is threatening or 'monstrous' and seeking out new perspectives beyond a dread of difference.

In other words, horror is a messy genre of friend and fiend, attraction and repulsion. Horror is all about blurred lines and ambivalent feelings. This is particularly true of contemporary horror, which is in the vanguard when it comes to exploring uncharted territory and unresolved issues. 'I'm not a fan of clearly cut lines between good and evil. There are layers to every human being,' says David Robert Mitchell,[8] whose film *It Follows* delves into sexual anxieties, and James Watkins, who made the 'hoodie horror' film *Eden Lake*, says that he admires movies which have a 'sense of queasiness and moral awkwardness ... where you're not sure what to think, what to feel, or what is right'.[9] Joss Whedon, co-writer of the self-conscious slasher film *The Cabin in the Woods*, describes a 'horror movie' as one that 'contains a meditation on the human condition, asking questions about our darkest selves that you know going in cannot be answered'.[10] Finally, playwright (and scenarist and director) Neil LaBute has said that he writes horrific scenes in order to 'scamper away from the wolves I hear in the darkness', but that 'sometimes I can't tell if I'm running toward the safety of the forest's edge or deeper into its centre'.[11]

At one point in the modern classic horror film *Don't Look Now*, the protagonist is asked, 'What is it that you fear?' The movie explores the possibilities: the foreigners of Venice, the female sex, the possibility of an afterlife in hell, his own unresolved guilt over the death of his daughter. My book asks the same question, examining horror films for what they can tell us about our fears. Some fears seem universal, such as those of disease, darkness and death – though different cultures adopt very different attitudes towards these. Other fears appear more specific to a time or place: eco-horror in an era increasingly cognizant of climate change and biological interconnectedness; body horror in a time of tattoos, piercings, plastic surgery, and digital manipulation of the human form; torture porn in an America shocked by revelations of 'extraordinary rendition' and 'enhanced interrogation'; and techno-horror in some Asian countries anxious about the effects of modernisation on traditional cultures.

Vampires have been with us for centuries, but 'every age embraces the vampire it needs',[12] and so *Let the Right One In* involves its tween bloodsucker in a present-day narrative about bullying. According to its Swedish screenwriter John Ajvide Lindqvist, 'even though I don't set out to write social commentary ... it comes as a side effect because ... horror, if taken seriously, becomes a form of criticism'.[13] Other twenty first century filmmakers agree. 'I am one of the directors who believes that genre is something you can use for communicating something important, more than just for having fun,' notes Marcin Wrona,[14] who made *Demon*, a horror film about how Poland is still haunted by the Holocaust. Scholar Brigid Cherry argues that '[h]orror films invariably reflect the social and political anxieties of the cultural moment',[15] and nowhere is this more true than in eco-horror, as can be seen in Larry Fessenden's 'global warming' ghost film, *The Last Winter*. Believing that 'horror as a genre is a responsibility' beyond mere entertainment,[16] Fessenden states that 'in my films I'm trying to use horror tropes to explore contemporary issues'.[17]

There are many ways that one could carve up the current state of horror, but I have chosen to divide this book into three main sections: 'nightmares', 'nations' and 'innovations'. 'Nightmares' looks at new manifestations of traditional fears, including cannibals, dolls, families, fathers, ghosts, haunted houses, holidays, mothers,

14

possession, sharks, succubae, vampires, werewolves, witches and zombies. Also considered are more contemporary anxieties such as dread of ambition, disabilities, home invasion, homosexuals and senior citizens. 'Nations' explores fright films from around the world, including Australia, Canada, Czechoslovakia, France, Germany, Hong Kong, Hungary, India, Japan, Norway, Poland, Russia, Serbia, South Korea, Spain and Sweden, as well as the United Kingdom and the United States. 'Innovations' focuses on the latest trends in terror, covering 3D horror, Asian horror and American remakes, body horror, eco-horror, found footage, neo-giallo, remakes of seventies horror, self-conscious slashers, techno-horror, teen romance, torture porn, and travesties and parodies. For each film examined, I provide the title, year of release and director, along with the principal stars and the roles they play. I then give an explanation of what each movie means, usually focusing on one or more of the most horrific scenes pertinent to its category. I often include quotes from the filmmakers themselves, who explain in their own words what they were trying to achieve. The book concludes with a list of books, videos and websites, which are recommended to those interested in further exploring the world of twenty first century horror films, along with notes and an index for handy reference.[18]

NIGHTMARES

AMBITION

American Psycho (2000)

Director: Mary Harron
Cast: Christian Bale (Bateman)

Serial killer Patrick Bateman plunges an axe into a man's face and uses a chainsaw to cut a woman's body in half. 'Basically, he's a monster and there's no explaining it,' says director Mary Harron.[19] Granted, to trace all of Bateman's crimes to one root cause would be absurdly reductive, as in Bateman's own glib explanation, 'Hey, I'm a child of divorce. Give me a break.' However, to claim that his actions are inexplicable is equally facile and problematic, for it risks a surrender to apathy (he's an insoluble mystery, so there's nothing we can do) or a demonisation of him (he's just inherently evil, so all we can do is destroy him). Interestingly, Bateman himself concludes at the end of the film that 'I gain no deeper knowledge of myself. No new knowledge can be extracted from my telling [of my crimes].' But is this true? A lack of one root cause does not mean that there aren't multiple, interrelated reasons for his bad behaviour.

It is New York City in the 1980s, a time when yuppies like Bateman are being encouraged to think that 'greed is good'. He and his fellow junior executives work for a Wall Street firm called Pierce & Pierce, a name that connects profit-seeking with stabbing. The cutthroat competition among these men is emphasised when, each time one of them tries to conquer the others by pulling out a better business card, we hear the sound of 'a sword being whipped out of a sheath', as Harron explains.[20] When Bateman later attacks his colleague with an axe, he is merely taking this business rivalry over which man has the most clout to its logical – albeit extreme – conclusion.

This avariciously materialistic environment tends to ruin Bateman's relationships with women. Purchasing magazines like *Playboy* and renting video porn, he comes to view women as sexual objects to be bought and consumed. When Bateman emerges from under the sheets after oral sex on a female, his mouth is bloody from having literally eaten her out. For Bateman, the meat market is not just a metaphor. He keeps a prostitute's severed head in his refrigerator, as if for late-night snacking. He has female corpses hanging in his closet like animal carcasses in a slaughterhouse. And he takes a bite out of a woman's leg before butchering her with a chainsaw, imitating what he saw done in a video of *The Texas Chain Saw Massacre*.

In a sense, Bateman is slavishly devoted to media images, even attempting to find his own identity in them. The problem is that no one can live up to the impossible ideal they represent. The escorts he hires for the night aren't blonde enough, smoke when they shouldn't, and fail to appreciate a fine chardonnay. Worse, they seem unimpressed by his big-shot job or the big biceps he flexes in the mirror during sex. Bateman needs the women he is with to be perfect so that they can serve as a reflection of him as the perfect man, and when they fail to live up to his media-driven standards, he takes it as an affront to his core being. His murderous rage at them is anger at himself for what he sees as his own inferior performance as a successful man.

'Something horrible is happening inside of me,' Bateman thinks, 'and I don't know why.' But, based on all the evidence in the film, we do.[21]

Starry Eyes (2014)

Directors: Kevin Kölsch and Dennis Widmyer
Cast: Alexandra Essoe (Sarah), Louis Dezseran (Producer), Fabianne
Therese (Erin), Pat Healy (Carl), Noah Segan (Danny), Shane Coffey (Poe)

Aspiring actress Sarah makes a Faustian deal with a devil-
worshipping cult and sells her soul to become a Hollywood star. Her
moral corruption shows itself as physical rot, with her hair and a tooth
falling out, blood coming from her mouth and crotch, and a stomach
ache that leads to her vomiting up maggots. She prostitutes herself
to a producer for a movie part and goes on a Charles Manson-style
rampage, murdering all her friends who served as her conscience
and tried to stop her. As co-director Dennis Widmyer says, his
movie is about 'ambition manifested as a monster. The idea that to
get what you want, how far will you go? What will you do and what
would that do to you mentally and physically?'[22]

This 'Hollywood horror' film certainly reveals how frightening
the success-driven Sarah becomes (its tagline is 'She would kill to
be famous'), but the more appalling horror may actually lie in the
supposedly normal people surrounding her. Sarah's friend Erin, also
a wannabe actress, 'jokes' about stealing roles from her and sending
in her own headshot for parts Sarah fails to get. At the restaurant
where Sarah works part-time, her boss, Carl, presents himself as a
respectable businessman running a family-friendly establishment,
but he also leers at her in her tight-fitting top, and the place he
presides over is called Big Taters (modelled on Hooters). Sarah's
male friends Danny and Poe – the first an aspiring filmmaker and
the latter more of a private pornographer – shoot videos of their
girlfriends cavorting in skimpy bikinis, and Poe grabs surreptitious
footage, which he calls 'Sick, Slutty Sarah', of her when she is
tearing off her clothes because she feels ill. In their exploitation
of her body, these two guys and her boss are not so very different
from the producer who subjects her to his satanic casting couch.
And why should Sarah have to pull some of her own hair out, as she

is asked to do at the audition, to show how committed she would be to a part? Why should any actress need to have sex with the producer, as Sarah is bid to do, in order to land a movie role? These are monstrous aspects of movie culture that must share a great deal of the blame for bringing out the monster in her. 'Let me see the real Sarah,' the producer says. 'Embrace who you are.' But they are the ones helping her to create this terrible creature and pushing her to become it. When Sarah slashes the envious and rivalrous Erin in the face, when she stabs sneakily invasive Poe in the back, and when she cuts her boyfriend, Danny, near the groin after he sleeps with Erin, Sarah is not without cause, for they have all helped to make her what she has become. When we first see Sarah at the beginning of the film, she is standing before her bedroom mirror and, despite looking model-perfect, pinching the flesh at her sides out of fear that she is fat – a fear that drives her murderous path to stardom, to be admired by millions on the silver screen. Did this fear really come from inside, or was it moulded by a culture that reduces women to their bodies and makes them feel inadequate?

The Neon Demon (2016)

Director: Nicolas Winding Refn
Cast: Elle Fanning (Jesse), Keanu Reeves (Hank), Abbey Lee (Sarah), Jena Malone (Ruby), Bella Heathcote (Gigi)

Sixteen-year-old Jesse, an aspiring fashion model, becomes the 'It' girl of the moment. 'You're going to be great,' her agent tells her. 'She has that "thing",' says her make-up artist. And a fashion mogul describes her as 'a diamond in a sea of glass'. But what is the 'It' that Jesse has? 'You can't put your finger on it,' says director Nicolas Winding Refn. 'You can't define it, you can't imitate it. That's what having "It" means.'[23] Some viewers of this film have noted that there doesn't seem to be anything particularly special about the way Jesse looks, other than her fresh face and youthful appearance, but that is precisely the point. Because Jesse is new on the fashion scene, characters project onto her their own ideal of what is beautiful. 'Beauty,' says Refn, 'really comes in the eye of the beholder,' and so 'people essentially make up their own interpretation of what [Jesse] may or may not look like.'[24] Unfortunately, rather than realising that Jesse's allure is the result of their own projected desire for perfection, the people around her start to envy her beauty and to reduce it to something merely physical, like youthful flesh, which they try to possess. 'Men want to sexualise youth,' Refn comments, and 'women want to consume it.'[25] Thus a motel manager named Hank tries to break into Jesse's room to eat some 'hard candy', and she has nightmares of him making her open her mouth wider and wider to swallow his knife. Hank then actually rapes the even younger girl – a 'real Lolita' – in the room right next to Jesse's.

When Jesse is chosen for a fashion shoot over rival Sarah, who was last season's 'It' girl, the older model smashes her own ageing image in the mirror. Jesse runs to help, but when she accidentally cuts herself on one of the mirror shards, Sarah sucks the blood from Jesse's hand as if trying to drink in her youthful vitality and good looks. 'Who wants sour milk when you can get fresh meat?', a jealous Sarah wonders, denigrating herself as an old cow and representing Jesse as a calf to be slaughtered. Sarah's words subtract the soul from beauty, leaving only its carnal dimension. There is a white statue of a female angel behind make-up artist Ruby when she praises Jesse for having 'such beautiful skin', but Ruby shows no regard for that spiritual side when she tries to force herself on the virginal Jesse, hungry for her flesh. Earlier, a live cougar had broken into Jesse's room, and in the scene after Ruby pounces on Jesse, the older woman is shown reflected in a mirror alongside a stuffed wildcat. When Ruby's advances are rejected, she goes to a morgue where, desperate in her desire, she kisses and fondles a female corpse that looks like Jesse. In a sense, this scene reveals what Ruby had done to Jesse, for in treating her beloved as nothing more than a body for her devouring kisses and mauling hands, Ruby had voided that flesh of spirit, reducing it to a kind of corpse. In her desire to possess Jesse's beautiful skin, Ruby had thought of nobody but herself.

Interestingly, Ruby's molestation of the corpse from chest to crotch is cross-cut with images of Jesse's fondling of her own breasts and genitals, and the two women climax at the same time. As opposed to Ruby and her rapacious narcissism, Jesse can be seen as exemplifying a healthy self-love. To another model's comment that 'nobody likes the way they look', Jesse's reply is 'I do'. Onstage during a fashion show with some other lookalike models, Jesse appears to be kissing them while simultaneously kissing her own reflection in a three-way mirror, as if she is able to balance self-love with regard for others. In other scenes, Jesse also appears to balance on the edge of a cliff overlooking Los Angeles, and at the end of a diving board above an empty swimming pool. Viewed from below, it looks as though she is half-flying, her beauty transcendent but also grounded in the flesh, a precarious balance of body and soul.

But Jesse's masturbation scene could also be viewed as one of vainglorious self-infatuation, and soon after, she uses the diving board as a platform to declare herself more beautiful than Ruby, who is standing below her in the empty pool. It would seem that Jesse is increasingly corrupted by the envious women who surround her, pulled into their egomania and jealous rivalry. Subsequently, Ruby, flanked by fashion models Sarah and Gigi, will push Jesse off that diving board, and her broken body dies on the concrete below. The three women then cannibalise Jesse's flesh, with Ruby bathing in her blood while watching Sarah and Gigi lick the remainder of it off their bodies in the shower – a nadir of narcissism and carnal appetite. Afterwards, Ruby lies naked in the moonlight with her legs spread, smiling as if about to give birth to herself as the image of her soulmate, Jesse. But while Ruby may imagine communing with Jesse's spirit, the fact is that she destroyed her beloved's beauty, emptying it of soul, and devoured her dead body. In the process, Ruby killed her own soul, so it is fitting that, rather than giving birth, she bleeds out from between her legs, with the departure of her vital spirit leaving her a corpse.

CANNIBALS

The Descent (2005)

Director: Neil Marshall
Cast: Shauna Macdonald (Sarah), Oliver Milburn (Paul), Alex Reid (Beth), Natalie Mendoza (Juno)

Sarah, her husband, Paul, and their young daughter are in a car collision and the latter two are killed, with Paul being impaled by a pole that flies off the other vehicle. One year later, Sarah goes on a spelunking expedition with some female friends, who hope to help her overcome her grief. But as they are headed towards their destination in the Appalachian Mountains, Sarah drives recklessly through the wooded area, which is similar to the one where the car accident occurred. Does she have a death wish prompted by survivor's guilt? Upon arriving at their cabin, Sarah imagines a pole breaking through window glass to spear her in the eye in the same way that her husband was killed, as though she remains haunted by the desire to join him.

Sarah descends into the mouth of the cave as if into an open grave, and after exploring the underground passageways for a while, she becomes trapped in a narrow tunnel and panics. 'The worst thing that could have happened to you has already happened and you're still here,' her friend Beth reassures her, but is Sarah scared of being buried alive or of her own longing for the grave? 'What it is about is a descent into madness,' writer-director Neil Marshall said of his film.[26] The caving expedition could provide the opportunity for Sarah to work through the trauma of the accident and move past her grief, but it could also be the occasion for a further decline into terminal melancholy and insanity. Despite being warned that the claustrophobic environment of the caves might induce 'panic attacks', 'paranoia' and 'hallucinations', Sarah begins to see savage predators crawling around in the tunnels. Marshall cautions us that 'maybe the crawlers are just a figment of Sarah's imagination'.[27] In one scene, Sarah thinks she sees her daughter from behind, but when the girl turns around, her face is that of a viciously threatening crawler. If Sarah does not learn how to deal with the death of her daughter, that loss will become a menace from beyond the grave, dragging her down with it.

In another scene, a frightened Sarah 'sees' a crawler, turns around quickly to escape, and is startled to find her friend Juno standing there. As if to rouse Sarah from her paranoia, Juno says, 'Look at me. There's nothing there.' Juno promises to help Sarah find a way out of the caves, but adds importantly that 'I can't do it unless you're with me'. Yet in order to join up with Juno, Sarah must move past fearing her as an enemy. Juno had betrayed Sarah by sleeping with her husband, Paul. In fact, Paul was lying to Sarah about this very adultery just before the car accident in which he died. Moreover, Juno effectively abandoned Sarah after the accident, never visiting her in the hospital. Now, on this caving expedition one year later, Juno makes repeated attempts to apologise, but she is continually rebuffed by Sarah, leading Juno to say, 'Why don't you try and find us a way through?' – referring to the caves and their troubled relationship.

However, what Sarah sees (or imagines) Juno doing in the caves only serves to increase her own paranoia. As Juno is defending herself against a crawler attack, she turns around quickly and accidentally sinks her pickaxe into Beth. Juno then leaves the wounded woman behind. A dying Beth later tells Sarah about the abandonment *and* about the affair Juno had with Paul, revealing that he had given Juno a 'Love Each Day' pendant. Juno's desertion of Beth reminds Sarah of when Juno abandoned *her* at the hospital, and the pickaxing of Beth brings back the impalement of Paul, for which Sarah blames Juno. And so, overcome by an insane rage at her friend's betrayals, Sarah skewers Juno's leg with a pickaxe and then abandons her to the deadly crawlers. In effect, Sarah has herself regressed to the primitive state of a crawler, striking savagely at others. Rather than inspiring her to 'Love Each Day', the memory of her husband becomes a reason to take revenge and cause the death of Juno. Thus, when Sarah finally manages to climb out of the caves and into the sun, her escape is revealed to be a deceptive dream. The sight of Juno's bloody ghost, representing Sarah's guilt over what she did to her friend, frightens her into waking up back in the cave. Forgiveness and compassion would have allowed Sarah to see the light; revenge has only dragged her down again. Showing that she still has some longing for humanity within her, Sarah is briefly comforted by a vision of her daughter and a birthday cake – before the candles go out and Sarah is left in the darkness with the other crawlers.

The Green Inferno (2013)

Director: Eli Roth
Cast: Antonieta Pari (Village Elder), Ramón Llao (Headhunter)

How can you make a cannibal movie in these culturally sensitive times? Writer-director Eli Roth's attempt is incoherent in interesting ways. When a group of student activists journeys to the Amazon to block the bulldozing of the rainforests and the destruction of indigenous peoples, they are captured by a local tribe. Horror-movie conventions dictate that the threat be made as scary as possible, so these natives are presented as repellently brutish and barbaric. With their bodies coated in red ochre, they look as though they have bathed in blood. The female village elder has a dead-white eye and strands of beads that look like snakes strung through her nose. The chief headhunter, painted a devilish black, has horn-like bones protruding from his nose and wears a collar composed of spiky teeth. Together, the two of them lead their tribe in committing atrocities on their student captives. While he is still alive, one student has his eyes gouged out and swallowed, his tongue cut off and consumed, and his limbs amputated prior to his torso being cooked in an oven. Village children delight in holding the flayed skin of a tattooed female student up against their bodies, and the headhunter enjoys playing with her severed arm and making faces at her flesh-stripped skull.

However, the movie emphasises that the tribespeople only attack because they mistake the students for the enemy (since, when captured, they were wearing construction uniforms in order to infiltrate the logging operation). Moreover, Roth has stressed how much the peaceful and polite natives in the village where he filmed *liked* portraying cannibals. 'They were so nice and they just loved what we were doing,' Roth comments. 'These [local] women were so great at cutting the body,' he says, adding, 'I love the kids biting here. It's so funny.'[28] Perhaps we have all reached such a stage of mutual respect (and sufficient food and shelter) that we can applaud the good time that the villagers may have had pretending to disembowel the students, but it is hard not to see the film's images of natives cannibalising whites as reinforcing racist stereotypes of indigenous tribes as savages. Positive accounts of happy attitudes behind the scenes and verbal justifications within the movie for the villagers' attacks hardly seem to compensate for our visceral reaction to the visuals of flesh-devouring brutes.

Why do the natives have to be devilish savages, and why does the Amazon have to be a 'green inferno'? Roth has an emotional investment in seeing the jungle as hell, in viewing its inhabitants as 'absolutely barbaric, primitive man',[29] because he wants to experience an 'adventurous, dangerous kind of filmmaking'[30] where he and his crew journey deep into the primordial jungle and where they 'could have died any number of times – there were floods, and there were rock-slides; there were tarantulas and snakes'.[31] And, for the characters at least, there were cannibals who could cook and eat them. One of the earliest inspirations for his horror films, Roth has said, was 'being Jewish and growing up hearing stories about the Holocaust. If you didn't finish your food, my parents would be like, "You could have been in an oven in Poland."'[32] The student activists are kept in a communal cage like a concentration camp, and some of them are taken to an oven. 'My God, I can smell my friend being cooked,' one says and ends up eating part of that person. Is *The Green Inferno* Roth's vicarious way of experiencing what it might have been like for his Jewish ancestors in the Nazi death camps? What terrible things would people be driven to do in order to survive? The tattooed pieces of skin are similar to inmate identification numbers, and one escaped character's remorse over leaving another behind in the cage is reminiscent of Holocaust survivor's guilt. When a tarantula threatens a male student's exposed penis and when the natives threaten the female students with genital mutilation, these can be seen as Roth's exploration of fears related to Jewish rites of circumcision. Finally, when a female captive is able to use a small flute passed down to her by her female ancestors in order to connect with the human compassion in one of her captors, we are reminded of the role that music played in the concentration camps as a means of sustaining hope.

DISABILITIES

The Quiet (2005)

Director: Jamie Babbit
Cast: Camilla Belle (Dot), Elisha Cuthbert (Nina), Martin Donovan (Nina's Father), Shawn Ashmore (Connor)

Dot hasn't spoken a word since age seven when her mother died. This traumatic or sympathetic muteness, her keeping as quiet as her mother in the grave, was then joined by a kind of deafness as Dot pretended – or convinced herself – that she couldn't hear in order to feel closer to her remaining parent, her deaf father. Years later, when her father dies, the now-teenaged Dot is adopted by her godparents. Their daughter, Nina, and her bitchy best friend torment and ostracise Dot at school, deeming her a 'freak' and a 'retard'. Cut off from her fellow students by their attitude towards her disability, Dot glides ghost-like down the school corridors in a deaf-mute daze. Divided from the living, she spends more time communing with the dead, playing Beethoven on the piano as she used to do for her father, who, like the deaf composer, could sense the instrument's vibrations.

If Dot is like a gothic heroine haunted by her past, then Nina is like the girl in a horror movie whose fear of a monster invading her bedroom comes true, for her father comes to her at night and insists on having sex with her. The man she trusted to love and care for her turns out to be a monster who imposes his selfish demands on her. Dot, whose continuing and creepily close attachment to her own father could also be seen as morbid and unhealthy, is especially attuned to Nina's suffering, and Nina tells her incestuous secret to Dot, finding her to be the perfect confidante because she 'cannot' hear and thus will not tell anyone else about it.

Dot also feels a growing likeness to – and liking for – a boy her age named Connor, who confides in her about his struggles with disability (attention deficit disorder) and his fears of sexual failure, assuming all the while that she is deaf. Dot agrees to make love with him, but when he then ignores her bodily needs and uses the occasion merely to prove himself a man, she later rejects him, prompting him to act possessively and domineeringly towards her, much as Nina's father does to Nina. Connor also discovers that Dot may have been capable of hearing the secrets he told her about himself, which causes him to feel ashamed of what he revealed and angry at her for deceiving him.

In the end, Nina helps Dot escape from Connor. In addition, as Nina's father is about to rape Nina for having finally rejected him, Dot, who has been playing the piano 'for' her deceased father, hears Nina's cries for help and strangles Nina's father with some piano wire. By banding together as 'sisters', Dot and Nina free themselves from their unhealthy attachment to their fathers, from the familial past that was haunting them. By attending to Nina's calls for help, Dot finds that she can hear her own.

The Darkness (2016)

Director: Greg McLean
Cast: David Mazouz (Mikey), Radha Mitchell (Mother), Kevin Bacon (Father), Lucy Fry (Sister), Judith McConnell (Grandmother)

Meet autistic tween Mikey. While camping with his family in the Grand Canyon, he wanders off, falls into a cavern, and steals some sacred stones, bringing them back to Los Angeles in his backpack. At night in his house, he takes out the stones, fondles them, and places them in a strange formation in front of his bedroom wall, an act which invites demons to use the wall as a portal to invade the family home. Mikey's inability to interact normally with his family led to his wandering off. His lack of safety awareness contributed to his fall. His obsessive focus on objects drew him to the stones, and his failure to understand society's rules made it easier for him to steal. Finally, his interest in unusual patterns and his peculiar sensitivity to his surroundings led to the rock formations and contributed to making him a conduit for evil forces.

As Mikey's parents 'discover' when they do some Internet research, 'Autistic Kids Are Magnets for Ghosts': 'Unseen beings like autistic children. Because they process information and see the world differently, autistic children are more likely to see strange things. They often witness activities way before anyone else in the home. They are more sensitive to nuances.'[33] With this dubious information, combined with the tagline of 'Evil comes home', the film plays on the idea of an autistic child being a kind of alien in our midst – affectless, weirdly remote, and seemingly attuned to paranormal frequencies. A charitable interpretation of the film would view it as making fun of our fear that autistic kids are especially susceptible to evil spirits, but it's hard not to see the movie as mired in old superstitions and misunderstandings about developmentally disabled people as being monstrous and threatening. When Mikey's mother is startled by his sudden appearance behind her in the attic, the fact that autistic children are often silent is made to seem creepy and frightening. When Mikey's father finds the walls and ceiling defaced with peculiar markings and sees Mikey smiling, the boy's inappropriate affect appears like an enjoyment of evil. Mikey's inability to recognise proper boundaries results in his spying on his sister in the shower and his leaving of strange handprints on her bed. Because he does not have our common awareness of danger, he sets the house on fire, and his lack of empathy leads him to kill his grandmother's cat. The film does not promote a better understanding of autistic kids when it makes them seem like incipient perverts, budding pyromaniacs, or serial killers in the making. In the alternate ending to the film, Mikey's repetitive behaviour and his obsession with numbers are linked to the evil spirits' destruction of the entire family, as the boy's counting turns out to be a countdown to their doom.

Fortunately, it is also possible to view this as a film about a family that scapegoats their autistic child, falsely accusing him as the cause of their own fears and tensions, until they learn better at the end. The foul odours, faucets that won't turn off, and laundry rising in ghostly shapes speak to the mother's fears of being a bad homemaker, though she blames them on Mikey. The father is an architect and so has a special dread of his house burning down – a fire he pins on Mikey. And when a dog somehow gets in and attacks the father's precious daughter, he charges absent-minded Mikey with having left the front door open. The bulimic daughter is extremely body conscious, which could make her anxious about being spied on in the shower, and it is interesting how her fear of being choked by strange hands relates to the times when she forces herself to vomit by sticking her own finger down her throat. With these suggestions that the family is projecting their own fears and blame onto Mikey, the film approaches an awareness that this autistic child has simply served as a catalyst, not a cause, as the stress of dealing with his disability exacerbates already existing tensions in the other characters. The film moves away from the supernatural (autistic kids as channelling evil spirits) and towards a psychological understanding of disabled children and 'demons'. If 'they bring out the darkness within people so [that] their victims destroy themselves or destroy each other', then this is because people scapegoat them as 'evil others' rather than recognising and solving their own problems. At the end of the film, Mikey's autism proves to be an advantage because he alone can return the sacred stones and placate the demons since he is the only one who is not afraid of them. What this suggests is that, unlike his family, who fear others because they blame them for their own problems, Mikey has not been socialised into those prejudices and dreadful projections. He is fearless because he senses that there are no 'others' and there are no demons. There is only us.[34]

DOLLS

Annabelle (2014)

Director: John R Leonetti
Cast: Ward Horton (John), Annabelle Wallis (Mia), Tree O'Toole (Annabelle), Alfre Woodard (Evelyn)

In late 1960s California, John and Mia are a young couple in love, living in the ideal suburban home and expecting a beautiful baby. Named after actress Mia Farrow who played the pregnant mother in *Rosemary's Baby* (1968), the character of Mia is plagued by many of the same maternal anxieties, which form the nightmarish flipside to her dream of motherhood. Childbirth can be a moment of life or death, and Mia's insistence that, if there is trouble during labour, the baby's life be saved at the expense of her own indicates an underlying fear that either mother or child might 'kill' the other during delivery. Another cause for concern is that, no matter how hard parents try to be loving and protective of their children, the kids may grow up feeling deprived and resentful, like their neighbours' teen daughter Annabelle who ran off to join a cult. Mia is also worried about her husband, John, who is completing med school and about to start his residency. Sometimes he is like the caring doctors she watches on the TV soap opera *General Hospital*, but at other times his solicitude seems to be a false front hiding his selfish and overbearing nature. When John presents her with a vintage doll in a white wedding dress, Mia says that the last time he said he had a gift for her, she ended up pregnant, a comment which relates the creepy doll to the baby in her womb, implanted there by her husband. (In *Rosemary's Baby*, as the wife has sex with her husband on the night she conceives, she imagines that he is replaced by the Devil thrusting on top of her, impregnating her with his evil spawn.)

Mia's mounting dread culminates in a scene where Annabelle, now a deranged cult member, joins forces with her Charles Manson-like boyfriend to kill her mother and then to invade Mia's home to come after her. The assault by Annabelle combines Mia's fear of being 'killed' by her baby during childbirth and her fear of being punished for her future failures as a parent by her grown-up daughter. When Annabelle's boyfriend stabs Mia's pregnant belly with a knife, the scene plays like a nightmarish version of intercourse with her husband, whose penetration of her implanted this baby that is causing her so much anxiety. Later, after the child is born, Mia will reach into the baby carriage only to be grabbed by the hand of an adult male demon, whose taloned fingers and phallic horns recall her fear of intercourse and inception. (In a real-life home invasion, members of the Charles Manson cult broke in and stabbed pregnant actress Sharon Tate, the wife of Roman Polanski, who had recently directed *Rosemary's Baby.*)

After grabbing the knife from her boyfriend but failing to kill Mia, Annabelle cuts her own throat, bleeding on the doll, which thus appears to be crying tears of blood. This 'blood connection' between Annabelle and the doll, which is also named Annabelle, worries Mia (who is played by actress Annabelle Wallis). After all, the teenage Annabelle was a 'nightmare daughter' who killed her mother, and a 'nightmare mother' who wanted to stab Mia in the womb. For these reasons, the doll becomes the locus of Mia's maternal and filial fears, reminding her of her own ambivalence regarding her infant daughter. The life-sized, cherub-faced doll looks like the perfect baby girl, but something is subtly wrong, whether that be her too-perfect porcelain skin, the artificial blush on her cheeks, or her beautiful blue eyes, which never blink. It's as though the doll is a creepy version of Mia's baby girl, a projection of the mother's fear that her daughter is less than ideal. Mia so wants the suburban dream that anything other than angelic perfection seems demonic. The devil doll's staring eyes and mocking laughter disturb Mia, who begins to act like a bad mother due to fear of being under attack, putting flies in her baby's milk bottle and overheating her bathwater (in deleted scenes). When Mia finds the doll in her daughter's crib, she bashes the little impostor against the crib rails and throws her to the floor, only to discover her actual daughter lying there, which prompts Mia to weep at the thought that she might have killed her own infant (who is fortunately revealed to be unharmed).

After nearly becoming a homicidal mother, Mia swings to the opposite extreme and decides to commit suicide in order to save her daughter. But despite these fraught blood relations, the movie eventually seems to realise that no mother or daughter should have to die so that the other might live. To move beyond this hysterical view of a world consisting of self-sacrificial angels or selfish devils, the movie creates another character, Evelyn, who accidentally did kill her own daughter and who pays the price for that death by killing herself in order to save Mia's baby girl. By acting out the two extremes of murder and self-martyrdom, Evelyn frees Mia to be a regular mother to her ordinary daughter, to have a mother-daughter relationship that isn't perfect but is good enough.

The Boy (2016)

Director: William Brent Bell
Cast: Lauren Cohan (Greta), Rupert Evans (Malcolm), Ben Robson (Cole), James Russell (Brahms)

When a young American named Greta takes a job as a nanny in an isolated English mansion, she discovers that the boy she is expected to tend is really a life-sized doll, an uncannily exact replica of an eight-year-old called Brahms who died years ago. While at first she jokingly dismisses him as a mere toy, Greta becomes increasingly unnerved by the creature's apparently animate behaviour, making her fear that the doll is alive or has been possessed by the spirit of the dead boy. As she is fixing her hair in a mirror, Greta hears a clattering behind her and runs to find Brahms's playthings strewn about the floor of his room. In another scene, Greta is looking into her bedroom mirror when she is unsettled by the sight of the boy doll propped up in bed behind her, apparently staring at her. Later, after brushing her teeth in her bathroom mirror, Greta walks to the bed and turns the doll's face away from her, only to have him turn it back! But this turns out to have been a nightmare she had while asleep. Greta is often troubled by sounds of a boy crying. One time when she runs to the doll to check on him, she sees a tear fall from his eye – but this is revealed to be from rainwater dripping from the ceiling.

The fact that so many of these 'creepy doll' moments have to do with mirror images of herself suggests that Greta is really being haunted by something within her own psyche. She recently lost a child to a miscarriage, and her unresolved grief may be the cause of her feeling that a dead boy has a claim on her, that she is still obligated to nurture this lifeless 'child', to help him and herself stop crying. However, by dressing, 'feeding' and reading to this substitute for her dead child, Greta is in danger of being dragged down into grief-stricken madness. When the boy doll 'steals' her dress to prevent her from going out on a date with a young man named Malcolm, this speaks to Greta's own inability to move on with her life, as she becomes enslaved by such rules as 'Never Leave Brahms Alone'.

The doll's 'jealousy' regarding Malcolm is also a reminder of Greta's possessive and abusive ex-boyfriend, Cole, whose violence towards her was what caused her miscarriage. When Greta imagines the doll spying on her in the shower or interrupting her intended lovemaking with Malcolm so that she must run and tend to the doll, she is being haunted by the memory of her lustful and selfish ex-lover. Indeed, Cole actually shows up to claim her, causing the doll child that Greta was holding to drop and break in a repetition of the miscarriage.

It turns out that the real Brahms did not die as a boy, but has been living inside the walls of the mansion, emerging in secret to manipulate the doll, which is why it seems alive. Now grown to be a young man, yet still wearing the mask of a boy, Brahms is the eerie embodiment of both Greta's fears: her still weirdly animate dead child and her possessive and domineering ex-lover. In retrospect, the strangely staring eyes of the doll do seem to make him a creepy combination of innocent boy and menacing man. 'He is sweet looking. I think he should look adorable, but [like] he has a knife hidden behind his back,' says director William Brent Bell.[35] In the end, when the hairy-chested Brahms, who is now a young man, forcibly pulls Greta towards his boy-masked face for a goodnight kiss, both the needy boy and the lustful male in him frighten her. 'I don't totally know if [she] is supposed to be his girlfriend or his mom – I think it's a messed-up in-between,' screenwriter Stacey Menear comments.[36] Interestingly, the delivery guy Malcolm, who is Greta's new love interest, isn't sure whether she should call him a 'grocery boy' or a 'grocery man'. Let us hope that she finds in him the best – and not the worst – of both.

FAMILIES

Insidious (2010)

Director: James Wan
Cast: Rose Byrne (Renai), Ty Simpkins (Dalton), Patrick Wilson (Josh), Barbara Hershey (Lorraine)

Renai is a young mother trying to have a career as a music composer. While seated at the piano where she is attempting to write a song (with the lyrics 'I'm gonna be somebody; I just can't be her today'), she suddenly hears a monstrous adult voice on the baby monitor, demanding 'I want it now!' Could some malevolent spirit be stalking her infant daughter, threatening to take her away? Or worse, is that what Renai herself secretly wants, the removal of her demanding child so that she can be left in peace to do her own work? While Renai is climbing a stepladder in the attic, one of its rungs breaks, and later her son, Dalton, falls from this same ladder, slipping into a coma. A box of Renai's music, which had earlier vanished, now reappears near the ladder. Why didn't she warn her family about the broken ladder? Did some dark part of her want her son to fall so that her music career could be restored to her?

If Renai is the evil entity menacing her son, this is a case of transgenerational haunting, for it has happened before: Renai's husband, Josh, was himself haunted by his own mother, Lorraine, when he was a boy. With Josh's father absent, Lorraine seems to have been her son's sole caretaker. This burden led to a resentment which, though mostly hidden, would occasionally reveal itself in odd behaviour, such as the fact that Lorraine rarely celebrated her son by taking photos of him. The few pictures that do exist show the ghostly image of an old woman – Lorraine herself – creeping towards young Josh in a menacing manner. This rage that builds up in women when they must give up their whole lives to tend to their children is what haunts the families of Lorraine and Renai, as symbolised by the ghost of a doll-perfect mother who suddenly stops her ironing in order to shoot her entire family. 'We wanted the ghosts to look like dolls, like relics from a different era, frozen in time, living the same loop over and over,' says screenwriter Leigh Whannell.[37]

If mothers can haunt us through generations, so, too, can fathers, for the former's rage at having to take on almost all of the parenting responsibilities is largely due to the latter's absence. Like his own father, Josh is mostly a non-presence in his children's lives, not even picking them up from school on the way home from work. Perhaps stunted by his own mother's resentment, Josh still seems like a boy in search of maternal solicitude, wanting Renai to write songs about him and preserving his baby face by plucking grey hairs and using wrinkle cream. Josh's frequent absences from home haunt his son, Dalton, whose own tendency to wander, which is described as an inheritance from his father, gets the boy into serious trouble because it leads to his fall and subsequent coma. The movie depicts Dalton as having been lured away by a male demon who wants to possess him. Dalton has sketched drawings of this demon, but Josh, absent father that he is, hasn't noticed them, perhaps because the demon is the dark side of Josh himself, the criminal neglect that is menacing his own son. Now Josh must be the father he never had and become fully present to his son in order to bring the boy back from the coma. Josh must stop his own immature wandering and behave responsibly so that the transgenerational haunting can end and his son can grow up to be a real father.

Where the Dead Go to Die (2012)

Director: Jimmy ScreamerClauz
Cast of voices: Jimmy ScreamerClauz (Labby), Joshua Michael Greene (Tommy), Ruby Larocca (Tommy's Mother and Sophia), Joey Smack (Tommy's Father and Ralph), Brandon Slagle (Sophia's Father)

Why make an animated cartoon that is not for children? First, this film's fantastically warped characters and crude computer graphics effectively represent the wild imaginations of its kiddie protagonists. Second, the animation allows the film to depict extreme forms of child abuse without having to damage any actual child actors. Finally, the disturbing distortions and jarring glitches in the rudimentary animation add to the sense that these troubled children's lives are not the happy idylls usually shown in kids' cartoons or other programming for young viewers. For example, the film offers a darkly comic parody of the TV series *Lassie* where, instead of the friendly collie dog that would help young Timmy, a black Labrador named Labby gives the wrong kind of aid to Tommy. Himself an 'unwanted' child, Tommy finds out that his mother is beset with another unwelcome pregnancy, and he hears his parents berating each other for their repeated failure to use birth control. Labby tells the boy that his mother is carrying the Antichrist and that any milk she might give this next baby is tainted because she used up all the good milk on Tommy. The demonic dog then proceeds to rip the foetus from her womb, while also biting off the penis and tearing out the throat of the father. Actually, however, the dog is merely a voice in Tommy's head, the part of his mind urging him to let loose his worst instincts, to respond in the most dysfunctional way to his dysfunctional family environment. It is really Tommy who kills his parents out of anger at them for not wanting him, and he who kills the baby out of sibling rivalry, believing that there is not enough of his mother's meagre love for both himself and a brother. But now that his mother is dead, Tommy misses her – and Labby is 'there' again to 'help'. Following the dog's instructions, Tommy has anal sex with Labby while Labby is having intercourse with the deceased mother. A more objective shot reveals that there is no Labby, but only Tommy moving between her legs. Tommy had imagined the presence of the dog in order to avoid facing the fact of his own incestuous desires. While one side of Tommy may want to bring his mother back by infusing new life into her, another part wants to satisfy his selfish lust.

Dysfunctional family dynamics are further explored in the story of another boy, Ralph, whose Siamese twin brother does not survive. In their grief, his parents blame Ralph for the death of his twin, leading the boy to believe that he was not loved as much as his brother. Ralph meets a girl named Sophia, whose father has been exploiting her by making her star in child pornography. At first, the troubled kids seem to find a safe haven in each other's company, with the boy feeling wanted by someone, and the girl glad to have somebody concerned about her feelings. Just as despair breeds despair with damaged parents having a deleterious effect on their children, so hope leads to hope as together the kids help each other imagine being freed from their family prisons, as symbolised when Ralph is able to release his bugs from glass jars so that they may live in Sophia's garden. But then Sophia's father gives Ralph one of her porn tapes, telling the boy that if he makes love with her, he could help her stop crying, and Labby whispers to Ralph that he could teach her what true love is. Confused by the father's lies and his own ambiguous urges (as voiced by the dog), Ralph has sex with Sophia while her father films them and masturbates. Ralph may want to believe that he's doing this for her, but his motives are increasingly selfish. Rationalising his own lust, he doesn't stop when she tells him to stop. And when she touches his twin brother's face (which is still attached to the side of Ralph's own head), Ralph's desire increases as if motivated by jealousy and possessiveness – two urges that often inflame the desire of porn viewers like Sophia's father. When Ralph shows a moment of concern that Sophia doesn't seem to be enjoying it, a panting Labby assures the boy that he should continue. Horrifyingly, the adults' corruption has now been fully internalised.

FATHERS

Sinister (2012)

Director: Scott Derrickson
Cast: Ethan Hawke (Ellison), Michael Hall D'Addario (Trevor), Clare Foley (Ashley), Nicholas King (The Boogeyman), Juliet Rylance (Tracy)

In an attic box, Ellison finds 8 mm home movies of families enjoying such all-American activities as mowing the lawn, playing on a tyre swing, partying by the pool, driving to a barbecue, and returning home to sleep safe and secure. Except that, for these families, the American Dream has turned nightmare, for their home movies are actually snuff films of being run over by the blades of a lawnmower, hanged from a tree, drowned in a pool, burned alive in their car, and stabbed in their beds. Something sinister has infiltrated these homes, and Ellison examines the found footage to see if he can determine the source of its uncanny creepiness, to pinpoint exactly where the familiar turned strange. Using his smartphone's camera, he digitises the 8 mm movies so that he can freeze-frame images and enlarge them on his computer. He also finds another box containing extended cuts of the films, which reveal that the cause of each family massacre was one of their own children. Ellison himself has a family, and he begins to notice uncanny correspondences between his own kids and the little killers in the home movies. He finds his 12-year-old son, Trevor, screaming inside a cardboard box like the one the films came in, and the boy later draws a sketch of the hanged family. School rumours about the murder, combined with night terrors, could account for Trevor's behaviour, or is the boy possessed? Soon after discovering Trevor in a box, Ellison sees a scorpion crawl out of one. Night noises turn out to have been caused by his seven-year-old daughter, Ashley, wandering lost in the dark, but later Ellison traces similar noises to their source in a snake rustling about in the attic. Are his son and daughter the proverbial 'viper in one's bosom'? Will he be betrayed by those closest to him? When Ashley paints a picture of the hanged family's daughter sitting on a tyre swing, Ellison fears that the ghost of this dead girl may possess Ashley to murder her own family.

Looking more closely at digitised images of the home-movie murders, Ellison discovers what appears to be a mysterious man behind each of the killer kids, exerting a baleful influence on them. In one shot, this boogeyman is reflected in a pool, watching a family drown, much as Ellison also views the murders, such as the stabbed family whose image is reflected in his eyeglasses as he peers at the film. Director and co-writer Scott Derrickson has described this as 'a horror film about a guy watching horror films'.[38] Ellison seems appalled by what he sees, but then why does he keep watching? Ellison is a true-crime writer. He is ostensibly viewing these films as research for a book, and he has moved his family into one of the houses where a murder occurred. At a certain point, just as Ellison is realising that each of the murdered families had also lived in a house where another such murder occurred, the frozen image of the boogeyman on the computer behind Ellison begins to move, turning to peer at him, but then turns back before Ellison can catch him looking. It is as though Ellison is starting to see that, when he views the boogeyman, he is staring at his own reflection, gradually discovering that he himself is the man having a baleful influence on his own children. Who took his kids to live at a former crime scene? 'My God, what on earth *possessed* you to move here?' his wife, Tracy, asks Ellison, noting that he often looks 'white as a ghost' (as does the boogeyman). Whose obsession with watching images of murder, combined with a failure to keep them locked away in his office, haunts his children to the point where they lose their way in the dark, suffer night terrors, and then begin to draw and enact such terrible crimes? There's 'something that's eating you up', Terry tells him, 'and whatever it is, it seems to be getting at Trevor as well'. At a key moment, Ellison sees ghosts of the killer kids all watching projected home movies of the murders. At first, the boogeyman is on-screen, watching and presiding over the crimes taking place there, but then the boogeyman is suddenly live and in Ellison's face – very close to him indeed, revealing the dark side of this all-American father.

Stoker (2013)

Director: Chan-wook Park
Cast: Mia Wasikowska (India), Dermot Mulroney (Richard), Matthew Goode (Charlie), David Alford (Reverend), Nicole Kidman (Mother), Alden Ehrenreich (Whip)

Described by writer Wentworth Miller as 'a horror film, a family drama and a psychological thriller, all wrapped up in one',[39] this movie begins with some highly improbable events in the life of a young woman named India. Richard, her father, dies, and Charlie, an uncle she has never seen before, appears at the funeral, which happens to occur on the same day that India turns 18. Each year, Charlie has mailed saddle shoes to her on her birthday, but this year, in person, he hands her a pair of high heels and begins to flirt seductively with her. India discovers a cache of letters revealing that Charlie has loved her from afar for years, but only now is he acting on that desire. During one scene, he plays a passionate piano duet with her while a spider creeps up her inner thigh.

None of this makes much sense in terms of realism, but if we consider these events from India's psychological perspective, there is a logic to them. It is Richard, her own ostensibly good father, who one day, as his daughter grows to be a woman, acts on his incestuous desire and molests India at the piano. Because she is unable to think of her father as bad, she splits him in two, imagining that her good father has died and that an evil uncle has taken his place. 'Have you ever seen a photograph of yourself taken when you didn't know you're being photographed, from an angle you don't get to see when you look in the mirror?' muses India. 'And you think, "That's me. That's also me."' Uncle Charlie *is* her father, Richard, viewed from another angle, a dark side of her father that she had never seen before. 'You look like my father,' she says to Charlie, and she discovers her father's wallet – containing a photo of him and herself – inside Charlie's suitcase. At the funeral, the reverend eulogises Richard as having been a 'family man', 'devoted husband' and 'loving father': 'a model to our town and of what it means to be a man who walks through the world with openness, honesty, and integrity'. But afterwards, Charlie (in the screenplay) presses her about her father: 'I want to know who he was to *you*, India ... I want to know what he was like behind closed doors, when the neighbours weren't watching ... That's when you get the real story. That's when you get the *truth*.'[40]

The trauma of incestuous contact just as she is coming of age threatens to bring out a dark side in India, too. Alternately fearful and sexually forward, she 'hates to be touched' – 'please leave before my mother wakes up,' she tells Charlie – but she also finds herself responding in kind to his advances. When her mother slow-dances with Charlie, who is wearing her father's belt, India jealously watches, just as he watches her as she interacts with boys after school. One boy, Whip, defends her from some lecherous louts, and she seems to feel some tenderness towards him, but then she bites his lip and he attempts to rape her – a turn from protector to molester that may remind her of her father. As Whip is on top of her, Charlie strangles the boy with her father's belt, and India later masturbates to the memory of this scene, climaxing at the moment when Charlie breaks the boy's neck. Because of the incest she has suffered, India has begun to associate desire with predation, sex with death.

However, in the end, just as Charlie is using that same belt to strangle her mother, India shoots him dead. Rather than giving in to her murderous desire to be with him, she protects her mother. Significantly, India has spent years on hunting trips with her father, who has taught her to wait until just the right moment to pull the trigger. It could be that, despite her father's incestuous advances, India has found a way to remember and internalise his good side, to live her life as a defender of others against the kinds of assaults she has suffered.

GHOSTS

The Sixth Sense (1999)

Director: M Night Shyamalan
Cast: Bruce Willis (Crowe), Olivia Williams (Anna), Donnie Wahlberg (Vincent), Haley Joel Osment (Cole), Toni Collette (Lynn)

Dr Crowe receives an award for his successes as a child psychologist, but he fears that work has led him to neglect his wife, Anna, and he is shot dead by a former patient, Vincent, who claims that the doctor has failed to help him. There then ensues a partial wish-fulfilment fantasy in which Crowe comes back as a ghost and is able to make at least symbolic amends for his past mistakes. Vincent is beyond help, but the doctor's spirit counsels and cures another boy like him, Cole. Crowe, who spends much of the movie in denial about being one of the ghosts ('They only see what they want to see; they don't know that they're dead'), finally faces the fact that he is deceased and thus can never really mend his relationship with his still-living wife. Nevertheless, Crowe comes to believe that if he whispers how much he loves her to Anna while she is asleep, his wife will sense his continued presence and be comforted by it. Earlier, Crowe's ghost has returned to their anniversary restaurant, but his spectral hand has been unable to meet hers across the table. He has also watched in jealous rage as Anna seems about to kiss a male co-worker. But in the end, Crowe reconciles himself to the reality that, despite the persistence of his spiritual presence, the absence of his flesh and blood means that her love for him will need to be enacted with another man who is physically present. Just as Crowe 'regained' his lost patient, Vincent, through another boy, Cole, so Anna will 'regain' her deceased husband, Crowe, through another man. It is in this complex sense that Crowe is right when he whispers to Anna, 'I didn't leave you.'

As for Cole, his father is absent due to a divorce, but the fact that the boy still wears the empty frames of his dad's eyeglasses is a sign of how much Cole wishes his father were there. As part of counselling

Cole, Crowe shows him the trick of the 'magic penny' which seems to vanish from the doctor's left hand to his right, then to disappear from that hand to his waistcoat pocket, and finally to return to his left hand, but the boy correctly surmises that the penny never really departed from Crowe's left hand. The penny seemed gone but was still present. When Cole's mother, Lynn, asks him about a missing pendant that had belonged to his now-deceased grandmother, the boy replies, 'Sometimes people think they lose things and they really didn't lose them. It just gets moved.' Later, Cole conveys a message from the ghost of his grandmother, who wants Lynn to know that – many years ago, back when they were both alive – she did attend Lynn's dance recital, even though Lynn may not have been able to see her standing in the back. Just as she was present then while seeming absent, so the grandmother, now deceased, is still there in spirit, even if not in body. Like the pendant and the penny, she never really left. As Cole says, 'Some magic's real.' When Crowe attends Cole's school play, the boy's absent father is there through Crowe, who embodies the dad's ever-present paternal spirit, the eyeglasses watching over the boy. Afterwards, Cole says to Crowe, 'I'm not going to see you anymore, am I?' With the boy's therapy completed for now, their doctor-patient relationship will end, and Crowe is dead and about to depart for the great beyond. Nevertheless, Crowe's spirit will remain as a guiding father-figure to the boy and a loving husband to his wife. Having made its accommodation with harsh truth (the dead are, in a very real sense, gone), the film allows us to believe that, in some meaningful and comforting way, we will still be able to see dead people.

The Woman in Black (2012)

Director: James Watkins
Cast: Daniel Radcliffe (Arthur), Sophie Stuckey (Arthur's Wife), Liz White (Woman in Black)

One of the highest-grossing UK horror films ever made, *The Woman in Black* is a 'weird fusion of a classical British ghost movie and J-horror,' says director James Watkins.[41] Arthur is a solicitor in Edwardian-era London. After his wife dies in childbirth, a son is delivered to him, but Arthur, unable to overcome his grief, has difficulty forming an attachment to the boy. To settle the accounts of an estate, Arthur travels to a remote country mansion, accessible only by a narrow causeway through a frequently flooded marsh. According to Daniel Radcliffe (who plays Arthur), 'It is a film about isolation, about how isolating death can be ... The island that the Eel Marsh House is on is metaphorically representing his mental state. He becomes increasingly isolated as the tide comes in and blocks off the island from the land.'[42] While occasionally visited by visions of his wife clothed in heavenly white, Arthur is also disturbed by sightings of a Woman in Black, whose mystery he dedicates himself to solving. As Radcliffe explains, 'Here's this guy who's lost his wife, goes to this house, and starts seeing the ghost of a dead woman. The reason he stays there and almost tries to find her is that in there is some hidden desire, or instinct, to get some sort of assurance that his wife is in a better place.'[43]

Each time the Woman in Black appears, some child in the nearby village is mysteriously compelled to commit suicide and then to linger in this world as a ghost. The deaths of the children seem connected to the four elements – drinking lye (water), setting oneself alight (fire), sinking into mud (earth), and jumping from a window (air) – as if to represent their souls' entrapment within the material realm. The film's very atmosphere, thick with fog and soggy marshland, emphasises this materiality. Watkins notes that 'the way the moisture hangs in the sky gives it a really heavy, foreboding sense',[44] and he says that when the land around the house is flooded, the 'water comes in' as 'a tide, but it comes up through the mud'.[45]

Arthur finds out that the Woman in Black is the ghost of a mother whose son has been taken from her and later drowned in a marshland accident. Since then, her ghost has been wreaking vengeance by taking away other people's children so as to inflict the same grief on them. Given that Eel Marsh House, with its flooded causeway, is a symbol of Arthur's grieving mind, increasingly cut off from the living, and given that his investigation of the ghost woman is driven by concerns about his deceased wife, it could be that the Woman in Black and the Woman in White (his wife) are psychologically interrelated. Like the ghost woman, Arthur's wife was a mother who had a son taken from her and given over to another (Arthur himself). Through a combination of widower's grief and survivor's guilt, could he not imagine her returning as a vengeful spirit to haunt him? Is not the Woman in Black a figment of that very fear? When Arthur digs the body of the ghost woman's dead son out of the muddy marshland and gives him back to her, Arthur is trying to make symbolic amends for the tragic fact that he and his son lived, while his wife did not. It is a metaphorical way of reuniting the son with the mother so that Arthur can mourn his wife's passing and continue living. But, unfortunately, Arthur's attempt at mourning gives way to terminal melancholy. In his mind, his wife will not be satisfied with a symbolic expression of sympathy, no matter how heartfelt. And so, in the end, his wife appears as the Woman in Black and causes their son to stand on some railroad tracks, and when Arthur goes to save him, both are killed by an oncoming train. Arthur ends his survivor's guilt and his sadness over having separated mother and son by bringing all three of them together again in death.

Nina Forever (2015)

Directors: Chris Blaine and Ben Blaine
Cast: Cian Barry (Rob), Abigail Hardingham (Holly), Fiona O'Shaughnessy (Nina), Sean Verey (Josh)

Among the unusual aspects of Rob, Holly and Nina's love triangle is the fact that Nina is dead. Having perished in a car crash, Nina nevertheless returns every time Rob and Holly try to make love, crawling out from under the covers or emerging from the mattress to join them in bed. Although she may seem like a jealous and possessive ex-girlfriend, the clingy Nina with her sticky blood is a manifestation of Rob's continuing attachment to his former lover due to his unresolved grief over her loss. As Nina states, 'This has nothing to do with me [as a malign spirit]. It's him.' Rob may want to love Holly, but as Nina says, 'It's me he can't forget.' When Holly kisses Nina and reaches out to pleasure her with a hand, welcoming her to their bed in an attempt to help Rob transition from his past partner to herself as the new one, this only makes things worse because it encourages his morbid obsession with his deceased ex. For Rob, who has already tried to kill himself so that he can join the dead Nina, sex has been contaminated by death. He can't think of making love to Holly without imagining Nina's bloody yet still alluring body drawing him in as it materialises from the mattress under Holly. Unable to stop seeing Nina's broken body in the bed where Holly is lying, Rob now connects intercourse with bleeding and bodily damage, and orgasm with dying, which is why Holly seems to break apart under his thrusting and why his climax seems to be shared by the expiring Nina.

If Nina is a sign of Rob's inability to detach from death and complete the mourning process, she is also evidence of a disturbance in Holly's own psyche. In training to be a paramedic, Holly is attracted to a man like Rob whose near-suicidal grief means that he is in desperate need of saving. Thus, while wanting to help Rob resolve his grief over Nina, Holly also wants Nina to continue to haunt Rob so that Holly's help will be required. In this sense, Holly is invested in Nina's continued presence, being as haunted by her as Rob is, paradoxically desiring Nina's ghost to keep on ruining Holly's relationship with Rob so that he will still need her to heal him. 'You've let me under your skin,' Nina says to Holly, and when Holly breaks up with Rob *because* he is getting better, Nina tells her, 'You're not ready for someone who doesn't need fixing.'

Working with her team as a paramedic, Holly goes to an accident scene where she succeeds in rescuing a car-crash victim who looks like Nina, holding the woman's hand until she can be transported to a hospital. Feeling exultant that they have saved someone's life, Holly has sex with a co-worker named Josh, but as he climaxes while glorying in his God-like omnipotence, Holly feels Nina's bleeding hands reaching for hers. It turns out that Holly does not have a saviour complex after all. Unlike Josh, she refuses to delude herself into thinking that her hands have some amazing power to heal. If she continues to see Nina's bloody and broken body, it is because Holly never loses touch with the reality of suffering. She *wants* to maintain the presence of death in her life in order to keep her compassionate connection with others through a shared sense of the body's fragility. In the end, when Rob asks her if she is going to be all right, Holly shakes her head 'no' while saying 'yeah'. Nina will haunt her for ever, but that's okay. Whereas death threatened to make Rob's life meaningless, it gives meaning to Holly's life.

HAUNTED HOUSES

Hell House (2001)

Director: George Ratliff

As one commentator put it, 'Where haunted houses promise to scare the bejeezus out of you, Hell Houses aim to scare you to Jesus.'[46] *Hell House* is a documentary about haunted houses designed by church groups to frighten visitors into having faith in God. Teens are led through a dark house where they can view tableaux of sinners suffering in this life and then being dragged to hell by demons. Unlike Disney's *The Haunted Mansion* with its innocuous and child-oriented chills, and unlike such immersive events as Underground Cinema's '28 Days Later' where the scares serve no clear purpose and where young adults end up drinking and partying among the zombie actors, *Hell House* instils fear with only one meaning in mind and it is deadly serious: to bring sinners to Christ, lest they lose their immortal souls and be damned for eternity.

The single-minded intent of the experience, its fundamentalist Christian message, makes *Hell House* the perfect exemplar of conservative horror, fear designed to ward off threats to a traditional way of life – drug-free, monogamous and heterosexual. It is fear aimed at enforcing a dichotomous view of the world, a separation between us (as saved) and them (lost souls). Thus, a man is shown dying of AIDS due to his 'homosexual lifestyle'; a woman bleeds out from a self-induced abortion following premarital sex; and another woman commits suicide after taking Rohypnol at a rave and being date-raped. All three are hauled off to hell to serve as a warning to watching visitors that a similar fate could befall them if they sin. Instead of inducing compassion for the suffering of these three unfortunates, the spectacle of their misery is meant to instil horror and aversion, to distance us from them and even to make us feel a certain sadistic glee at their supposedly just demise. Interestingly, one member of the church is able to show great sympathy for his son when the boy is afflicted with a seizure due to cerebral palsy. If only he could feel a similar empathy for the three victims in his haunted-house tableaux. In times past, his son's shaking body might have been feared as a sign of demonic possession, and there are people today who may be alarmed by the sight of this man and his congregation when their bodies convulse and they speak in tongues – people who might see them as possessed by something other than the Holy Spirit. Yet they do not judge him. Would that this man were able to extend a similar compassion to those he condemns out of fear. 'And now abideth faith, hope, charity, these three; but the greatest of these is charity.'

The Others (2001)

Director: Alejandro Amenábar
Cast: Nicole Kidman (Grace), Alakina Mann (Anne), James Bentley (Nicholas)

It is 1945 on the island of Jersey, where Grace, her eight-year-old daughter, Anne, and her younger son, Nicholas, live in an isolated mansion. Because the children have a rare skin disorder that would cause them to suffocate if they were exposed to daylight, Grace insists on keeping the windows shrouded and the doors locked to preserve the darkness. Disturbing sounds and displaced objects begin to make the family fear that the house is haunted by ghosts of its former inhabitants. However, it is eventually revealed that Grace and her children *are* the ghosts haunting a new family trying to make the house their home.

Some viewers may think that, for much of the movie, Grace and her kids are unaware of being dead, but this is incorrect. They do know, but are in denial. Feeling deserted by her husband when he went off to war and in despair at the thought that he would almost certainly never return, Grace felt that she and her family had nothing left to live for, so she smothered her children with a pillow and then shot herself. But the realisation of what she has done is too painful, so instead of acknowledging their deaths and her own, she imagines that God has given her a second chance to be a good mother and not to give up. Now she protects her children with a fanatical devotion to their safety, but what Grace is really doing is shielding herself from the terrible truth of her misdeed. She keeps everyone in darkness so that this truth will not come to light. When Anne tells her that she senses mysterious intruders (the new family) in the house, Grace warns her that children who lie will be condemned to a limbo of eternal pain. Yet it is Grace herself who is lying, and by refusing to recognise their own deaths, she has sentenced her family to endless suffering in a limbo between life and death. Insisting that 'there are no intruders here', Grace enforces silence on the subject by ordering Anne to 'stop breathing!'. Thus, Grace's overprotectiveness smothers Anne again, repeating what she did with the pillow. Perhaps Grace suffocated her children before killing herself so that they would not have to go on living with the feeling of having been abandoned by their mother, as Grace felt she was by her husband. But in fact, by drawing her children so smotheringly close to her for their 'protection', she really ended up enforcing her own despair on them, making them give up on life.

Slowly, Grace begins to acknowledge that there are others present in the house, but she wilfully mistakes them for enemy entities appearing to attack her family. When Anne puts on a white dress and moans like a ghost, Grace 'sees' the spectre of an old woman trying to possess her daughter. Grace rushes to protect Anne by strangling the old woman, but in the process she chokes her own daughter. Grace herself is the ghostly woman possessing Anne, grabbing hold of her so that she will not speak the truth about how her own mother smothered her. In another scene, Grace enters a room with furniture and unidentified objects covered in white sheets. When she lifts off one of these sheets, afraid of the ghost that might lie beneath, Grace is spooked by the sight of her own face in a mirror.

Ultimately, Grace admits that she committed infanticide and suicide, and she begs her children for forgiveness. The fact that Anne and Nicholas can now stand, alongside Grace, in the sunlight without being harmed suggests that they can accept the truth and still forgive their mother. But as a mother who killed her own children, even if it was out of a loving desire to protect them, Grace cannot be sure of a place in heaven, yet neither does she feel that she deserves to be damned to hell. And so, rather than finding a new home above or below, the spirits of Grace and her children continue to haunt this house – at least until such time as a higher grace might be granted to them.

Crimson Peak (2015)

Director: Guillermo del Toro
Cast: Mia Wasikowska (Edith), Tom Hiddleston (Thomas), Jessica Chastain (Lucille)

In the early 1900s, a sheltered American named Edith falls for Thomas, a dashing aristocrat, who takes her away to England to live in his grand but decaying family mansion. As in many gothic romances, the film centres on a young bride's anxieties regarding her new husband. The ghost of Edith's mother warns her, 'Beware of Crimson Peak,' which turns out to be 'the top of a mountain, a peak that, when it snows, turns blood red' because of the crimson clay seeping up into the white snow from the ground below, as writer-director Guillermo del Toro explains.[47] Thomas has developed a steam-powered drill by which to bore into the red clay and mine it for ore, and the crimson flowing from this rift not only stains the snow, it also bleeds up from below the house to darken Edith's white dress. Representing both the husband's phallus and the bride's sex, Crimson Peak is a figure for Edith's fear of intercourse and defloration, of what will happen to the virgin on her wedding night. Another concern common to brides is the thought of other women her husband might have bedded and who might have a prior claim on him. Is he still tied to someone from his past, or even worse, will Edith become just another in a long line of foolish females he has seduced and abandoned? Thomas, she discovers to her horror, has been marrying women for their money and then having them murdered – slain by his sister, Lucille, with whom he is in an ongoing incestuous relationship. The bodies of Thomas's past wives are hidden in a room beneath the house, sunk in cauldrons of clay from which they rise as blood-red ghosts to scare Edith with the sight of the fate that might befall her.

But Crimson Peak is a twenty first century gothic, and so the film allows Edith to conquer her fears of men and sex. As del Toro says, 'Rarely do gothic romances function without the heroine needing to be kept away from sexuality in order to remain pure for the tale, and to survive. That's one of the things I wanted to break on Crimson. The main character can have sex and still be strong, and still be able to survive and triumph.'[48] On the night their marriage is consummated, Edith makes passionate love with Thomas and – nothing horrible happens. She is neither injured nor abandoned. The film rewards her physical courage and psychological strength by granting her a reformed Thomas, who now appears as a faithful and protective husband who tries to defend her against his murderously jealous sister. In a sense, the Thomas of her nightmares is replaced by the husband of her dreams because the former was a mere fiction of her anxieties, which have finally been overcome.

HOLIDAYS

Trick 'r Treat (2007)

Director: Michael Dougherty
Cast: Brett Kelly (Charlie), Dylan Baker (Steven), Connor Levins (Billy), Quinn Lord (Sam), Anna Paquin (Laurie), Lauren Lee Smith (Laurie's Sister), Samm Todd (Rhonda), Britt McKillip (Macy), Jean-Luc Bilodeau (Schrader)

On Halloween night, red-headed Charlie, an overweight boy in an orange T-shirt, knocks over pumpkins and steals extra candy. As punishment, he is fed a poisoned candy bar by school principal Steven, who has had enough of misbehaving kids. Then, just as we think that Steven is about to bring a knife down upon his own rebellious, red-headed son, Billy, it turns out that the boy is actually helping his father with some ritual carving, but what they are cutting up is not a pumpkin, but Charlie's severed head. The film suggests that, in order to avoid becoming a victim like Charlie, Billy attempts to join his father and become the aggressor. According to writer-director Michael Dougherty, 'Halloween was about appeasing the dead. It was believed to be the one night when the barrier between the living and the dead was thinnest, allowing … supernatural beings to walk amongst us'; 'costumes were worn as a way of disguising yourself as one of them.'[49] In order to save himself from his monstrous father, Billy 'disguises' himself as a monster, but the risk of such a disguise is that it may stick, becoming his permanent self. 'Don't forget to help me with the eyes,' Billy tells Steven. If Billy joins his father in cutting out the eyes – the most human part – of Charlie, who is Billy's red-headed double, then the son will truly have been shaped into a soulless monster. 'Let's carve a scary face this time,' Billy says, but the face he carves won't ward off evil; it will become his own evil face.

Billy will become like Sam, a ghost child wearing orange pyjamas and a round burlap mask like a pumpkin head. When the mask is taken off, Sam's deformed face is revealed to resemble that of a demonic jack-o'-lantern, the facial flesh itself having permanently taken on that shape. Dougherty notes that jack-'o-lanterns have their origin in bonfires that the ancient Celts would set 'to protect themselves from evil spirits let loose on All Hallows' Eve'. The power of these pumpkin heads is 'rooted in the desire to harness a little bit of evil'[50] as a defence against the greater evil of the threatening ghouls, but what if the evil that is harnessed ends up harnessing the self?

In another scene, virginal Laurie, costumed as Little Red Riding Hood, is accosted by a masked man in the woods who threatens her with rapacious bites, but she turns the tables on this wolfish predator. Trapping him in her little-girl's red cloak, she has his fake fangs pulled out, thus making him the vulnerable 'female'. She then performs a striptease, removing her costume and womanly skin to reveal a she-wolf underneath that tears off *his* clothes and bites *his* neck. Laurie's female empowerment is impressive, but hasn't she herself become an animalistic rapist? In order to avoid being prey, does she have to become a predator? 'Just be yourself,' Laurie's she-wolf sister advises, encouraging her to attack, but we must wonder if this is the self that Laurie really wants to be.

Meanwhile, an autistic girl named Rhonda goes with Macy, Schrader and some other kids to an abandoned rock quarry where, years before, some special-needs children were killed in a school-bus crash partially engineered by parents who no longer wanted them. As the present-day kids stumble around in the dark, Schrader says, 'I think I found a dead retard,' and Macy replies, 'That's me, asshole.' Perhaps defending against their own fear of being unwanted and abandoned, the kids pretend to be child zombies come back from the grave to scare 'Rhonda the retard', who ends up frightened and alone at the bottom of the quarry. Thus, these kids, instead of empathising with the dead, end up repeating their victimisation on Rhonda. When the real child zombies come to attack the kids, Rhonda refuses to save them, even turning her back on Schrader, the only one who had earlier shown any potentially loving interest in her or concern about how she was being treated. In leaving him to die with the others, Rhonda removes any last chance he had to change for the better, while possibly losing her own last chance as well, for she then turns to put on her witch's hat, having become as evil as the costume she wears.

Krampus (2015)

Director: Michael Dougherty
Cast: Emjay Anthony (Max), Luke Hawker (Krampus), Conchata Ferrell (Dorothy)

'I love horror films,' says director Michael Dougherty, who insists that *Krampus* is 'definitely part of that genre, but I really think we're genre-defying in that we're mixing heavy elements of horror and humour and Christmas'.[51] Arguing that Christmas has become 'too commercial and saccharine and kid-oriented', Dougherty is 'adding a dash of [a] mischievous dark side' by bringing in Krampus,[52] an 'actual ancient legend about a horned and cloven-hooved pagan demon who steals naughty children'.[53] All kids know that there is a dark side to Santa, the letters of whose name, rearranged, spell Satan. Santa's arrival down the chimney is, minus the benevolence, a home-invasion scenario. Any child rewarded for niceness could just as plausibly be punished for having been naughty. Santa's diabolical double, Krampus, visits 12-year-old Max because the boy, as he grows older, is losing his belief in Santa Claus and his faith in the stability of his family, which once seemed to embody the Christmas-card ideal. Now his father overworks; his parents fight; and his sister is off with her boyfriend (what if she never came back?). Christmas is darkened by Krampus in much the way that Max's formerly close-knit suburban family is haunted by the possibility of becoming like their dysfunctional, lower-class relatives who, when they come to visit, bicker, spout bigotries, and leave their own baby outside in the car. Krampus is like Santa's white-trash cousin. But Max's crass relatives, as a result of their hard-knock existence, are also better at facing the fact that the world isn't always a holiday idyll. 'We're fucked,' Aunt Dorothy says when

Krampus attacks. 'I'm old enough to know when life is coming at you with his pants down.'

Krampus, with his devilish horns, serpent's tongue, and taloned hands, is the Santa Claws who grabs hold of a boy who no longer believes in a benign Saint Nick, and Krampus's evil minions provide equal evidence of a faith that has turned: snowmen who were left out in the cold mount a sneak attack; gingerbread-man cookies bite back; a discarded toy jack-in-the box swallows children between its razor-sharp teeth. 'All this might be my fault,' Max thinks, considering that his lack of the Christmas spirit may have led these traditionally happy signs of the holiday to go bad. In a last-ditch leap of faith, Max pleads with Krampus to take his life and spare that of the others – an act of Christ-like self-sacrifice which, rather than bringing about salvation, merely prompts Krampus to throw the boy down into a fiery pit to join all the others! But a subsequent shot of Max waking up on Christmas morning to find his entire family safe and sound would seem to indicate that it has all been a bad dream – until the camera pulls back to reveal everyone encased in a snow globe within the grip of Krampus's claw. This ending suggests that, at least in this world, faith may not always be enough to defeat evil.

HOME INVASION

The Strangers (2008)

Director: Bryan Bertino
Cast: Scott Speedman (James), Liv Tyler (Kristen), Gemma Ward (Dollface), Laura Margolis (Pin-Up Girl), Kip Weeks (Masked Man)

It has been said that the strangers' attack on the young couple in this film is random and motiveless. It *is* scary to think that we could be besieged from anywhere at any time without any apparent reason, but so what? We all already know this to be true. A motiveless crime is not very interesting, and watching a helpless couple being tortured for 90 minutes is an exercise in masochism (or sadism). Fortunately, this film appears to have been crafted in a way that makes it more intellectually intriguing and humanly involving, for the attackers seem to be external manifestations of the couple's own increasing distance from each other. In other words, 'the strangers' are really the couple themselves.

At a friend's wedding party where James is a groomsman and Kristen a bridesmaid, he proposes marriage, but she turns him down, saying that she is 'just not ready yet'. When the couple then go to spend the night at an isolated vacation house, they grow more and more estranged, unable to celebrate their engagement as he had planned. At one point, just as they are about to make love and possibly reunite ('You are my girl,' James says), a doll-masked woman interrupts them by knocking at the door and asking, 'Is Tamara here?' When told no, Dollface presses the question: 'Are you sure?' If Tamara is James's former girlfriend (later manifested in the film as a woman in a pin-up girl mask), then Dollface's question could represent Kristen's doubts about whether he really does love her and her alone. Kristen sees a man in a burlap-sack mask staring at her from outside and then cowers at the sound of footsteps approaching her inside the house, but they turn out to belong to James. She spies the Masked Man sitting at a table with candles and champagne glasses – the same table James sat at earlier when he was depressed (and angry?) about her rejection of his proposal. Late in the film, James himself will emerge from a burlap bag, as if he were the Masked Man.

At one point, James feels a woman's hand on his shoulder and turns to find that it's Kristen's. Later, he senses a similar hand, but this one belongs to a threatening masked woman. As he is backing into the house and away from a shadowy female figure, he is startled by what he fears is an attack from behind, but it's Kristen. In this confusion between outside and inside, strange and homey, masked marauder and familiar face, the film suggests that James and Kristen are spooking themselves, each afraid of how different the other might turn out to be from who they originally thought. When James searches the house for a masked woman who may have got inside, he looks in the same rose-petal-scattered bed and bathtub where Kristen had lain earlier – the bride who is now not to be. Kristen sees Dollface standing at a table and touching the engagement-ring box, just as she herself did earlier. After she turned down his proposal, James had asked her what they should do, and Kristen answered, 'I don't know.' James asks the same question about the strangers' attack, and she repeats that reply. The attack *is* their fear of a ruined relationship and their attempt to face it and figure out what to do. 'It's just us and them,' James says, but it's really just he and she.

In the end, the couple are tied to chairs with her in her bridesmaid's gown and him in his groomsman's tuxedo. Kristen, wearing the engagement ring, turns to James and says, 'I love you.' As if cued by this declaration, Dollface drops her knife, and the strangers take off their masks (though we don't see their faces). Could it be that the couple's love for each other is strong enough to save them? However, the male stranger proceeds to plunge a knife into James. 'Look at my face,' Kristen begs James and he does, but a female stranger then stabs her. It would appear that, despite their new-found trust, they still do not *recognise* their loving selves. They do not have sufficient faith in each other or themselves for their relationship to survive. According to some of the song lyrics heard in the film, 'When we're all through … we're [either] killed or cured.' Unfortunately, it is not the latter.

The Purge (2013)

Director: James DeMonaco
Cast: Ethan Hawke (James), Edwin Hodge (Injured Man), Rhys Wakefield (Mob Leader), Adelaide Kane (Zoey), Tony Oller (Henry)

In a near-future America, on one night of every year, people are permitted to commit all kinds of violence, even murder, with impunity. Allowing citizens to 'release the beast' – all their pent-up hatred and aggression – in this way makes them better able to remain peaceful throughout the rest of the year. Moreover, on 'purge night', the affluent remain safe within their gated communities. As suburban homeowner James reassures his family, 'I know bad things do happen tonight, but we can afford protection, so we'll be fine, just like always.' It is only the poor and needy who are open to attack, and the eradication of these 'non-contributing' members of society helps to 'unburden' the economy. Sound like the perfect plan for a utopia? Here are three reasons why it's not:

1. You can't just behave like a beast one night and then go back to being a civilised human. When an injured man takes refuge in James's house, the leader of the rampaging mob outside demands that James hand over the 'dirty, homeless pig' to be slaughtered. The leader describes his gang as 'ready to violate, annihilate, and cleanse our souls'. He means that they will be purer if they get rid of that 'dirty' man, but what the leader's words unwittingly reveal is that, if they murder this man, they will 'violate' and 'annihilate' their own 'souls', destroying their humanity. One female gang member strokes a machete. In love with violence, she is in danger of cutting herself. Another thug mimes shooting himself in the head with the gun he is holding, which is what he will metaphorically be doing if he guns down the injured man. The mob's leader brags about the murders they are committing, but if they are so proud of their violence, why do they all wear masks? After all, on this night they have immunity from prosecution for their killings. Could it be that they don't really want to be *seen* behaving like vicious beasts, that they have some residual conscience regarding their crimes?

2. Possessive materialism and competitive capitalism will rebound on the rich. James loves his daughter, Zoey, in the way he loves his luxurious house – as signs of his wealth and accomplishment. Mirroring James, Zoey's boyfriend, Henry, also desires to possess her. A hungry growling is his way of saying 'I love you'. When Zoey hears the story of a man whose love was so powerful it could kill people, she comments that the man should cut off his own penis. It is clear that she feels threatened by the grasping 'love' of the males around her. James's possessiveness, which results in his disapproval of Zoey's boyfriend, backfires when Henry fires a gun

at him on purge night. James's 'hoarding' of his daughter brings on Henry's envy and violence. James's desirable house was paid for by his earnings as a top salesman of home security systems, many of which he sold to people in his surrounding community. But, in a telling irony, his own security system isn't enough to protect him against the wrath of his envious neighbours, who come to kill James and his family and to take away his grand possessions in a literal example of cutthroat competition. 'You made so much money off of us and then you stuck it in our faces,' one of them accuses, and now James must reap what he has sown.

3. James thinks of himself as separate from the predatory violence that occurs on purge night, as he and his family sit safely within their well-secured home while more impoverished people are hunted down outside. But in the competitive capitalist system of which James is a part, poorer persons are killed off every day, only this occurs more slowly and less directly than on purge night, as resources are gradually removed from less fortunate citizens in order to benefit the wealthy like himself. The systemic violence of a rapacious economy is still a form of violence, even if it succeeds in distancing its perpetrators, like James, from their victims. In addition, by profiting from the home security systems that make purge night possible (the rich would never allow such rampages if they themselves went unprotected), James is most definitely a part of the predation that is happening to others outside. He, too, is 'making a killing' off them. When the injured homeless man seeks a safe haven in James's home and he has to decide whether to personally hand this man over to the mob that wants to kill him, James can no longer deny his own responsibility for the lives of the less fortunate. Finally forced to face the systemic violence that he and his family have been participating in and benefiting from, James decides that, morally, he can no longer afford to be part of it. James would rather give up his life in defence of this man than risk losing his own soul.

HOMOPHOBIA

Jeepers Creepers (2001)

Director: Victor Salva
Cast: Justin Long (Darry), Gina Philips (Trish), Jonathan Breck (The Creeper), Patricia Belcher (Jezelle)

While on a car trip home from college for spring break, Darry and his sister, Trish, play a road game. Spotting a vanity licence plate (6A 4EVR), he reads it as 'Gay Fever' or 'Gay Forever', whereas she offers the more likely 'Sexy Forever'. In conversation with his sister, Darry shows particular interest in her former boyfriend ('Mister Poli-Sci Track-Team Guy') and later in a 'strip-o-gram' hunky cop who catches her eye, while nothing is said about Darry himself having a girlfriend. When Trish notices the 'rosy pink jockey shorts' in Darry's gym bag, he explains that some of his friends dyed them as a prank, and she jokes that 'maybe they know something about you that you don't'. Indeed, the evidence for Darry's hidden homosexuality is mounting. When a truck begins to tailgate them, Darry comments, 'He's coming up right on our ass,' adding 'Fuck me – go!' when they are rear-ended. Later, Darry uses a pair of his pink jockey shorts to tie down the broken trunk of their car.

In these ways, the film begins to suggest that what stalks Darry is the fear that he might be gay. Darry's homophobia is then projected outwards as he imagines a queer monster lusting after him. Thus, while the brother and sister are seeking help inside a diner, the driver of the truck that rear-ended them breaks into their parked car and starts sniffing Darry's dirty laundry. 'And now he even knows my name,' Darry says when he recovers his labelled underwear. Significantly, the Creeper (as the monstrous driver comes to be called) has singled out Darry for attention rather than the female Trish. As gay writer-director Victor Salva has said, 'Let the guys be the object of desire for a while. It fits my sensibilities better.'[54] Speaking to a psychic named Jezelle Gay(!) Hartman, Darry says, 'You know, don't you? ... You know who it wants.' Jezelle tells him,

'There's something in fear, something it can smell, something that tells it if there's anything inside someone that it might like.' It is Darry's homophobia that attracts the Creeper to him, because that fear is a sign of repressed desire as well as dread. 'I've dreamed this,' Jezelle says, and the Creeper is both Darry's worst nightmare and his most hidden wish.

After Darry spies the Creeper stuffing a sheet-wrapped figure down a sewer pipe, he insists on returning to the scene. This is ostensibly to check if someone needs help, but Trish questions why Darry is drawn back, suggesting that he 'wants a little adventure' and desires to 'see if there's something nasty at the end of that pipe'. Darry peers inside and ends up falling down the pipe, as if through an anal passageway. At the bottom, Darry finds a dying boy inside the sheet with a wound cut into his stomach. The boy prefigures Darry's own future, as Jezelle has foreseen him with his shirt having been 'torn just above a small rose tattoo on [his] stomach', and in *Jeepers Creepers 2* we find out that the Creeper does extract the skin containing the rose tattoo around Darry's navel. Here the various images – the rear-ended car, the pink jockey shorts, the rose-tattooed navel, the torn shirt – all combine to represent Darry's fear of anal intercourse as a deadly rape.

And yet the ending of *Jeepers Creepers* is intriguingly equivocal. When the Creeper puts his mouth near Darry's and sniffs the boy's sweaty face, Darry has reason to fear, for earlier he had watched while the Creeper cut off a male cop's head and then French-kissed the tongue out of it. Now, the Creeper grabs Darry from behind and, pressed up against him, smells the boy's neck, as the tendrils on the monster's lizard-like head grow erect. It is the moment of maximum fright because the very thing that Darry has most dreaded is now, metaphorically, being done to him. 'I don't know if it's a demon or a devil or just some hungry thing from some dark place,' the psychic had said, but it could be that the Creeper only looks satanic because Darry is afraid of the hunger inside himself. As the Creeper flies away with the boy in his grasp, they are backgrounded by the moon, as if this terrible embrace were also a romantic clinch. And, in the film's final shot, we see that the Creeper has removed the skin of Darry's face and placed it over his own so that his eyes peer out. Or whose eyes are they? The end reveals that, behind the mask of Darry's fear, there was his desire for the Creeper. The gay Creeper was Darry all along, his homosexuality hiding behind his homophobia. Referring to Justin Long, who plays Darry, Salva has said, 'That is Justin [whose eyes we see] as the Creeper looking out at us through Justin as Darry [in the end]'.

Juan of the Dead (Juan de los muertos) (2011)

Director: Alejandro Brugués
Cast: Alexis Díaz de Villegas (Juan), Jorge Molina (Lazaro), Jazz Vilá (China), Eliecer Ramírez (Primo)

In *Juan of the Dead*, the fear of a zombie attack serves as a metaphor for homophobia. Juan and his friends Lazaro, China and Primo are ostensibly united against the predatory ghouls, but in fact gay panic about his buddies afflicts Juan as much as the zombies do. In one scene where the men are assailed by the monsters, the lights go out and a cry is heard – 'Don't touch my ass!' – as if friend and foe had become indistinguishable in the dark. During a search-and-destroy mission, Primo, a hulking gay bodybuilder, tells Juan to 'step aside' because 'this is a man's job'. Yet, at this very moment, Primo, who wears a blindfold because he faints at the sight of blood, is grabbed by a ghoul. Primo's gayness is thus associated with effeminate fear and mere posing as a strong man. When Primo's lover, the male-to-female transgendered China, makes a disparaging remark about the size of Lazaro's male member, the insulted man cringes in embarrassment that his virility might be inferior to that of a campy queen – one who shrieked in fright at the sight of a cockroach. It is as though, by associating with gays, straight men dread being rendered soft and vulnerable, infected by a contagious weakness. In a scene where the friends run afoul of the military and are handcuffed naked together in the back of a troop truck, China flirts with a soldier, who grows increasingly more macho in 'self-defence'. The men's fear of being in such close physical proximity to each other eventually erupts when – a nightmare come true – one of the naked passengers turns predatory and lunges open-mouthed at the others. After escaping, Juan gazes in horror at the bite on China's inner thigh, terrified that he himself will be 'unmanned' when this effeminate gay attacks him. Juan's fight to free himself from being handcuffed to China is filmed as an ironic dance, deadly rather than romantic. Dismissing his friend as 'a fucking pain in the ass', Juan finally asserts his masculine dominance by beating China to a pulp with a paddle, much as he later uses a paddle to pound another zombie down onto a pipe the man has sat on, calling him a 'sodomite!' Although Juan had earlier told his friends that they weren't there 'to see who's got a bigger one', by the end of the film he is standing with his paddle upraised and grabbing his crotch, a triumphantly hetero hero.

The film is clearly as anti-gay as it is anti-ghoul, but it may also be open to alternative readings. This horror-movie spoof tends to mock Juan's machismo, representing it as a desperate exaggeration while exposing his homosexual panic as ludicrously overblown. Furthermore, the gay China and Primo are shown to be effective zombie-fighters, the former deftly wielding a slingshot and the latter using his bare hands to break necks in scenes where we are expected to admire their 'manly' capabilities. Perhaps most interestingly, the film has Lazaro, when he thinks he has been bitten and is about to turn into a zombie, declare his heretofore hidden love for Juan and ask to fellate him – a request that Juan overcomes his homophobia to grant, unzipping his fly. While it is true that Lazaro goes on to say that the request was a joke and to laughingly call Juan a 'faggot', this potentially homoerotic moment between two best friends suggests that, at some level, one male coming at another with an open mouth may be as much desired as it is feared. Lazaro may be a homo-zombie, but Juan, for love of his friend, is okay with being 'turned'.

MOTHERS

Inside (A l'intérieur) (2007)

Directors: Alexandre Bustillo and Julien Maury
Cast: Alysson Paradis (Sarah), Béatrice Dalle (The Woman), François-Régis Marchasson (Jean-Pierre)

Pregnant Sarah is in a car crash in which her husband, seated beside her, is killed. Afterwards, she sinks into a suicidal depression, losing all interest in her own life and that of her soon-to-be-born baby. On the night before she is to go to the hospital for the delivery, she is stalked and then attacked by a mysterious woman who seems to want to stab her in the womb with scissors. This stranger – known only as 'The Woman' in the credits – first appears right after Sarah wakes up from a nightmare, but in reality Sarah is still dreaming. The Woman is a fantasy projection of Sarah herself, a kind of dark double. This is how the Woman can be outside the house and then suddenly, inexplicably, inside: she is within Sarah's own mind. This is why the Woman and Sarah look so much alike: they both have long, dark hair and round faces; they both end up covered in blood, with similarly placed wounds; and they are both filmed as window or mirror reflections of one another – that is, when they are not indistinguishable shadowy figures. The Woman claims to have been a pregnant passenger in the car that Sarah crashed into. Really? Is it not more likely that she is Sarah's imaginary double?

As a grief-stricken widow unable to bear the thought that she would rather die than go on living, even if that means taking her baby with her, Sarah splits off that deadly portion of her psyche, creating a murderous doppelganger who appears to come from outside to threaten her and her child. Yet deep down, by providing herself with such an antagonist, Sarah is trying to reawaken her own will to survive and reconnect with the people around her, most importantly by saving the life of her baby. Thus, the Woman's first appearance is as a person who rings Sarah's doorbell, asking for help – the same request of others that Sarah unconsciously senses she must make. Earlier, Sarah's boss, Jean-Pierre, a potential love interest following the death of her husband, is brushed off by her, and when he comes to her house that night, the Woman stabs him in the groin and face until he is dead. By permanently removing this man from her life, the Woman shows Sarah how much she really did want a relationship. Similarly, Sarah has been dismissive of her own mother, claiming that she prefers to have dinner alone that night, and when her mother stops by, the Woman contrives to have Sarah kill her 'by mistake' with a knitting needle – the same needle Sarah has been using to make clothes for her baby. Once her mother is gone, Sarah misses her terribly, realising how much she did need that maternal connection. While one half of Sarah – the side represented by the Woman – may wish that she had never been born or loved a man if the result was to be that she would end up as a pregnant widow, the murder of her mother and of a future romantic partner shocks her into seeing that death and disconnection are not what she really wants.

Sarah's nightmarish realisations occur on Christmas Eve. At one point in the fight to protect her unborn baby, Sarah has her hand pinned to a wall by scissors wielded by the Woman, and later Sarah lies bloody and spreadeagled in bed. The references to Christ's stigmata and his suffering on the cross show how the Woman's persecution has brought out Sarah's spirit of self-sacrifice. In the end, the two adversaries become allies – after all, they are actually the same woman – when Sarah, by saying, 'It's stuck,' prompts the Woman to perform a caesarean section and cut the baby out of her, even though Sarah knows full well that this is likely to mean her own death. In the nightmare, Sarah thus demonstrates a willingness to give her own life for her child. In the end, when Sarah is shown eviscerated and dead while the Woman sits cradling the baby, we can see bloody murder and the theft of a child. Or we can consider that Sarah, having imagined making the ultimate sacrifice, has proven herself worthy to be a mother and is now rewarded with a vision of herself – as the Woman – with her baby in her arms.

The Babadook (2014)

Director: Jennifer Kent
Cast: Essie Davis (Amelia), Noah Wiseman (Samuel), Tim Purcell (The Babadook), Ben Winspear (Oskar)

'If it's in a word or it's in a look, you can't get rid of the Babadook.' When Amelia reads to her son, Samuel, the story of *Mister Babadook*, the spindly, charcoal-black title character seems to emerge from the pop-up book to terrify the six-year-old boy. Rather than soothing her son to sleep, this bedtime storybook character only increases his fear, making reality into a living nightmare soon shared by his mother, too. 'Wake up, Mommy,' he tells her. 'But you're the one who's asleep,' she tries to convince him and herself. Samuel's fear of the Babadook results in terrible behavioural problems that turn his frantic, sleep-deprived mother against her own son, whom she verbally abuses. This horror film explores 'a big taboo subject' – 'mothers who can't love their kids', according to writer-director Jennifer Kent.[55] Unable to cope with her son's shrieks of terror and defensive-aggressive actions, the mother herself begins to exhibit monstrous behaviour in reaction to her son's.

So what is the Babadook? In the film's backstory, Amelia's husband, Oskar, has been killed in a car accident as he is driving her to the hospital for Samuel to be born. Since the Babadook seems to wear Oskar's clothes, one meaning of this monster could be that he represents Samuel's fear that his mother will be taken from him as his father was. 'I don't want you to die,' the boy tells her. The Babadook could also be Amelia's unresolved grief over her husband, a melancholy that threatens to pull her and her son into death after him. 'We can be together,' she imagines Oskar saying; 'you just need to bring me the boy'. Since Oskar perished on the same day Samuel was born, the Babadook may also embody her terrible tendency to blame her son for her husband's demise. 'You don't know how many times I wished it was you, not him, that died,' she tells Samuel. And the horrible idea that the husband's death was somehow triggered by the son's birth may be an extreme version of a more common fear: that once a child is born, a wife will have to give up all romance with her husband to devote herself entirely to maternal care of her son. In the film, the widowed Amelia's wistful watching of television romances and her surreptitious self-pleasuring with a vibrator are both interrupted by the need to tend to her terrified son.

While the Babadook book may seem to be an avenue for fear to pop up into the world, the story also serves as 'a warning of what's to come if Amelia doesn't face this thing'[56] – her unresolved grief and unreasoning anger at Samuel over her husband's death. 'The more you deny, the stronger I get,' the Babadook says, and Amelia reads in the book about herself as the incarnation of the monster, strangling Samuel and then cutting her own throat. It is only by acknowledging the despairing widow and monstrous mother she has become that Amelia can quell the creature – not by denying its existence within her, but by recognising her own rage and deathward-tending depression and dealing with them. This healing process is figured in a scene of Amelia embracing and protecting her son from the Babadook, while leaving a bowl of worms to lessen the monster's hunger for fear.

Spring (2014)

Directors: Justin Benson and Aaron Moorhead
Cast: Lou Taylor Pucci (Evan), Nadia Hilker (Louise), Francesco Carnelutti (Angelo)

While travelling in Italy, Evan meets Louise, the woman of his dreams. There is only one problem: she is a 2,000-year-old monster who, every 20 years, finds a man to impregnate her and gives birth to a new version of herself, using his DNA. If he is still with her at the time of her rebirth and transformation, she will kill him with one of her tentacles. Evan must convince her not to transform, but to give up eternity and fall in love so that they can spend one human lifetime together. If he fails in the attempt, he will die.

Before going to Italy, Evan has spent the last several years caring for his mother, who has eventually died of cancer. Evan's romance with Louise is shadowed by horror because this new relationship is affected by his mother's dying. While he deeply loved his mother, Evan had to put his own life on hold while tending to her, and now that she has passed, his melancholy over her loss threatens to drag him down to death with her, preventing him from beginning life anew with another woman. This is why Louise's skin rots like that of his cancer-ridden mother and why he finds himself tending to her sickness (her current body is failing) rather than romancing her. In his own mind, Evan is still at his dying mother's bedside. Immediately following his mother's funeral, a friend suggests that Evan use his grief with girls in order to get a 'sympathy fuck', but the attempt to reinvigorate himself through sex fails. When Evan asks his friend to stay over, the man replies that he does not want to sleep in the mother's deathbed – and Evan may feel the same.

Now Evan is in Italy, but when he looks at Louise, he still sees his mother. Louise is a young woman, but she is revealed to be years older than he. Variously equipped with claws, fangs and tentacles, she is a monstrous combination of biological life-forms, an evolutionary soup of all past creatures – an oceanic Mother Nature who gives life but who also takes it back into herself, as Evan fears his mother will do with him, pulling him psychologically back into her body to die with her. Evan begins working for Angelo, a man so attached to his wife that, when she dies, he cannot bring himself to date anyone else but only gazes forlornly out at the ocean. Will Evan's continued ties to his dead mother similarly prevent him from seeing the young Louise? To be with her, Evan must conquer the association in his own mind between physical closeness to a woman and the threat of bodily decay and destruction. When another guy from the US speaks of females as 'octopussy', tries to have sex with Louise, and then is killed by her, Evan seems to see his worst fears confirmed. But Evan is not like that 'ugly American' tourist; he is committed to staying with Louise and overcoming his own immaturity. As if expressing Evan's own terror when he was at his mother's bedside, Louise says, 'I don't want to die and I don't want to watch anyone die.' Yet Evan himself is beginning to draw on inner strength. 'I've seen what happens to you,' he tells Louise (and his mother). 'I mean, I've seen this at its worst, right? And I can deal with that part.' Finding the courage to face illness, Evan is eventually able to confront death as well, to love his mother and to let her go, to find that closeness matters *because* it will eventually end. Because life is finite, 'there's motivation to make every second count', he tells Louise. And that is the way every horror romance should end.[57]

Evolution (2015)

Director: Lucile Hadzihalilovic
Cast: Max Brebant (Nicolas), Julie-Marie Parmentier (Mother), Roxane Duran (Stella)

Nicolas, a prepubescent boy in red swim trunks, dives into the sea and is mesmerised by the waving fronds of multicoloured fauna on the ocean floor – before being startled by the sight below him of a dead boy with a red starfish on his belly. 'I like to have this ambiguity, this element that it's both beautiful and repulsive, frightening and attractive,' says writer-director Lucile Hadzihalilovic,[58] who has described *Evolution* as 'the nightmare of a ten-year-old child unable to tear himself free of the "maternal waters"'.[59] The sea fronds are like the enfolding arms of a mother, wonderfully comforting but also potentially dangerous, for they threaten to drown the boy if he fails to grow up and separate himself from her amniotic embrace. (In French, *mer* [sea] and *mère* [mother] are homonyms.) The drowned boy with the red starfish gripping his belly is Nicolas's own fear that his mother's womb could become a watery tomb. In his bed at night, Nicolas dreams of a starfish reaching out one of its tentacles to grip his navel, and in another scene, the boy uses a rock to break off one of the creature's five arms. In this way, Nicolas attempts to cut the umbilical cord tying him to his mother, to differentiate himself as a land-dwelling boy from his marine and maternal origins. A nightmare vision of his mother writhing with other women on the seashore, their bodies joined to form a starfish shape, shows us his fear of female flesh as something from which he must extricate himself in order to evolve. Nicolas imagines caesarean sections which result in stillborn babies – those who were unable to make the transition from amniotic fluid to land. In his feverish mind, a woman sticks his navel with a needle, extracting blood from him, as if she were a mother feeding off her own son rather than nurturing him to become independent. The navel penetration could also be a child's way of imagining how babies are made, for after his belly button is fertilised, Nicolas is given an ultrasound and eventually gives birth in what is perhaps an attempt to deliver himself into the world.

As part of his growth into manhood, Nicolas begins to sketch drawings of a nurse, Stella, whose curls of red hair around her head he depicts as being like the wavy arms surrounding the centre of a starfish. The drawing, which the boy hides in his bed for his own viewing pleasure, shows Nicolas evolving from nature to culture even as he also transitions from his mother to a potential lover. In the film's final scene, Stella wraps her arms and legs around the boy while putting her mouth to his as the two of them swim underwater, surrounded by the swaying of sea fronds. At once beautiful and frightening, the scene depicts the boy's fear of drowning in a woman's watery embrace while simultaneously showing his desire for the kiss of life. In fact, Stella proves to be more mermaid than siren, for by breathing air into Nicolas, she enables him to survive underwater until she can bring him to a boat that is headed towards land and a city inhabited by men. And so Hadzihalilovic concludes her film about 'relationships to childbirth and the journey through puberty, seen here through the dark lens of a fantastic tale'.[60]

POSSESSION

The Possession (2012)

Director: Ole Bornedal
Cast: Natasha Calis (Em), Jeffrey Dean Morgan (Father), Kyra Sedgwick (Mother), Matisyahu (Exorcist)

'It's not my little girl any more ... It's this thing looking back at me ... Tell me she's still in there.' What parents haven't had these thoughts about their growing daughter, whether or not she's actually been possessed by a demon? Kids can make life a living hell, particularly ones that are acting out in reaction to their parents splitting up. 'The supernatural and divorce are intertwined, a metaphor,' say screenwriters Juliet Snowden and Stiles White, explaining, 'The daughter was possessed because ultimately the children are the victims of a divorce.'[61] Pre-teen daughter Em opens a demon box alone because her neglectful father is too busy on the phone to tend to her. She slips a ring from the box on to her finger, binding her to the malicious spirit, because her parents' marriage bond is broken. Shuttled between her overprotective mother and her negligent father, Em becomes a demon child with mood swings between the two extremes. While her germaphobic mother insists that shoes be removed so as not to track bacteria into the home, her father buys a house near the woods, resulting in an insect infestation where a swarm of moths flies down into Em's mouth. Dietary restrictions make Em a vegetarian while at her mother's house, but she gorges on pizza when staying with her permissive father. Schizophrenically torn between the two, Em stabs her father in the hand with a fork, eats raw meat from the fridge in front of her mother, and sees two fingers inside her throat while looking in the bathroom mirror, as if she were a binge-and-purge bulimic. Em overeats with ravenous hunger at a diner to show her father that she is starving for his affection, and she breaks table glasses and plates for her barefoot mother to step on to show her that rigid etiquette rules and hypervigilance cannot protect one from everything. In the end,

Em's mother learns to take a risk by allowing her daughter to be brought to an exorcist, and Em's father shows he cares by offering up his body in place of his daughter's for the demon to possess. The evil spirit departs from this family at the same time that the father and mother are reunited, and Em sits down to eat some pancakes with a healthy – not monstrous – appetite.

The Conjuring (2013)

Director: James Wan
Cast: Lili Taylor (Carolyn), Joseph Bishara (Bathsheba), Vera Farmiga (Lorraine), Joey King (Christine), Hayley McFarland (Nancy), Shanley Caswell (Andrea), Mackenzie Foy (Cindy), Kyla Deaver (April), Sterling Jerins (Judy)

Carolyn, her husband and their five daughters move to a remote farmhouse in rural Rhode Island. Noting that 'pretty much all of the family' is 'female', director James Wan has said that this 'gave the movie a very sort of feminine edge to it, and ... a very maternal quality'.[62] Indeed, this film is largely about the hidden horror of being a mother – a role that society pressures women to see as a privilege and a pleasure. The farmhouse was once inhabited by a mother named Bathsheba who killed her seven-day-old baby in front of the fireplace and then hanged herself. Any woman who would strike so directly and inexplicably at the sacred ideal of hearth and home must be a witch making a sacrifice to prove her love for Satan, but we might consider whether a constantly crying infant and post-partum depression might have had something to do with it.

'How could a mother kill her own child?' Carolyn asks Lorraine, a paranormal investigator who is herself a mother and who is called in to help when Bathsheba's ghost tries to possess Carolyn and induce her to kill her own daughters. Christine feels someone grab her foot in bed; Nancy is dragged by her hair across the kitchen; Andrea has a demonic woman leap on her from the top of a wardrobe; Cindy hears a spirit voice say that 'it wants my family dead'; and April sees the ghost of a previously murdered child in a mirror and is herself almost stabbed with scissors by her mother, Carolyn. Why do these safe domestic spaces – the nurturing kitchen, the womb-like bed and wardrobe – threaten to become a tomb? How can items associated with maternal care – scissors for cutting hair, a vanity mirror for putting on make-up – suddenly turn so deadly? The witch is said to target for possession 'the one who's the most psychologically vulnerable', so it seems strange that Carolyn would be chosen, since she appears to be such a blissfully happy and confident mother. However, it could be precisely because she so thoroughly represses all her anxiety and dissatisfaction that these feelings creep up on her and nearly take hold of her entirely. Her husband is an underpaid trucker whose long-hauls leave Carolyn as the sole parent at home with five daughters to shelter and feed with very little money. The icy draughts that blow through the house and the foul odours of rotten meat show her fear of being unable to protect and provide for her family. Her daughters complain about the new house, annoy and worry her with their games of hide and clap, and interrupt what few attempts at love-making she is able to share with her husband. Through it all, Carolyn maintains a smile on her face, but the buried rage and resentment eventually come out and she attacks her family like a woman possessed by an evil spirit.

In one scene, Carolyn seems happy folding laundry for her kids while her husband is away, but the song on the radio – 'the night fills my lonely place' – suggests a certain discontent with the domestic life of a mother. Later, the paranormal investigator, Lorraine, is gathering laundry from a clothes line when a ghostly form appears in one of the sheets – a scare that seems to come from within the very doing of a maternal task. A mother herself, Lorraine is also susceptible to psychic invasion by the filicidal Bathsheba, as if Lorraine, too, harbours some unacknowledged ill will towards her own daughter, Judy. It may be that Lorraine resents Judy for making her feel guilty about spending so much time away from home on her investigative work. 'I miss you,' Judy tells her mother and has them exchange necklaces ('This way we'll always be together'), but instead of serving as a kind of umbilical cord to maintain a positive maternal connection, Lorraine's necklace is used by the witch as a conduit to harm the daughter through the mother. Thus, Judy is haunted by the sight of malicious Bathsheba brushing a creepy doll's hair – a demonic repetition of the loving way Lorraine would brush Judy's hair, suggesting a latent menace within Lorraine towards her daughter. A further explanation for this menace can be found if we look at a prior paranormal investigation involving a farmer who, after being molested as a child by his father, became possessed ('a dark spirit made its home in this man') and turned into a killer of his own family. Lorraine has been particularly traumatised by this case, having seen something terrible in the farmer that she won't talk about. Could it be that his case reminded her of when she, too, was abused as a child, instilling fear in her that she might grow up to become an abuser of her own daughter? Society must allow mothers to recognise that, like everyone else, they have troubled histories and present-day reasons for resentment. Otherwise, they will continue to be haunted and possessed by these dark feelings and visit them upon their own children.

SENIOR CITIZENS

Bubba Ho-Tep (2002)

Director: Don Coscarelli
Cast: Bruce Campbell (Sebastian/Elvis), Edith Jefferson (Elderly Woman), Larry Pennell (Kemosabe), Ossie Davis (Jack)

In the town of Mud Creek, Texas, Sebastian is wasting away along with other senior citizens being warehoused in a retirement home before their corpses are carted off to a funeral home. Lacking in élan and vitality, increasingly dispirited by the daily round of eating and excreting, Sebastian has begun to wonder whether there is 'anything to life other than food [and] shit'. Enter the figure of what Sebastian most fears, the total reduction of self to mere body: an Egyptian mummy that sucks old people's souls out of their anuses and then expels the residue down the toilet. Sebastian, who spends most of his time lying in bed in a state of torpor, is scared that the mummy will 'violate' him while he is asleep. The mummy's own slumber was disturbed when his tomb was desecrated and his body placed in the back of a vehicle, from which it ended up being dropped into a creek, much as the senior citizens of Mud Creek are driven away and dumped after they die. The mummy's curse is the curse of being old: entombed in decaying flesh, more and more immobilised, and eventually buried and forgotten.

Rather than wallow in self-pity or fall into apathy, Sebastian has to stand up and fight for life. He begins by doing battle with the mummy's vanguards, some giant scarab beetles, whose threat he is initially inclined to dismiss: 'Big damn bugs, all right? ... [But] what do I care? I got a growth on my pecker.' The fact that, after defeating one of these ugly black cockroaches, Sebastian gets an erection for the first time in years suggests that the fight has enabled him to overcome his fear of impotence and penile cancer. Interestingly, unlike Sebastian, an elderly female resident of the rest home succumbs to a beetle attack. Earlier, we saw her steal some eyeglasses from a helpless fellow resident in an iron lung, and then she is gorging ecstatically on stolen chocolates when a beetle crawls under the bedcovers and up between her legs. Her defeat implies that masturbatory self-indulgence and preying on others weaker than oneself are not effective ways of dealing with old age.

For the right kind of inspiration, Sebastian turns to Kemosabe, a male retiree with the courage to put on a black mask and fire his six-shooters at the soul-sucking Egyptian mummy. And, just as this Tonto masquerades as his friend and hero, the Lone Ranger, so an African-American man named Jack is infused with the spirit of civil rights leader Jack Kennedy when he himself combats the mummy. Seeing his fellow senior citizens put up a fight, Sebastian, an Elvis impersonator, is moved to become the King he has 'always fantasised being', that 'two-fisted Hound Dog' who could 'out-strum, outrace, out-fight, and outwit the bad guys'. No longer bedridden, Sebastian/Elvis mobilises with the aid of a walker and a motorised wheelchair. Refusing to be wasted without a fight, he confronts that 'undead sack of shit', the mummy. And, if 'small souls are those that don't have much fire for life', he proves he has a big soul by setting fire to the mummy. He reclaims his dignity from the undead.

Drag Me to Hell (2009)

Director: Sam Raimi
Cast: Lorna Raver (Ganush), Alison Lohman (Christine), David Paymer (Jacks), Justin Long (Fiancé), Reggie Lee (Coworker)

An aged gypsy woman named Ganush applies for a mortgage extension to save her house from being repossessed, but loan officer Christine decides to deny it. Ambitious Christine, in line for a promotion, wants to prove her worth to Jacks, the male bank manager, and so she chooses profit over compassion. In a sense, she sides with 'father' Jacks against 'mother' Ganush. When the proud gypsy woman falls to her knees and grasps Christine's hands to beg her for the loan, Christine backs away, horrified, creating a spectacle of misery that is witnessed by everyone in the bank and which Ganush considers to be a public shaming. Though Jacks approves of Christine's cold-hearted calculation in refusing the loan, Ganush takes revenge by placing a witch's curse on her and by returning to haunt her throughout the film.

But is Ganush a witch or does a guilty Christine just see her that way? The film explores Christine's gerontophobia by having this gypsy woman embody a number of anxieties associated with growing old. This poor, foreign, decrepit female is everything that Christine fears to be, and yet the movie keeps reminding her that, as much as she might idealise wealth, whiteness and youthful strength (qualities she finds in male father figures), Christine – like everybody else – has a body subject to impoverishment, embarrassment, decay and death (weaknesses linked to the mother). Ganush has a thick Hungarian accent marking her as foreign, but Christine, who grew up on a Midwest farm, is also marked by her regional speech, even though she practises with language tapes to try to fit in. Ganush cannot help taking out her false teeth so that she can gum some candies at the bank – an appetite Christine views as grotesque because she, who was once 'pork queen' at the country fair, fears becoming fat again and no longer slim and successful. Christine's farm-girl roots show when she brings a harvest cake, which she made with eggs laid by geese, on a visit to meet her fiancé's patrician parents. Feeling their disdain for her humble background and having just admitted that she has an alcoholic mother, Christine looks down to see Ganush's glass eye staring up at her from inside the cake. Ganush is the embarrassing mother Christine can't leave behind, the bodily weakness that she is heir to in the same way that no one can escape being born of mortal flesh. Christine is disgusted when Ganush coughs up phlegm at the bank, yet Christine herself later gets a nosebleed and is publicly shamed when the blood splatters on her boss. Ganush's yellowed fingernails appear claw-like and her false teeth seem sharp *because* Christine fears being dragged down into a world of decay and devoured by death. When Ganush's corpse vomits maggots into Christine's mouth, and when the old woman's cadaver rolls over on top of her in a grave, it is the threat of her own decomposition and demise that is really haunting Christine.

And yet acknowledging bodily weakness can enable spiritual strength, for it is our shared sense of vulnerability that leads to compassion. Christine realises this in the end when she extends sympathy to a coworker and refuses to sacrifice him to save herself, thus making up for her shameful scapegoating of Ganush.

The Visit (2015)

Director: M Night Shyamalan
Cast: Olivia DeJonge (Becca), Ed Oxenbould (Tyler), Deanna Dunagan (Nana), Peter McRobbie (Pop Pop)

Teenage Becca and her younger brother, Tyler, journey to a remote Pennsylvania farmhouse to visit their grandparents, Nana and Pop Pop, whom they have never seen before. Although the kids are at first comforted by Nana's chicken pot pies and fresh-baked cookies, her crawling around at night and her projectile vomiting make them fear she is possessed. Similarly, the calming effect of Pop Pop's folksy chats and quaint wood-chopping tends to be offset by his Alzheimer's-fuelled paranoia and his sudden attacks on innocent people. In the opinion of one critic, *The Visit* is 'a prime candidate for the most gerontophobic film ever made': 'the movie's fear of the elderly is pathological ... It uses dirty adult nappies as a source of hideous threat. Memory loss is presented as freaky, good for a scare ... Essentially it presents old people ... as if they're already dead: smelly nightmares looming up at you in their soiled nightclothes.'[63] But the fact is that many kids (and adults) *are* frightened by old people. Perhaps the film could be accused of exacerbating this fear, but it seems intended to have the opposite effect: it is horror cinema as exposure therapy, subjecting audience members to movie doses of terror so that they can face their fears in the theatre and then live a more anxiety-free life with their actual grandparents.

The movie's characters are the means by which we vicariously confront our gerontophobia. Twelve-year-old Tyler keeps his emotions bottled up inside. Apart from the misogynistic rap songs he uses to defend himself against feeling rejected by older girls, he keeps a lid on all anger and despondency. His elderly grandfather, who was fired from his job and who suicidally 'cleans' his rifle, forces Tyler to acknowledge his own depression over feelings of inadequacy. The boy has been suppressing his rage out of fear of the monster he might become should he let it out. When Pop Pop rubs his dirty adult diaper in Tyler's face, the anal-retentive boy must confront the 'incontinence' he fears in himself. Tyler finally lets it all out when he tackles his grandfather, thereby proving that he can channel his rage into effective action, unlike the time he froze on the football field. Tyler doesn't have to be afraid of his grandfather any more because he need no longer fear himself.

As for Becca, she sees in Nana the spectre of her own miserable loneliness and anger at feeling trapped. Sometimes Nana sits alone in her rocking chair, wrapping her scarf suffocatingly around her face. At other times, she almost literally climbs the walls, growling and baring her teeth like a werewolf. Becca feels forgotten by her father, who divorced her mother and left the family. Due to the lack of his approval, Becca has been unable to look at herself in the mirror, fearing the lonely girl she might see there, abandoned because of her worthlessness. Becca does not want to end up as a lonely old woman, confined to her house with only domestic chores to do. When Nana asks her to climb inside the oven to clean it and then shuts the door, this fairy-tale image of Gretel in the witch's oven forces Becca to confront her fear of being swallowed up by a life of domestic drudgery. Later, Becca peers into a mirror where she sees Nana's lost and rage-filled face coming up behind her own, the spitting image of what she most fears she might become. Breaking the mirror to grab one of its shards and then turning to confront Nana face-to-face, Becca is able to use the shard to defeat the spectre of her nightmarish future self. By independently realising that she is indeed worthy of love and approval, Becca can stop projecting her fears onto her grandmother. Only by looking at herself can she conquer her gerontophobia.

SHARKS

Open Water (2003)

Director: Chris Kentis
Cast: Blanchard Ryan (Susan), Daniel Travis (Daniel)

While on a scuba-diving vacation in the Caribbean, young couple Susan and Daniel are accidentally abandoned at sea. We shudder with them throughout a fearfully long day and night as, floating in their life vests, they wait in hope that their absence will be noticed and a search team sent to rescue them before they are set upon and devoured by sharks. This watery world is not their home. There is water everywhere, but not a drop to drink. They can breathe the air above, but if they inhale in the depths below, they will drown. Glimpses of dorsal fins fill them with terror, but visibility under the ocean's surface is poor, so they live in constant fear of a sudden shark attack. They do not know where these ancient sea-creatures are, what they will do or why.

The prospect of violent death is frightening, but so, too, is the incomprehensibility of these alien creatures, who are but one part of an entire ocean environment that is unknown and beyond their control. 'I can't stand not knowing what is under me,' Susan says. Cast adrift in this vast sea so devoid of humans or humane behaviour (the film's original title was *Blue Desert*), the couple confronts both 'nothing that is not there and the nothing that is'.[64] They are brought to the terrifying realisation that the structures that give their life meaning do not signify in the same way for the creatures in this alien environment, just as the conventions that usually govern films do not necessarily pertain to this one. The couple can swim or stay put, remember or forget some coral landmark, wave their arms as a distress signal or remain motionless – the ocean appears indifferent either way. The sharks do not seem to care whether it is day or night, whether the couple get along or fight, whether fear or bravery is exhibited in the face of death. After blaming each other for their situation and panicking as the sun goes down and the sharks attack, the two show courage, offering reassurance and love to one another, and eventually dawn breaks. But none of this stops the sharks from killing Daniel, as the morning sun rises to reveal his dead body. The survival gear they have, the knowledge gleaned from watching TV documentaries, the knife that Daniel brandishes – these are of no avail against the sharks, nor is any of the other human technology successful, for the helicopter and speedboats mobilised to rescue them all fail to do so. Unlike in most movies, love and courage are not rewarded. Man-made explosives blow up the shark in *Jaws*, but here humans don't triumph against these denizens of the deep.

Yet there are few scenes more poignant than the ones of Susan and Daniel floating together through this nightmare side by side, with her hand on his shoulder or with him being held by her. Doesn't their ability to draw together in the face of probable and then certain death speak to the value of human love? In the end, when Susan removes her life vest and sinks below the waves, it may be because she fears that the sharks will be coming for her and she does not want to share Daniel's fate. Or it could be a testament to the connection she had with her lover that she does not want to go on living without him.

SUCCUBAE

Jennifer's Body (2009)

Director: Karyn Kusama
Cast: Megan Fox (Jennifer), Amanda Seyfried (Needy), Johnny Simmons (Chip), Joshua Emerson (Jonas)

High-school cheerleader Jennifer turns succuba and begins seducing and slaying her male classmates. Why? The most likely answer is revenge for a rape. Four members of an indie band, intent on sacrificing a virgin to Satan in exchange for fame and fortune, lure Jennifer into the woods where they stab her repeatedly with a knife – an act that is filmed to resemble a gang rape. Desire for vengeance then turns Jennifer into a distaff version of her male predators, as she leads innocent guys into the woods where she uses her monster mouth to bite out their necks and feed on the flesh of their bellies. Traumatised by her rapists' knife, Jennifer fights back by becoming a castrating *vagina dentata*, driven by their violence to the opposite extreme. And, just as the band members assaulted her in order to live up to the media image of successful rock stars as 'ladykillers', so Jennifer preys on guys because she sees her serial conquests as building up her image of irresistible feminine allure. 'She's eating boys,' Jennifer's friend Needy says. 'They, like, make her really pretty and glow-y, and her hair looks amazing.' According to screenwriter Diablo Cody, 'Jennifer is a product of a culture that pressures girls to be skinny, beautiful, and just like movie stars.'[65] It also seems significant that the boys Jennifer kills are ones Needy has shown some romantic interest in, so another reason for Jennifer's slayings may be competition with her best friend. Indeed, Jennifer's murderous assertions of independence may be mere cover for the fact that she is really just as needing of love and approval as her friend, especially given that, when Jennifer doesn't kill, the only consequence is that she ends up looking as lonely and imperfect as any other girl.

But perhaps the real reason Jennifer is killing guys is not to take them away from Needy, but instead to eliminate them so she can have Needy for herself. The two girls have had a 'sandbox love' since they used to 'play boyfriend-girlfriend' together as children, and they are still close friends despite the social division that would normally separate a 'babe' like Jennifer from a Needy 'dork' – so close that an observing classmate calls them 'lesbigay'. When Jennifer lures Needy's boyfriend, Chip, away by telling him that Needy has been unfaithful, the lie has a kernel of truth in it: Needy *has* been unfaithful – to Jennifer with Chip. When Jennifer masturbates Jonas, a jock she plans to kill, asking him if he misses his slain football buddy, the reference to same-sex desire suggests that Jennifer's slaying of Jonas is related to her longing for Needy. Needy, too, seems to be struggling with repressed desire for her friend. When the two hold hands at a rock concert, Needy drops Jennifer's hand when she sees her looking at the lead male singer, and a mysterious fire breaks out, reflected in Needy's glasses, as though her jealous rage had somehow started it. When Needy has sex with Chip, she looks up to see blood forming a heart shape in the ceiling while she telepathically senses that, in another location, Jennifer is feeding on one of her male prey. Needy's terror at that slaughter occurs simultaneously with her orgasm, as if she is excited along with Jennifer by the elimination of the men separating them. Jennifer's monstrous mouth has a strange fascination for Needy; she is both drawn to the female sex and afraid of her friend's and her own lesbian desire. (Jennifer's vaginal maw is like the 'Devil's Kettle' whirlpool which threatens – or promises? – to draw people into a bottomless vortex.)

Finally, in a scene that blends girlish play and erotic attraction, Jennifer leans over and begins kissing Needy, who gradually responds with reciprocated passion as the two make out in bed.

But Needy is unable to accept sexual desire as continuous with female friendship. Succumbing to homophobia, she ultimately and violently rejects Jennifer's advances, ripping the heart-shaped BFF locket from her friend's neck and stabbing her in the heart with a knife. Even before Jennifer is stabbed (an act which resembles the band's knife-rape of her), all the life seems to go out of her when Needy tears off that locket, for it seems her friend's love is all that she really lived for.[66]

Under the Skin (2013)

Director: Jonathan Glazer
Cast: Scarlett Johansson (The Woman)

A predatory alien, disguised to look as beautiful as a Hollywood actress (in fact, Scarlett Johansson), cruises the streets of Scotland in a van, luring unsuspecting men to take a ride with her. (In truth, many of the men were regular Glaswegian guys unaware that their conversations with this woman were being filmed by hidden cameras. They gave their consent afterwards.) The banal dialogue of the males' pick-up lines – 'I think you are gorgeous'; 'I'm all alone; you're all alone' – shows how formulaic and superficial these interactions are. Given that the men are so attracted to the external trappings of femininity, all it takes is some red lipstick, a fur coat, and black undergarments to draw them in. After being driven to a trysting site, one guy walks all around her, fascinated by her dark hair, her lips and her eyes, entranced by her appearance. At a different place, another man follows her as if mesmerised by the sight of her flesh as she performs a striptease in front of him. So driven is he by the desire to possess her body that he does not notice himself sinking into a sticky black substance. Submerged within the viscous liquid, this man with an erect penis reaches his hand up to try to touch the woman above, who has been able to walk on the liquid's surface like Christ walking on water. With these images, the film suggests that the man's sexual pursuit may ultimately be a desire for something higher, an emotional or spiritual connection beyond the merely physical. However, by viewing women mostly as bodies to be consumed, the man becomes mired in his own lust, sinking down to the purely physical level and unable to rise above that. The man then implodes, his innards sucked out of his skin where they run down a chute to be processed as food for the aliens. Having reduced women to sexual objects, to flesh at a meat market, the man has also done the same thing to himself, so it is fitting that he comes to such a beastly end.[67]

It Follows (2014)

Director: David Robert Mitchell
Cast: Maika Monroe (Jay), Jake Weary (Hugh), Daniel Zovatto (Greg), Keir Gilchrist (Paul)

In an eighties slasher film, teenage sex was often met with death at the hands of a Freddy or Jason, who represented paternal punishment or the teens' own guilt doing them in. It was Reagan-era repression killing the sixties spirit of free love. In *It Follows*, after a movie date, a young woman named Jay makes love with Hugh in the back seat of his car, but then this seemingly amiable guy turns nasty, saying that their intercourse has cursed her: she will die unless she has sex with someone else, thereby passing the curse on to him. Beyond the fear of sexually transmitted diseases as potentially fatal in the age of HIV-AIDS, this movie also deals with romantic teens finding that adult disillusionment can be psychologically deadly. As Jay muses after her back-seat tryst with Hugh, 'I used to daydream about being old enough to go on dates and drive around with friends in cars … It was never about going anywhere really, just having some sort of freedom, I guess. Now that we're old enough, where the hell do we go?' The It that relentlessly stalks these teens is the fear that growing up will mean the death of their romantic hopes and dreams. That is why Its movement seems so slow and inevitable, stealthily creeping up on them. It is based on a 'recurring nightmare' that writer-director David Robert Mitchell had as a child: 'the feeling that something was coming and would always be coming was very disturbing'.[68]

When Jay sleeps with Greg, a boy who does not love her, he is promptly stalked and murdered by It, which takes the form of his divorced and lonely mother who forces sex on him. Greg is killed by fear of a potential future of adult acrimony and desperate desire. Despite an awareness of Greg's cursed demise, Jay's friend Paul then offers to combat It and have intercourse with her. Paul and Jay have known each other since they were kids, but younger Paul cannot tell if the sexually mature Jay is 'a girl or a monster'. For her part, Jay does not know whether Paul's offer to sleep with her is altruistic or merely a cover for his own lust. 'I want to help,' he says. 'Do you?' is her dubious reply. After all, when they were still children, 'horndog' Paul went on to kiss Jay's sister right after kissing her. But the fact that Paul determines to battle It in the same pool where he and Jay had their first kiss suggests he may still have the innocence and hope necessary to combat adult disillusionment. Perhaps Paul's belief in love can inspire a renewed faith in the near-terminally jaded Jay? After the two have sex, they are shown walking hand in hand down a tree-lined suburban street, as in the romantic 'image' Jay used to have 'of myself holding hands with a really cute guy'. A glimpse behind them suggests that someone or some*thing* may be following them, but perhaps their belief in each other will be enough to quell their unconscious fear of failed love. While 'Jay opens herself up to danger through sex ... sex is the one way in which she can free herself from that danger', according to Mitchell; 'love and sex are two ways in which we can – at least temporarily – push death away'.[69]

VAMPIRES

Dracula: Pages from a Virgin's Diary (2001)

Director: Guy Maddin
Cast: Zhang Wei-Qiang (Dracula), CindyMarie Small (Mina), Johnny Wright (Harker), Tara Birtwhistle (Lucy), David Moroni (Van Helsing)

This revisionist version of Bram Stoker's classic narrative presents excellent examples of 'hypocrisy horror', a kind of scapegoating where authority figures abuse their power and punish others for acts they themselves would commit. As in the original novel set in the late Victorian era, four male characters try to prevent two women from being preyed upon by the vampire, but here the men are really trying to repress the liberating force of female desire, as the women want to be bitten and freed from the males' possessive control. As director Guy Maddin puts it, 'I don't even think Dracula exists. He's just the embodiment of female lust and male jealousy.'[70] Dracula is punished for exciting the women beyond the bounds of feminine propriety and for lusting after them in ways that Victorian gentlemen want – but are not allowed – to do, at least not publicly. Thus, when Mina reads the diary account of how her fiancé, Harker, succumbed to the bloodlust of some female vampires, she kneels and brazenly opens his trousers, but he rejects her advances. Enforcing the double standard by which men can clandestinely satisfy their lust with prostitutes while ladies must demur, Harker has Mina wrap up the diary in a nun's veil, using repression to keep her pure. Similarly, when Lucy wonders, 'Why can't a woman marry three men?' her suitors are horrified, for convention dictates that only one of them should get to possess her. Nevertheless, while her fiancé is sidelined, the other three all pump their blood into her body through a tube. This transfusion is also a penetration, which suggests a sexual rivalry over her and foreshadows the later scene where they will all pierce her with their stakes.

Earlier, the ringleader, Van Helsing, had 'examined' Lucy for signs of vampirism by sticking a tongue depressor in her mouth, feeling her chest and checking under her dress. Then, while peering voyeuristically through binoculars at Dracula's appetitive affection for Mina, Van Helsing cranks a wind-up flashlight near his crotch. When Dracula strips off some of Mina's undergarments, Van Helsing moves to cover them up. While this act may appear to be about preserving modesty, it also allows him to 'get to molest her by putting his own coat over the top' of her underthings, as Maddin points out.[71] Finally, after diverting most of his sexual energy into violence and proving his superior prowess by spearing Dracula, Van Helsing surreptitiously picks up Mina's undergarments and slips them into his coat. This is presumably so that he can indulge in private the very same desires he just destroyed Dracula for displaying.

Byzantium (2012)

Director: Neil Jordan
Cast: Gemma Arterton (Clara), Jonny Lee Miller (Ruthven), Saoirse Ronan (Eleanor), Caleb Landry Jones (Frank)

Over 200 years ago, a working-class girl named Clara is raped and forced into prostitution by Ruthven, a military officer. When Clara discovers that she is dying of tuberculosis contracted from men in the bordello, she saves her own life (in a sense) by seizing the opportunity to become a vampire. The buxom Clara still dresses in cleavage-revealing outfits and fishnet stockings, but now she uses her feminine wiles 'to punish those who prey on the weak' and 'to curb the power of men'. Luring lustful males to her, she deploys an elongating thumbnail ('the pointed nails of justice') to penetrate their neck veins and feed off *them* before they can exploit her. But rather than being a dispassionate dispenser of justice, Clara seems trapped by her own desire to take revenge, to appropriate the men's phallic power and rape them with it. Director Neil Jordan has described 'this thumbnail that grows' as being 'like a strange erection' that is more 'terrifying' and 'sexual' than fangs.[72] In his view, Clara has 'a rather shocking ability to use her sexuality and to treat killing as a kind of orgasm'.[73] The fact that 'morbidly sexy' Clara is condemned to an eternity of feeding off men suggests that she has not freed herself from their baleful influence, but is still caught up in a dynamic of wounding and revenge.

Clara has a daughter, Eleanor, whom she tries to protect by sending her to a convent-like orphanage, but when Ruthven rapes Eleanor, giving her terminal syphilis, Clara 'saves' her daughter by making her a vampire. Clara sets herself up as a madam running a brothel, but she assures Eleanor, 'It's all right, angel. I'll make sure you're not involved.' In this way, the mother tries to preserve her daughter's 'angelic' purity, keeping her away from all 'demonic' sexuality. To Clara, this means all men, and so she also tries to separate Eleanor from her potential boyfriend, Frank. Unlike the hot-blooded, rapacious Ruthven, Frank, who is pale from leukaemia, poses no clear threat, yet Clara feels she cannot take any chances with her daughter, who is made to fear that any sexual contact with Frank 'would be fatal'. And so, if the mother is overly embroiled in the hot world of deadly passions, the daughter is exiled to the cold world of forced abstinence and loneliness. As Eleanor tells Frank, 'That's me, where light barely penetrates and it's cold … Everything outside of time is cold.'

In the end, Clara is able to find a male vampire who uses his sword to chop off another bloodsucking male's head in order to save her. With this, the film suggests that there are still some men out there who are willing to defy the patriarchal order and curb their own voracious desires. As for Eleanor, she finds warmth in the blood of her boyfriend Frank, turning him into a vampire, but her act is not that of a predator who wounds in order not to be violated. Instead, believing in his gentle love for her, she 'saves' him as he is dying of leukaemia so that the two of them can be passionate *and caring* companions throughout eternity.

Only Lovers Left Alive (2013)

Director: Jim Jarmusch
Cast: Tom Hiddleston (Adam), Tilda Swinton (Eve), John Hurt (Christopher Marlowe), Mia Wasikowska (Ava)

Having survived as the undead for centuries, vampires Adam and Eve have developed a deep appreciation for the best in this world, all of the arts and sciences that make life worth living. In addition, their heightened sensitivity to the world around them has led to an ecological understanding of how everything on Earth is interdependent, as in the 'spooky action at a distance' of entangled particles as taught by quantum mechanics. In the film's opening, Adam wakes up in Detroit and Eve awakes in Tangiers, but a spinning overhead shot merges both of them with a vinyl record revolving on a turntable. Though they are thousands of miles apart, the two are still connected by their shared love of music. By contrast, Adam calls humans 'zombies' because they walk through life with their senses deadened to the wonders of the world, viewing music only as a means to make money and greedily fighting over and using up the Earth's resources – first, oil, and now, in the era of global warming, water. More humane than the humans, Adam and Eve do not prey on others but instead purchase their blood from black-market blood banks because they realise what a precious resource it is. For the electricity needed to power his guitars, Adam has built his own generator modelled on the dynamo of Nikola Tesla, whose revolutionary scientific ideas were allegedly suppressed by unimaginative and greedy power companies. 'If we had followed Tesla, we'd have free energy all over the fucking planet,' says writer-director Jim Jarmusch.[74]

Everywhere Adam looks, he sees humans wastefully depleting the world's resources, not only oil and water but even their own blood. Adam's friend, the vampire Christopher Marlowe, will no longer be capable of writing great works because his blood supply has been contaminated by humans who took too many drugs. And then there are the unevolved vampires like Eve's sister, Ava, who sinks her fangs into Adam's assistant, greedily draining the young man of all life. Adam sinks into a suicidal depression, planning to kill himself by firing a wooden bullet into his heart, but Eve crosses the miles that separate them to come to his rescue. As the two ancient vampires watch a pair of young human lovers kiss, they bare their fangs and move in on them. Have the vampires given in to their worst selves, feeding on and sacrificing others for their own survival? Or, inspired by the young lovers' embrace, have Adam and Eve decided not to kill, but to turn the human couple into immortals like themselves, living on through them and the power of love? Do they become a vampire Adam and Eve, founding a new race of evolved beings who know that, in the end, only lovers will be left alive? As Jarmusch has said, 'I'm not making a vampire story. I'm making a love story and they happen to be vampires.'[75]

WEREWOLVES

Red Riding Hood (2011)

Director: Catherine Hardwicke
Cast: Amanda Seyfried (Valerie), Shiloh Fernandez (Peter), Alexandria Maillot (Lucie), Billy Burke (Cesaire)

Back in mediaeval times, Valerie is about to accept Peter's invitation to come away with him when her elopement is stopped by news that her sister, Lucie, has been killed by a werewolf. The lycanthrope had drawn Lucie into the woods by forging a note from the man she loved. Now this same nightmarish creature appears to Valerie and tries to get her to come away with him. It turns out that the werewolf is really the girls' father, Cesaire, and his stealth attacks on them would seem to be a metaphor for molestation. Distanced from his wife who has been unfaithful, Cesaire grows too close to his daughters. 'I have been so disrespected,' he says. 'I have settled for far less than I deserve.' He first preys on Lucie, giving her the love bite he deludedly thinks of as a gift ('By birthright, the gift would go to my eldest daughter'), and then he turns to Valerie as the next in line for his wolfish attentions. Appearing only at night, his face transformed by beastly desire, Cesaire is barely recognisable to Valerie as her father – a fact she also represses as too awful to acknowledge. But sometimes, during her daylight hours, she seems to half-remember and realise the truth. At a festival, when she sees a drunken reveller pretending to hump her father who is passed out on the ground, she pulls the man off him, and her father says, 'You're my good girl. I'm so sorry.' In this rare moment, he would seem to be apologising for what he has done to her.

Later, in a monologue intended as a boast but which is also part confession, Cesaire says, 'Valerie, come with me … One bite and you'll be like me … It's a gift my father gave to me that now I give to you.' Having been preyed upon by his own father, Cesaire is the abused become the abuser, threatening to pass along a distorted view of love as lustful violation. And Valerie, as is sometimes the case with incest survivors, must fight the tendency to feel ashamed or to blame herself: 'Maybe the wolf knew something I didn't,' she worries. 'Maybe there was something dark in me.' Because of her father's actions, Valerie has also grown fearful of all men as potential marauders – even of her beloved Peter, which is why she does not follow his urging to come away with him, since it reminds her too much of her father's. Peter does help Valerie expose and defeat her werewolf father – 'You're not so terrifying when the sun is up' – but by having Peter bitten in the fight, the movie acknowledges that he, too, could give way to rapacious desire. 'When the moon rises, I'll be like him, a beast,' Peter fears, and so he leaves her, vowing not to return until he has matured enough to keep his desire within consensual bounds.

Jack & Diane (2012)

Director: Bradley Rust Gray
Cast: Riley Keough (Jack), Juno Temple (Diane)

A mash-up of teen romance, coming-out tale and horror, this lesbian werewolf film has the tagline 'Love is a monster'. Jack is a tough-talking skater girl who wears cut-off jeans and metal-band T-shirts. Diane is a fragile pixie in a babydoll dress. When Jack, butch and brash, comes on to Diane, the inexperienced girl is initially hesitant. 'Do you like sushi?' Jack asks. 'I don't know,' Diane says and then spits it out. When Jack tries to engage in phone sex, the voice on the other end of the line says, 'I'm not gay,' and claims to be Diane's identical twin sister, Karen. Later, Jack watches a web porn video in which 'Karen' was drugged and taken sexual advantage of by some unscrupulous men. 'I told her she should say it was me [who was attacked],' Diane reports, and we suspect that in fact it was – that Diane herself was the victim. Such experiences go some way towards explaining why Diane is so reluctant to make herself vulnerable again. The nosebleeds she gets around Jack signify Diane's fearful anticipation of getting hurt. When Jack slips off Diane's underwear in bed and adopts a position above her, Diane is reminded of what the men in the video did to 'Karen' and so pushes Jack away.

But Diane is not just afraid of being victimised by rapacious passion. She is equally frightened by her own ferocious desire, which, once unleashed, might become all-consuming. When Diane gets excited, she imagines herself transforming into a ravenous monster that rips out and devours Jack's heart. It is as though, having repressed her sapphic passion for so long, Diane fears it will leap forth with uncontrollable strength if she lets it out. It could also be that homophobia leads her to dread her own same-sex desire as something monstrous. Even as she links her lover's name to hers by writing 'jackanddiane' in her notebook, Diane also has nightmare visions of coarse female hairs braiding together and coiling around slimy viscera – an image that shows her inner turmoil over what lesbian love might mean. Luckily, no-nonsense Jack has a knack for allaying Diane's fears with erotic humour that assumes a reciprocal and healthy desire. When Diane tells her that 'I dreamed I ate you', Jack's response is 'That's nice.'

Yet Jack, too, is subject to her own personal form of dread, which comes true when Diane plans to leave her in order to go study abroad. 'You've taken my insides and I'm not myself any more, and it's just so evil,' Jack accuses. In an expression of her wounded rage, Jack's nose starts to bleed and *she* now imagines *herself* as a monster devouring Diane – the vicious version of something Jack told her earlier: 'I just want to unzip my body and put you in there.' The movie suggests that the two women can transform the monster back into romance, but only by admitting their shared vulnerability and their matching rage to feed the beast.[76]

WITCHES

Antichrist (2009)

Director: Lars von Trier
Cast: Willem Dafoe (He), Charlotte Gainsbourg (She)

When this film's title appears, its final *t* is in the form of the female symbol: *Antichris♀*. In the movie, a woman smashes a man's testicles with a block of wood, masturbates him until he ejaculates blood, and bolts a grindstone to his leg after drilling a hole through his flesh. The film won a special 'anti-prize' at Cannes for being 'the most misogynist movie from the self-proclaimed biggest director in the world'.[77] Is the horror in this movie merely an example of the director's gynophobia run amok, or can the film be seen as having more feminist implications?

'He' and 'She' – the two are only identified as such in the credits – are a present-day couple living in Seattle. Studying the notorious witch-hunting manual known as the *Malleus Maleficarum*, she is writing a feminist thesis decrying the patriarchal persecution of women as witches. One day, as she is making love with her husband, their son opens his baby gate and falls out of a window to his death. She blames herself for putting her own sex drive above her son's safety. The couple travel to a cabin in an Edenic, wooded setting, but her self-accusations, combined with her grief and despair over her son's loss, infect her view of nature, which she now sees as 'Satan's church'. The hundreds of acorns that fall and die just so that one can take root and allow the tree to propagate, the baby chick that falls from its nest and is then devoured by a predatory bird – these sights remind her of her own negligence as Mother Nature, her own lust which led her to disregard her falling son. This jaundiced view of herself and her surroundings proves contagious for her husband, too. 'I see her anxiety spreading to nature and to him,' says writer-director Lars von Trier.[78] In one scene, the husband watches a stillborn fawn dropping from the womb of a deer. He begins to blame his wife for the death of their son. The wife's guilt is further fed by her reading of the witch-hunting manual. Rather than defending women, she now condemns herself and all females as servants of the Devil, forces for evil in the world. Believing that Eve's lust caused the Fall of Adam and all mankind, she begs her husband to hit her during sex, to punish her sin. In effect castrating him and then cutting off her own clitoris, she tries to bring an end to Mother Nature's mindless propagation, the physical desire that she now equates with death after the fall of her son.

Her desperate acts are a cry for help – something her husband, even though he is a psychotherapist, fails to see. Instead of bringing her back to reality through love, he lets his fear triumph, himself becoming infected by her belief that she is a witch. Acting like one of the inquisitors and torturers in the *Malleus Maleficarum*, he strangles her to death and then sets fire to her body, thus hanging and burning her as a witch. But in the film's final image he sees hundreds of faceless women approaching him – all the anonymous women from the past whose pleas for help were ignored or misunderstood, one of whom was his wife. This film has not forgotten them.

The Witch (2015)

Director: Robert Eggers
Cast: Harvey Scrimshaw (Caleb), Anya Taylor-Joy (Thomasin), Kate Dickie (Mother)

A Puritan family in seventeenth-century New England ekes out a meagre living on the edge of a wooded wilderness. To survive, all they have is each other and their trust in God. However, believing so fervently that everyone is a sinner and that wolves may come in sheep's clothing, they let their faith turn to paranoid fear and suspicion. Accusing each other of being in league with the Devil, they fall into mutual recriminations and tear their own family apart. But what may be most interesting about *The Witch* is the way the title figure becomes an outlet not just for fears, but for unspeakable desires.

Teenage son Caleb talks of seeking delicious apples and takes sneak peeks at the breasts of his older sister, Thomasin. When caught looking, he is ashamed, but she understands his growing desires and laughs them off as natural and innocent. In adolescent play, he tickles her around the bodice and she pretends to chomp down on his head as if it were an apple. But Caleb's sense of guilt, ingrained from years of strict religious instruction, is not so easily overcome. Out in the forest, he imagines a buxom young woman who first leans in to kiss him and then grabs his head to pull him towards her with a withered arm. Caleb is at war with himself, his budding sexual interest at odds with his belief that all such desires are prohibited as evil. Returning home to his family, he writhes naked in bed before their horrified eyes, vomiting up a poisoned apple – he has clearly tasted of the forbidden fruit – and screaming that he is being oppressed by a witch: 'She's upon me! ... Sin, sin, sin! ... She desires of my blood!' Caleb blames himself for his own openness to her seduction and is afraid he may be damned: 'My Lord, my Jesus, save me! I am thine enemy, wallowing in the blood and filth of my sins!' The witch is thus a projection of what Caleb most desires and fears. Touchingly and yet tragically, he resolves the conflict between wish and prohibition by simultaneously dying and imagining himself as saved through an ecstatic reunion with God. 'My Lord, my Lord, kiss me with the kisses of thy mouth,' he says, adding, 'How lovely art thou, thy embrace,' as he wraps his arms around himself and falls back in bed, dead.

His sister, Thomasin, fights her own battle between guilt-induced worry and what she secretly wants. As a good Christian daughter, she is expected to be a mother-in-training, performing chores around the house and tending to baby Samuel whenever her mother hands him to her. She must remain on the farm and never venture into the woods. But, partly owing to her mother's strict standards and constant criticism, Thomasin feels increasingly confined in a role that does not seem to suit her. She worries that she will make an inadequate mother – fears that manifest themselves when a goat she is milking produces blood, when an egg she drops reveals a dead chick, and when the baby inexplicably vanishes on her watch. We see a witch carry Samuel off into the woods and then smear the baby's blood all over her naked body as an unguent enabling her to fly into the sky. This is surely the last thing Thomasin wanted to have happen, and yet, after being relentlessly blamed for the baby's disappearance ('She stole Sam ... she gave him to the Devil in the wood'), the girl succumbs to madness, fantasising that she is a witch in order to release herself from religious guilt. How many times has Thomasin secretly wished not to have to gather those eggs or milk that goat? Didn't some hidden part of her want to abandon that fussy baby and leave that family farm behind for ever? Now she imagines the Devil speaking to her to ask, 'Wouldst thou like to see the world?' She unlaces her bodice and slips out of her dress, 'freeing herself of the confines of Puritan society', according to writer-director Robert Eggers.[79] Walking naked into the woods, Thomasin joins the witches there, opening herself up to their evil influence, her face ecstatic and insane as she flies away from everything.

ZOMBIES

28 Days Later (2002)

Director: Danny Boyle
Cast: Cillian Murphy (Jim), Christopher Eccleston (West), Naomie Harris (Selena)

Rethinking zombies for the twenty first century, this film has no slow-stalking ghouls, but twitchy and fast-moving humans infected with a 'rage' virus, which is spread through vicious bites, vomited blood or arterial spray. Because it so closely resembles actual outbreaks of AIDS, SARS, Ebola and rabies, as well as disturbing instances of road rage and air rage, this film's zombie plague is frighteningly rooted in reality. Rage is often a reaction to failed attempts at love. Civilised humans act with kindness and generosity, but these can open one up to potential attack. The movie begins when animal activists free a captive chimpanzee to end its suffering in an experimental laboratory, but the ape attacks, having been infected by the rage virus and now spreading it. Their caring act makes them – and us – vulnerable. Jim, the film's protagonist, awakes from a 28-day coma to wander the empty streets of London, which seems entirely depopulated. Rephrasing Sartre's 'Hell is other people', director Danny Boyle has said, 'Hell is no people, really. When you're truly, truly alone, it's a terrible thing.'[80] So Jim reaches out, calling 'Hello?' – only to be assailed by an infected child, whom he then batters to death in self-defence.

Humans that are bitten become infected with rage like the zombies, but the more insidious threat posed by these creatures is that, in the very process of fighting them, we can become as rage-filled, vicious and paranoid-aggressive as they are. As part of the war against the zombies, an army officer named West keeps an infected black soldier in chains as an 'experiment' to see how long it takes him to starve to death. By holding this man captive like an ape in a laboratory or like a slave, West treats him as subhuman, while showing himself to be primitive and barbaric. It is West's *response* to the zombies as much as it is the zombies themselves that threatens to destroy the human race, leading to its devolution. West and his soldiers *enjoy* gunning down and blowing up zombies, using the creatures' attack as an excuse to unleash their own aggression. And, in fighting against one of these soldiers whose aggression has raged out of control, Jim finds himself becoming nearly indistinguishable from the soldiers or the zombies as he bashes the soldier's head against a wall and gouges out his eyes. In fact, Jim's companion, Selena, fears he has become infected, but rather than engaging in a pre-emptive strike born of paranoia and killing him with her machete, she waits a moment, giving him a chance to show that he is still human. Metaphorically, it is her willingness to trust him, even though it makes her vulnerable, that allows him to recover his humanity and restrain his violent impulses. The film ends with Jim and Selena reaching out to the rest of the world by unfurling a big sign, letter by letter, so that HELL becomes HELLO. This trust is the only thing that will really stop our regression into barbarism brought on by the rage virus.

Otto; or, Up with Dead People (2008)

Director: Bruce LaBruce
Cast: Jey Crisfar (Otto), Katharina Klewinghaus (Medea)

In this horror/art/porn film, zombies are a metaphor with multiple meanings. Emo-teen Otto, sporting a hoodie, striped sweater and black tie, has the pale-faced, zoned-out look of heroin chic. He is a parody of the goth youths who have 'a kind of macabre and morbid, almost romantic view of death', says writer-director Bruce LaBruce.[81] At the same time, though, Otto is meant to be a serious and sympathetic portrayal of a boy who has been 'so traumatised by all the hostility and negativity directed at him for being a homosexual that he perceives himself as a zombie, as dead'.[82] According to Medea, the radical filmmaker who wants to cast Otto in a movie, the living also persecute zombies like Otto because they find in him 'an echo of their own somnambulistic, conformist behaviour', a reminder of their robotic work routines and their mindless consumption of corporate products. Otto's zombie-like behaviour is an exaggeration of, and a protest against, conformist heterosexual society.

But when Otto turns to gay culture, he finds a similar homogenising pressure there. While on a train, he sits across from a conservative gay couple who, having assimilated to the norm, mock Otto's pretty-boy appearance. As LaBruce has said, 'The most reviled thing culturally even within the gay community ... is extreme effeminacy in men,'[83] and so, to counteract this bigotry, he 'wanted to make [Otto] a zombie who was a misfit, a sissy'.[84] A local gay bar presents Otto with nothing but macho skinhead clones in bomber jackets and brand-name shoes. When one guy remarks that 'it's *so* dead' in there, he inadvertently comments on the lifeless conformity of the scene. The name of the bar is Flesh, and Otto also finds that gay cruising, which may involve sex with strangers and an attraction to body parts as much as to persons, can be 'kind of sad' in its zombie-like sameness and alienation. 'If you've ever cruised a public toilet or a bathhouse, it's like *Night of the Living Dead*. You've got people in this zombie-like trance, in dark shadows with disembodied body parts,' says LaBruce.[85]

However, he hastens to add that 'all of it can be quite fun and exciting!'[86] Here LaBruce flips the zombie metaphor around again to suggest that such anonymous gay sex can have positive potential. Medea is making a 'politico-porno-zombie' movie in which gay ghouls assault hetero men and, in a kind of cannibalistic sex orgy, turn them into an army of the undead like themselves. The film mocks by making literal the heterosexist fear of a 'gay plague', whereby homosexuals seduce and recruit straight males while also spreading disease and death to them. Another scene in Medea's movie shows a gay male zombie eating another's intestines and then sexually penetrating the stomach wound – an exciting experience which they both enjoy. Here LaBruce defies the heterosexist presumption that vaginal intercourse is the only proper way to pleasure. Two years later, LaBruce would continue this project of 'exploring more orifices in unexpected places' with *L.A. Zombie* (2010),[87] in which a homeless gay ghoul brings a series of dying male strangers back to life by having sex in and then ejaculating over their various wounds. Calling it 'zombie gorn with a heart',[88] LaBruce notes that his life-affirming form of 'splatter' horror 'reversed this negative idea of AIDS or gay sex as toxic, poisonous'.[89]

Yet, despite some pleasingly promiscuous encounters, Otto does not feel entirely at home in the world of anonymous sex, and even though he has an erotic encounter with one particular love interest, the more traditional ideal of forming a romantic couple does not seem to suit him either. Much as 'undead' zombies are neither living nor dead, so the misfit Otto seems to occupy a place 'in between' gay and straight cultures without conforming to trends in either one. Perhaps this is why, at the end of the film, Otto remains unsure of his destination. And yet, backgrounded by a queer rainbow, he goes in search of someone who will embrace his unique difference.

World War Z (2013)

Director: Marc Forster
Cast: Brad Pitt (Gerry)

World War Z is a zombie movie that sends mixed messages. Director Marc Forster has lamented the fact that people today 'live in constant fear', noting that 'the government' creates 'scenarios people fear, because ultimately through fear you can control people'. He adds, 'I wish we could live in a world where there would be no fear.'[90] A horror movie about the threat of a zombie apocalypse is not likely to bring about that world. Especially when characters speculate that the zombie plague may stem from an 'outbreak of rabies in Taiwan' or from 'the organ trade in Germany', the film could be accused of divisive fear-mongering. But perhaps fear can be harnessed to prompt positive action for the general good. As one character says, 'The problem with most people is that they don't believe something can happen until it already has.' If this film can stir us to believe in and fight a worldwide zombie epidemic, what about global warming? Unfortunately, the battle to reduce carbon dioxide emissions doesn't look as spectacular in 3D IMAX as zombie-blasting action.

At least the film's hero, Gerry, is a crisis investigator working for the United Nations rather than for any one country's government or military, and his globetrotting quest to find a way to curb the zombie outbreak is a veritable model of international cooperation, involving persons of many different ethnicities and faiths. Of course, a white American male is still at the centre of it all, and he is the one who leads his family to safety, figures out the virus's weakness, and risks death in an ultimately successful attempt to save the world. About midway through the movie, Gerry has an idea about how humanity might fight the virus. So why doesn't he tell his boss about his hunch when he has him on the phone? That way, if Gerry were to die, others could test his idea, and the world wouldn't have to die with him. It's never exactly clear what Gerry does for a living, but perhaps the question should be, 'What doesn't he do?' as, throughout the movie, he proves capable of doing everything. By contrast, the other characters all have pronounced weaknesses, from the Latino father whose stubbornness endangers his own family, to the black South African official who fails to keep Gerry's family under safe protection, to the British-Indian intellectual who accidentally shoots himself, to the Italian scientist whose kicking of a can almost draws the zombies to attack them. Gerry himself seems flawless, serenely aiding others, as when he helps his daughter breathe during an asthma attack or when he tells a female Israeli soldier to take big breaths while he disinfects the stump of her amputated arm. Why couldn't Gerry be the one who needs an inhaler, or the one who has to have his arm chopped off to prevent a zombie infection? The movie says that we all need to help each other because problems are global now – but mostly we need one man like Gerry to save us.

NATIONS

AUSTRALIA

Wolf Creek (2005)

Director: Greg McLean
Cast: Cassandra Magrath (Liz), Kestie Morassi (Kristy), Nathan Phillips (Ben), John Jarratt (Mick)

Two young British tourists, Liz and Kristy, are on a car trip across the Australian Outback with Ben, a native Aussie, when the three of them are kidnapped and tortured by a crazed hunter named Mick. Or at least this is the story given to police by Ben, who is, significantly, the only one who survives to tell the tale. During the entire time the two women were being tormented, Ben claims he was unable to help them because he had been nailed to a wooden cross. It is hard to imagine anyone more innocent than a crucified Christ figure. Despite wearing camo trousers, a black T-shirt and dark sunglasses, Ben presents himself as a guileless, goofy guy. In his account of events before the kidnapping, not just one but *both* women are sexually interested in him. When they stop at a place called Emu Creek, Ben seems offended at hearing some crude locals make rapacious remarks about Liz and Kristy, whereas Mick later shows himself to be a leering misogynist and murderer. However, visible behind Ben as he is gassing up his car is the truck belonging to Mick. 'Mick' is really part of Ben, his other side (as hinted at by the two-headed emu they see on their travels), his dark side that sometimes takes him over (as in the solar eclipse they also see). Like Ben, Mick initially presents himself as a nice guy – helpful, charming and funny. But his 'Crocodile' Dundee act is a façade concealing a vicious predator (like the man-eating crocodile in *Rogue*, writer-director Greg McLean's next film after *Wolf Creek*). Mick's dual nature is a clue to the fact that it is really Ben who has an alter ego: Mick.

Despite Ben's cover story, traces of the truth can be detected in the narrative he recounts. In this tale, Ben imitates the voice of evil Darth Vader telling Luke, 'I am your father.' Ben lunges after the two women, pretending to be a monster. And when 'Mick' stabs Liz through the back with a knife, he does so from the car's back seat where we earlier saw Ben, who also has a knife. (Ben tells the police that his is a small penknife, not a hunter's bowie knife like Mick's.) Ben weaves a confusing and elaborate story, speculating that Mick's motive for murder could be social, psychological, natural and/or supernatural. The lights on Mick's truck are reminiscent of UFO sightings, and Mick's evil deeds are somehow associated with a meteorite crater. The primal landscape of the Outback could have made Mick into a savage hunter, though his sniper rifle suggests that he may have picked up his predatory instincts in Vietnam, where he learned the trick of severing spinal cords so that his captives aren't able to escape. These captives tend to be patronising tourists who invade his native land, so his killings could be seen as an attempt to protect his territory. All these explanations prove mesmerising in their particularity as we are drawn into the elusive mystery that is Mick, while being distracted from the thought that Ben could be the murderer. The police hold Ben in custody for four months of questioning before releasing him as cleared of suspicion. Perhaps they should have held him longer.

CANADA

Pontypool (2008)

Director: Bruce McDonald
Cast: Stephen McHattie (Mazzy), Rick Roberts (Ken), Georgina Reilly (Laurel-Ann), Louise Houle (Sydney), Hannah Fleming (Farraj)

Pontypool has ghouls who try to chew their way through the mouths of people, but in this film, the zombie plague is not spread through bites. It is transmitted through sound bites – infected words that, once heard and understood, drive the listener mad and induce an insane aggression. Accordingly, replacing the 'frontal assaults' of 'gore' and 'action' typical of today's zombie films, *Pontypool* has us 'experience the terror and the chaos through the radio and through [audio] communication devices ... because sometimes our best special effects are created by our imaginations', as director Bruce McDonald has explained.[91]

Talk radio host Mazzy wages a war of words against conventional language, since its falsehood and hypocrisy are making people sick. When weatherman Ken calls in his report from the 'sunshine chopper' ('it's always brighter above the clouds'), Mazzy discovers that Ken is phoning from his car, not a helicopter, with news that is dark indeed. Not only is there an infected teenage boy, but Ken's claims that he is trying to help him are belied by the 'screaming baby' sounds coming from the kid as Ken approaches, revealing that Ken is in fact a paedophile. Scholars have noted that Canadian horror films often expose people's 'ridiculous need to hide violence and perversion behind the veil of good conduct and respectability',[92] showing how 'superficial rationalism, prudence, and level-headedness' can 'collapse like a house of cards under the pressures of repressed lust, anger, and madness'.[93] Like the word 'typo' hidden within the town name of Pontypool, the verbal virus spreading among the townspeople points to their underlying flaws, revealing harsh facts about them that they have sought to cover up with lies or half-truths. After returning from service in Afghanistan, radio technician

Laurel-Ann has been lauded as the town's 'homecoming hero', but buried guilt over acts she committed in the war, a sense that she is no longer fully 'there' as a moral person, begins to manifest itself as a strange stuttering: 'Mr Mazzy's missing ... I'm Missy Mazzy ... I don't miss Mr Mazzy. I'm not missing any more.' In the end, unable to deal openly with her war experiences ('the situation I brought back in my head'), Laurel-Ann becomes crazily violent and then commits suicide.

Radio show producer Sydney ends up having to kill a zombie girl named Farraj, whose name connects her with child casualties of the foreign war in which Laurel-Ann fought. Like Laurel-Ann, Sydney denies her guilt ('I didn't kill the kid'), but the result of this attempt at linguistic cover-up is that she becomes infected with the verbal virus and begins to obsessively repeat the word 'kill'. Earlier, Sydney has verbally infected her own daughter by telling her that the only reason she didn't phone her earlier was that the lines were tied up: 'Honey, I didn't forget to call you. I just couldn't get through, sweetheart.' Even though Sydney has been warned that the disease can be spread by using 'terms of endearment such as "honey" or "sweetheart"', she ends up contaminating her child by speaking these words in a less than entirely truthful context. However, unlike Laurel-Ann, Sydney is saved from suicide by Mazzy. First, he insists that she fully disclose her guilt and make a confession: 'My name is Sydney Briar and today I killed a girl.' Then he has her do penance and receive forgiveness. 'Kill is kiss,' he says, and when she says, 'Kill me,' he kisses her. Thus Sydney offers her life as punishment for the wrong she has done, and receives a forgiving kiss. In the process, Mazzy cures her of the verbal virus, overcoming her obsessive repetition of the word 'kill' by having her own up to its true meaning and realise that she is capable of moving beyond it.

CZECHOSLOVAKIA

Lunacy (Šílení) (2005)

Director: Jan Švankmajer
Cast: Pavel Liška (Jean), Jan Tříska (Marquis), Martin Huba (Coulmiere),
Anna Geislerová (Charlota)

Created by Czech surrealist Jan Švankmajer, this 'philosophical horror' film uses dread as a means to debate such issues as the right relation between freedom and restraint or the proper balance between the body and the mind. Jean is a young man who fears he will go insane, like his mother who recently died in an asylum. He suffers from a recurring nightmare in which two attendants drag him away in a straitjacket. Jean meets the Marquis, who has overcome his own obsession – that of premature burial – by having himself buried alive with tools enabling him to break out of his tomb. The Marquis suggests a similar therapy for Jean, that he check himself into an insane asylum, realising he is sane and can leave any time. The mind must live with the thought of potential madness, just as the body must live in spite of its imminent decomposition and death. But what if Jean's stay in the asylum fails to restore his peace of mind, driving him instead towards insanity? Is Jean's self-incarceration a move towards freedom or a trap?

The Marquis, in the name of freedom, lives a life of blasphemy and licentiousness, pounding nails into a Christ statue and engaging in an orgy on a church altar. Crying out for punishment, he rails at God for being absent and allowing humans to yield to such temptations. If there is a God, the Marquis says that He must be a sadist who enjoys seeing virgins raped – an event that serves as the climax to the church orgy. Despite his proclamations, the Marquis is not free: the vicious sex he has is driven by a desire to overcome religious guilt or to have an authority figure set moral limits. Such a figure appears to arrive in the person of Coulmiere, a psychiatrist who believes in strict supervision and corporeal punishment for the asylum inmates, one of whom turns out to be the Marquis, a madman who thinks he's de Sade. The mind must surveil and discipline the body so as to keep it within healthy bounds. Yet Coulmiere is not really an exemplar of proper control. Not only are his methods of punishment extreme – they include whipping, blinding and the cutting out of tongues – but he takes pleasure in the inmates' pain while also abusing his authority to secretly sleep with female patients. In his failure to achieve a right relation between the mind and the body, Coulmiere is no more healthy than the Marquis. Both are unbalanced.

With these men as his guides, it is no wonder that Jean struggles to retain his sanity and maintain his well-being. For this, he turns to Charlota, the woman whose love he hopes will free him from the insane asylum. But the Marquis has filled Jean's head with notions of women as lacking minds or any sense of morality; women are greedy, flesh-devouring whores who will sell themselves to anyone for survival, just as Mother Nature will mate with any male in order to ensure the continuation of all flesh. The Marquis's misogyny prompts Jean to have a fearful vision of what sex with Charlota might be like: two severed beef tongues licking each other lasciviously and then bestially copulating. This is later followed by another nightmare, also a stop-motion animation, of hens pecking at meat from a grinder and laying eggs, which crack open to reveal more red meat that goes back up into the grinder for the hens to peck at. This final nightmare of indiscriminately eaten and endlessly regenerated flesh is cued when Jean catches sight of Charlota about to fellate Coulmiere and then perhaps become pregnant. Importantly, Jean isn't sure of what he sees – Charlota could be innocent and faithful to him – but, in his weakness, Jean lets dread get the better of him, jumping to the worst possible conclusion. Having lost faith in the woman he loves, Jean goes insane, ending up as the straitjacketed inmate he has most feared becoming.

FRANCE

In My Skin (Dans ma peau) (2002)

Director: Marina de Van
Cast: Marina de Van (Esther)

Focused on the horror of self-harming, this New French Extremist film follows a young woman named Esther as she becomes increasingly obsessed with a leg wound, compelled to scratch at and cut into it, to drink her own blood, and to cannibalise her flesh. Why? One scene of Esther in her office shows her correcting a typo – one to do with the word 'alternatively' – when suddenly she has the urge to cut herself. Could it be that, even though Esther is a successful market analyst about to receive a promotion, she hates this job and wishes for something else – an alternative? At a business dinner, just when she is under the most pressure to keep up appearances, Esther's arm goes numb, tries to mess up her plate, and detaches itself so that it appears to be lying severed on the table. The dinner-table conversation at the time refers to a hand gesture that, though intended as elegant, might be interpreted as a sign of refusal. One part of Esther is rejecting this career, wanting to create the kind of social embarrassment that gets her fired. In another scene, Esther is withdrawing money she plans to use in her future life with her boyfriend, but she suddenly stops upon seeing pieces of her own cut-off skin in her wallet. Despite the appearance of a perfect romance, her self-mutilation is a way of telling herself that she may not really want to marry this man. Though consciously she would deny it, Esther is feeling constrained and hurt by his expectations of her, much as she is suffering from the pressure to conform in her job. Self-laceration becomes her way of acknowledging the pain she has actually been feeling all along. When Esther first injured her leg, it was by accident at night as she was stumbling around in a garden still under construction. Disturbingly, she did not even notice until later that she had hurt herself. She starts cutting in order to break through her own numbness to the pain of living a life that society has mapped out for her and that does not seem freely chosen. She begins to see herself as a project under construction, whose destiny she can have a hand in shaping.

Withdrawing from her boyfriend and holing up in a hotel room, Esther engages in an illicit affair – with her own body. Grimaces of pain turn to expressions of ecstasy as she finds sensual pleasure in self-inflicted lacerations, getting back in touch with her corporeal self. She experiences 'the desire of fusing with her own body as if it were another object that is driving her to feel it and to try to mix with it, to ingest it, to suck it, to be pleasured by it', according to writer-director Marina de Van,[94] who also plays Esther. Pulling her leg up to her face, Esther licks her wound, as if to heal it. Curled up in a foetal position, she regresses to an infantile state while also attempting to mother herself into a rebirth. But the danger of focusing so exclusively on herself and her body parts is that she might lose any connection with the social whole that holds her together. Is it possible for her to be herself and yet also to be what society expects of her? After her self-fragmentation, Esther looks into a mirror and 'sees herself as a whole body, and more than a body … she actually sees a face, a look, a person,' de Van says.[95] Appearing determined, Esther makes herself presentable and leaves the hotel room, presumably to return to her boyfriend and her job. But then we see her still in that room, where she has mourned some cut-off skin of hers which has died. Esther may rejoin society, but only at the expense of a part of herself – the part she must give up to fit in.

GERMANY

Wetlands (Feuchtgebiete) (2013)

Director: David Wnendt
Cast: Carla Juri (Helen), Meret Becker (Mother)

Wetlands is a coming-of-age comedy with gross-out elements that tip it over into horror. Helen finds herself in a proctology ward when a shaving accident, combined with pressure from a haemorrhoid, leads to an infected anal lesion, necessitating an operation. During her recovery, the young woman enjoys recalling the times when she would scratch her anus, finger her nasal mucus, and taste her vaginal discharge. To attract men, she would let odours emanate from her unwashed vulva and dab vaginal secretions behind her ears like perfume. To express solidarity with her girlfriend, the two would exchange and reinsert bloody tampons. 'You always laugh loudest at the things that scare you the most,' thinks Helen in the book on which this film is based,[96] and her uninhibited embrace of all the body's substances acts as a kind of exposure therapy, helping us to overcome disgust at natural functions. As Helen explores her own physical being, sampling its tastes and smells, she learns to know her body and to accept herself as a woman. 'I have very healthy pussy flora,' she exclaims, comparing the varied consistency of her 'pussy mucus' to 'olive oil' and 'cottage cheese' and finding it delectable either way. Helen's celebration of her natural self is also defiance of her cleanliness-obsessed mother, who has tried to impose on her daughter an oppressive hygiene regime. Novelist Charlotte Roche has said that she was inspired to write the book because too often she found 'the mothers teaching the daughters that the vagina is something dirty'. She cites the example of her own grandmother 'teaching [her] mother to lie in bed with her hands on the blanket so she didn't touch herself'.[97]

However, it sometimes seems as though Helen's acts of bodily rebellion against her mother's prudery and propriety are less than truly liberating. Her mother's worst fear is to be caught wearing dirty underwear if she must be taken to the hospital, and so Helen lies in the hospital bed with her rear end exposed after the anal operation. To prove she is immune to humiliation, Helen becomes an exhibitionist. In defiance of her germaphobic mother, Helen wades barefoot through waste water in public lavatories. While her mother always squats to urinate, Helen sits directly on the soiled toilet seat and wipes her bare bottom and exposed genitals around on it. It is one thing to counteract the myth that all bacteria are harmful, but Helen's risk-taking behaviour seems to move beyond raunchy self-empowerment, becoming pathological and self-destructive. One reason that Helen tries to be so physically fearless is her concern that her mother's body phobia is an inherited mental illness, passed on from grandmother to mother and now, Helen worries, to her. Helen imagines this oppressive inheritance as a turkey gobbling up a duck swallowing a chicken, and she connects this roasting turducken to the time when she found her mother holding her baby brother with both their heads in the kitchen oven. The idea that her mother could fear the outside world so much that she would take her own children 'back into her body' and kill them explains why Helen is so determined to embrace her own flesh, even to the point of insisting that the bloody piece of skin surgically removed from her anus be returned to her. But the more Helen fights to differentiate herself from her body-obsessed mother, the more crazily like her she becomes.

HONG KONG

Dumplings (Jiao zi) (2004)

Director: Fruit Chan
Cast: Miki Yeung (Kate), Tony Ka-Fai Leung (Mr Li), Pauline Lau (Secretary), Miriam Chin Wah Yeung (Mrs Li), Bai Ling (Mei)

The horror in *Dumplings* concerns women's suffering under patriarchal domination. Schoolgirl Kate is raped by her father, who chooses sex with his underage daughter over having relations with his wife. Similarly, in a quasi-incestuous attempt to rejuvenate himself, middle-aged businessman Mr Li sleeps with his young secretary, neglecting his spouse. In what amounts to a kind of cannibalism of youth, these men believe that if they indulge their sexual appetite for tender flesh, they will consume their lovers' vitality, thereby halting their own ageing process. This superstitious belief, rooted in a desperate fear of their own bodies' ageing and death, essentially turns the men into predatory paedophiles. In their immaturity, these men prize the body over emotion or spirit.

Their superficiality has a tragic effect on women like Mrs Li. Since she is a trophy wife valued only for her physical beauty, Mrs Li becomes desperate to restore her fading good looks, so she turns to Mei, a former-doctor-turned-cook who procures aborted foetuses which she uses as meat for dumplings that supposedly have restorative powers. 'You'll soon regain your youth and the heart of your man,' Mei promises, but Mrs Li will never win her husband's heart because he is a resolute materialist, a consumer of flesh rather than a lover of sentiment. Nevertheless, Mrs Li eats the foetal dumplings. The fact that her red fingernails and lipsticked mouth match the red meat, combined with the sound of bones cracking between her chomping teeth, accentuates that this is an act of cannibalism. Even worse, the meat she is consuming comes from the foetus of incest victim Kate, who bleeds to death after the abortion, so Mrs Li can be seen as continuing the father's original abuse of this young woman by further preying on her.

Mrs Li then pays her husband's now-pregnant mistress to abort the embryo to make more meat, letting jealousy of the mistress's and the unborn child's youth drive her to it. So dependent is Mrs Li on her husband's approval of her good looks that she kills his own offspring in an effort to maintain her youthful appearance rather than nurturing the child as a parent should. In the film's final scene, as Mrs Li brings the meat cleaver down upon the foetus, blood splashes onto her face, implying that she damages her own soul as she cuts into that flesh. This self-destruction is even more apparent in the shorter, alternate version of the film (included as part of the horror-movie anthology *Three ... Extremes*), where Mrs Li herself becomes pregnant and then uses a metal wire to abort her own foetus, planning to consume it. Mrs Li has in effect become her own rapist, violating herself and her foetus in her effort to stay young for her husband. As she bleeds out in the bathtub, some blood also drips from her mouth and she snakes her tongue out to lick it up. By consuming her own child, Mrs Li is essentially eating herself up. Her husband's obsession with youth and beauty has made her into a monster.

HUNGARY

Taxidermia (Der Ausstopfer) (2006)

Director: György Pálfi
Cast: Csaba Czene (Morosgoványi), Gábor Máté (Oreg), Gergö Trócsányi (Kálmán), Adél Stanczel (Gizi), Marc Bischoff (Lajos)

Taxidermia is a 'body horror' film that is simultaneously a critical commentary on three eras of Hungarian history: fascism, communism and capitalism. During World War Two, Morosgoványi is a common soldier who is relentlessly dominated and demeaned by his lieutenant, Oreg, who commands him to scrub the outhouse and muck out the stables. Oreg considers himself above such gross manual labour, strengthening his sense of superiority by treating Morosgoványi as if he were no better than the pig he is ordered to tend. Though Oreg has a similarly low opinion of women, whose 'cunts' he considers 'ugly' and 'unwashed' like a 'pig', the lieutenant nevertheless exults in his sole possession of a wife and two nubile daughters, whom lonely Morosgoványi can only watch longingly from afar. In one voyeuristic scene, as the soldier attempts to find some satisfaction by poking his erection through a greased hole in the barn while spying on the daughters, a rooster pecks at his protruding member. This dominance of one cock by another is a metaphor for the vicious pecking order Oreg maintains over his subordinate. That Morosgoványi desires to reconnect with innocent love and to transcend his degradation can be seen from the fantasy he has of asking a young girl to 'put magic stars … in the sky' by stroking him until his ejaculate flies upwards. And when Oreg's wife appears to come to the young soldier for the loving attention her misogynistic husband won't give her, Morosgoványi briefly imagines finding spiritual fulfilment through intercourse with her body, saying, 'Let's grunt together because life's too short,' as she urges on his thrusting. It is at this point that Morosgoványi wakes from his fantasy to discover himself having sex with a pig, for which transgression he is shot by Oreg – destroyed by the lieutenant's despotic rule and body phobia.

In the film's next segment, set in the 1960s, Kálmán is a champion eater whose shovelling of food into his mouth shows the country's willingness to swallow any and all socialist propaganda, though at one point he does develop lockjaw in symbolic protest against the 'shit' he is being fed. Later, his wife, Gizi, endangers her pregnancy by speed-eating vast quantities of red caviar from a star-shaped bowl in order to impress some Russian dignitaries and gain the special privileges granted only to those favoured by Communist Party officials. Even though competitive consumption just makes the Hungarian Kálmán feel inferior to the Soviets who keep winning first place, he continues eating until his body is obscenely bloated, and he has nothing but contempt for his scrawny son, Lajos.

The film's final segment takes place in present-day capitalist Hungary, where the emaciated Lajos cannot seem to bulk up despite the abundant food on the supermarket shelves, suggesting that he remains starved for affection in this new economy of isolated individualists. Perhaps in reaction to his father's attempt to dominate through obesity, Lajos is withdrawn and anorexic. Neither can establish a healthy relation to his body or to the social body surrounding him. In the end, Lajos employs an elaborate machine to eviscerate his organs, to sew up his skin, and to cut off his head. His taxidermied body stands as an accusation against a consumer society that left him feeling emotionally empty. Instead of finding personal fulfilment in this new land of plenty, he feels more hollow and anonymous than ever.

INDIA

Ghost (Bhoot) (2003)

Director: Ram Gopal Varma
Cast: Ajay Devgn (Vishal), Urmila Matondkar (Swati), Barkha Madan (Manjeet), Sabir Masani (Doorman), Fardeen Khan (Sanjay), Victor Banerjee (Doctor)

Near the beginning of this Hindi 'high-rise horror' film, newlyweds Vishal and Swati stand and look up admiringly at the 12-storey building where they will be living in a designer apartment on the top floor. The yuppie couple has secured this upscale domestic space for their new home, and, at first, it and their relationship both seem idyllic. But the apartment is haunted, and Swati soon finds herself possessed by the ghost of a woman named Manjeet, a former tenant who fell from the balcony to her death. Manjeet's dark presence reveals the hidden underside of Swati's seemingly sunny life, the abyss into which this happy wife is in danger of falling. An early sign that her marriage may not be all it's built up to be comes when Swati discovers that her husband has kept the apartment's dark past a secret from her, not caring that she might be interested in the suffering of the previous occupant. Then there is the fact that Vishal, who works long hours, often leaves her alone and unprotected. As a result, instead of her husband riding up in the elevator, a thuggish doorman ascends and creeps up behind her inside the apartment. This is uncomfortably close to what happened to Manjeet when a lustful man named Sanjay came up behind her – and she fell off the balcony while resisting his rape attempt.

When Vishal and Swati have sex on the stairs of their split-level apartment, their coupling is consensual and the height of passion they reach seems mutual, but there is some implication that he is using her for his selfish pleasure rather than really fulfilling her needs. Their sex scene ends with a shot of Swati reflected in a mirror, and Manjeet's ghost will soon 'emerge' from a mirror near Swati, as if revealing the dissatisfied side of this supposedly contented wife. From the way Swati cuddles a doll she finds in the apartment, it is clear that she wants a child, but her husband, despite enjoying sex with her, has not given her one. The doll once belonged to the son of Manjeet, who was deprived of her boy when Sanjay had him killed (so as not to leave a living witness to Sanjay's ultimately deadly assault on Manjeet). In a later scene, when Vishal comes up behind Swati while she is standing at a window, she starts to fight him as if in self-defence. Swati has been possessed by Manjeet, who is 'reliving' the assault by Sanjay, but the movie keeps suggesting that the way Vishal treats Swati is not as different from Sanjay's treatment of Manjeet as we might first have thought.

To stop her fighting, Vishal ties Swati to their bed and then summons a doctor to cure her illness. But what his wife needs is not forced confinement (which includes penetration by the doctor's needle) or the presumption that she is sick. She needs Vishal to listen to her concerns about him, anxieties about the male mistreatment of women which are haunting her and expressing themselves in the form of Manjeet's rage. In the film's finale, which takes place in an underground parking garage beneath the apartment complex, Manjeet has the possessed Swati suspend Sanjay above some iron spikes that are sticking out of the building's foundation, threatening him until he admits his misdeeds. Now that the hidden underside of Swati's marriage has also been revealed, will Vishal recognise his own faults before he or his wife has to take the fall for them?

Hisss (2010)

Director: Jennifer Lynch
Cast: Mallika Sherawat (Nagin)

Hollywood meets Bollywood in this film written and directed by David Lynch's daughter Jennifer, but filmed in India by a largely indigenous crew. Rooted in local myth, the film is focused on Nagin, a snake woman worshipped as a fertility goddess but also feared as a force of nature who can take revenge when wronged, using her fanged mouth as a *vagina dentata* to bite and swallow her enemies. In one of the movie's quieter moments, Nagin, now in human form, sheds her sari and climbs naked up a lamp post. This scene has been criticised for being sexually exploitative, with reviewers condemning its 'gratuitous' nudity[98] and even comparing Nagin's climb to that of 'a stripper pole dancing'.[99] However, a closer look reveals deeper meaning. Nagin has been forced to leave the jungle forest and journey to the city to rescue her kidnapped mate, the cobra king, but she longs to return with him to her home. The director's outline of scenes charts Nagin's progress: 'i) Jungle, ii) Swamp Area, iii) Deserted Road (lamp post), iv) Vikram House'.[100]

The curvy lamp post that Nagin climbs is located between trees on the left and houses to the right, and it arches back towards the trees. Nagin's climb shows her having moved towards the human habitations of the city but ultimately wanting to turn back to nature. Before her ascent, Nagin discards the cloth wrap she has been wearing, shedding her human clothes to return to her bare skin. She wraps her arms and legs around the lamp post. Its pole has a mottled texture making it resemble a tree branch, linking her limbs to the tree limbs she loves. The pole's texture is also similar to a snake's, and as she straddles it throughout her climb, it's as though she imagines making love with her missing mate. (Later in the film, she will lie on an actual tree branch, and take the king cobra between her legs and mate with him.) After Nagin has mounted the pole and moved out along its horizontal portion to the lamp, she hangs her head back so it receives the light, while a tear falls from her eye. We hear a female vocalist sing a melancholy love song and we briefly see a full moon. This street light is the closest thing she has to a romantic moon, just as this lamp post is to a tree. Together, they remind her of her beloved and her home – of her true nature as a snake woman.

IRAN

Under the Shadow (2016)

Director: Babak Anvari
Cast: Narges Rashidi (Shideh), Bobby Naderi (Iraj), Avin Manshadi (Dorsa)

Shideh is a young wife, mother and medical student living in 1980s Tehran during the Iran-Iraq War. The movie begins with a university administrator informing her that, due to her past political activism, she will no longer be allowed to continue her studies to become a doctor. And this is just the first of many patriarchal forces arrayed against her, forces which gradually seem so pervasive and overwhelming that they take on an almost supernatural power.

Her husband Iraj, himself a doctor, tells her that the forced end to her studies may be 'for the best' because now she can devote herself solely to domestic duties. Then, even after he has left to be a medic on the war's front lines, she receives strange phone calls from him, filled with crackling static, where he berates her for being a bad mother. It is as though his constant criticism of her has become a ghostly voice in her head, undermining her belief in herself. The authoritarian male voices from loudspeakers, the blaring of the air-raid sirens, and the phallic missile that strikes the roof of her building all invade Shideh's world to the point where she begins to succumb to paranoid madness, imagining that a djinn – an evil spirit that rides the wind – has intruded upon her home and peace of mind, threatening her safety and sanity. When Shideh flees her apartment in terror, clutching her six-year-old daughter, Dorsa, in her arms, military police do not offer to help her. Instead, they arrest her for not wearing the hijab or veil required by religious law, reminding her that she could be whipped for so 'shamelessly exposing' herself. Shideh is eventually freed and returns home, but the trauma of such religious intolerance affects her so strongly that its oppression now seems ubiquitous and inescapable. She imagines a hijab-wearing demon lady who wants to possess and smother Dorsa, for Shideh fears she will not be able to save her own child from a life of sexist restrictions.

When Shideh starts to see patriarchal oppression as a demonic power, this may seem like a terrible mistake born of uncontrollable fear and increasing despair at her own helplessness. But, in fact, viewing social forces as supernatural ultimately serves as a way to get a handle on them, symbolically localising them so they can appear manageable. As Shideh battles a ghostly, floating hijab to rescue her daughter from its suffocating confines, she gives all the oppressive forces around her a shape she can struggle with, an imaginary form she can fight. When there seems to be no realistic way to prevent her daughter from being possessed by a restrictive religious regime, Shideh can hallucinate an evil djinn who steals Dorsa's doll so that Shideh can rescue it, patch it up and give it back to her daughter, symbolically saving her child from the regime's grasp. By seeing amorphous social forces embodied as a definable demon, Shideh is able to stand up to them, refusing to surrender her daughter to their evil influence or to be scared out of her own home. For Shideh, a belief in demons is what keeps her strong and sane.

JAPAN

(see 'Techno-Horror' and 'Asian Horror and American Remakes')

NORWAY

Dead Snow (Død snø) (2009)

Director: Tommy Wirkola
Cast: Bjørn Sundquist (Village Elder), Vegar Hoel (Martin)

With Nazi zombies rising from the snow to attack some youths on a skiing vacation, this Norwegian zom-com exploits its country's particular landscape and history to interesting effect. What initially appears as a beautiful setting for sledding, snowball fights and sex turns out to be a vast expanse of empty whiteness, freezing and isolated from human help. Snow also serves as an effective backdrop for the film's gory splatstick, with the red arterial spray standing out against the white as zombies are bloodily dispatched with knives, axes, chainsaws and, in one especially ludicrous moment, a snowmobile's grinding engine. All this humour tends to undercut the horror's potentially serious message about the need to acknowledge the past in order to avoid repeating it. In the backstory, Nazis occupied Norway during World War Two, torturing the villagers, who then rose up in violent opposition to their oppressors, killing them or driving them off into the snow where they became zombies. A village elder tells the vacationing youths of these past 'events that people prefer to keep quiet about', but they pay no heed, self-involved as they are in the hedonistic pleasures of partying and sex. As a result of such ignorance, history repeats itself. When the Gestapo ghouls attack, the youths are at first victimised like the locals of yore and then, in fighting back, they turn mindlessly violent, themselves gleefully stabbing, slicing and machine-gunning their enemies just as the Nazis had done. Despite being warned to 'not get bitten' or 'you'll be infected' and 'become like them', this is exactly what happens. When one youth, Martin, is bitten in the arm, his solution is to amputate it, but the violence he commits in doing so shows that he has been infected. His very attempt to distance himself from the Nazis proves his connection to them. In the sequel, *Dead Snow 2* (*Død snø 2*, 2014), a zombie arm will be grafted on to Martin's torso and he will attack others with it. His failure to recognise his own aggressive impulses makes it hard for him to stop unconsciously acting them out. He himself becomes a Nazi zombie.

POLAND

Demon (2015)

Director: Marcin Wrona
Cast: Itay Tiran (Peter), Agnieszka Żulewska (Zaneta), Włodzimierz Press (Professor), Maria Dębska (Hana), Andrzej Grabowski (Father), Tomasz Ziętek (Ronaldo), Tomasz Schuchardt (Jasny)

English engineer Peter travels to his bride-to-be's home village in rural Poland, where they plan to marry and live in the house she has inherited from her grandfather. On the night before their nuptials, Peter, who has been excavating the ancestral land, digs up a human skeleton. The next day, the wedding festivities take a strange turn when Peter stomps on his champagne glass (a Jewish tradition), rather than throwing it over his shoulder in the Polish way, and begins speaking Yiddish in a feminine-sounding voice. Instead of dancing with his bride, Zaneta, he convulses wildly and arches his back as though someone is about to leap out of his body. It turns out that Peter has been possessed by a dybbuk or restless spirit. As a professor at the wedding explains, 'In Jewish tradition, the soul of a dead person can cling to a living one in order to carry out what death interrupted.'

The spirit that has laid claim to Peter is that of a former bride-to-be, Hana, who was deprived of her groom decades ago when she mysteriously vanished on the eve of her wedding. What actually happened is obscure due to the family's attempts to keep their past buried, but it seems likely that the Jewish Hana was murdered by Zaneta's grandfather so that he could steal her land. He covered up his crimes by spreading the false rumour that she had been taken away to a Nazi concentration camp. Though many Poles resisted the Nazis during World War Two, there were others who collaborated with them and benefited from their anti-Semitic purges. Hana, the ghost bride who will not stay buried, returns to expose this Polish family's shameful secret. 'The whole country's built on corpses,' Zaneta's father blurts out at one point, half-admitting that his native land is haunted by the Holocaust, but then he determines to cover it all up again, saying 'We must forget what we didn't see here.' Like the Jewish Hana, English Peter (who is played by an Israeli actor) is thought of as an outsider by this Polish family. Peter worries that Zaneta is 'more in love with this place than she is with me', and we notice that she hesitates during her marriage vows to take him as her husband. Though Zaneta's father says that the old 'have to make room for the young', he seems loath to give up his daughter or his land to this 'foreigner'. And then there is a jealous rival, Ronaldo, who wants Peter gone so that he can claim Zaneta for himself, and who may even have slipped Peter something to make him deathly ill.

Peter's possession by Hana, interrupting his wedding, may also reveal his own buried reasons for wanting to prevent the marriage between himself and Zaneta. Peter has long been best friends with Zaneta's brother, Jasny, with whom he seems to have a very physical relationship of close masculine camaraderie. Peter seems melancholy about the impending loss of that relationship due to marriage, saying, 'I'm not Python any more [Jasny's phallic name for him]; I'm Piotr [the name he is called by Zaneta].' When Peter is about to have sex with Zaneta, he is interrupted by the noise of Jasny using a digger machine in the area where Hana's body was unearthed, as if to reveal Peter's buried 'feminine' desire for

Jasny. It is said of Hana that she 'only loved one Polish boy'. Could this be true of Peter as well? Hana's possession of Peter involves a woman in a man's body, and he begins to evince feminine speech and mannerisms as if he were transgendered. The professor has said that when the dybbuk or ghost bride possesses Peter, this provides 'a chance for it to purge itself, but also to purge the soul of the possessed one'. If the ghost bride's long-buried desires come to light, perhaps Peter's do as well.

RUSSIA

Night Watch (Nochnoy dozor) (2004)

Director: Timur Bekmambetov
Cast: Konstantin Khabensky (Anton), Rimma Markova (Witch), Dima Martynov (Yegor), Anna Slyu (Tiger Cub), Aleksandr Samoylenko (Bear), Galina Tyunina (Owl Woman), Viktor Verzhbitsky (Zavulon)

In mediaeval times, the forces of Light battle the forces of Darkness until, realising that they are equal in strength, they call a truce, on condition that each is allowed to monitor and punish the other for violations. This fragile truce is a metaphor for the precarious balance between good and evil in every individual, which could tip at any moment towards either side. Consider Anton, who, in 1992 Moscow, believes that his girlfriend has left him because she is carrying another man's baby. Anton consults a witch and, after drinking a potion composed of his own blood, pays her to cause a miscarriage in a desperate attempt to get his girlfriend back. Anton's egotism and possessiveness not only damage the woman he loves, they also threaten to destroy his own bloodline, for the foetus is in fact his. Anton's act is thus potentially self-consuming, but luckily the baby lives.

Anton is a vampire, but as one of the forces of Light, he lives off animal blood, unlike the Dark vampires who prey on humans. Nevertheless, Anton sometimes struggles to keep his own bloodlust in check. In a 2004 scene where an innocent kid named

Yegor is being used as human bait to catch some Dark vampires, Anton follows the boy down into the metro like a paedophile stalking his prey. Attracted to the young blood coursing in Yegor's veins, Anton comes close to sinking his fangs into the boy, but is suddenly interrupted. Later, he finds out that Yegor is not some stranger, but Anton's own 12-year-old son. If Anton had sucked the life out of him, he would in effect have been draining his own blood. With this warning, the film promotes the view that all men are blood brothers and that the old have a duty to protect the young, as a father should do for his own son.

Anton then goes about proving himself worthy of this paternal responsibility. He teams up with two shape-shifters, Tiger Cub and Bear, were-animals who have redirected their natural viciousness towards fierce protection of humans from evil. Anton also frees a woman who was trapped in an owl, releasing her from her prison of predatory instincts, much as he is trying to liberate himself from his vampiric hunger. In the film's final scene, Anton manages to fight off a female vampire before she can bite Yegor. Anton then does battle with Zavulon, the leader of the Dark Ones, but just as Anton is about to strike his foe, Zavulon makes it appear as though Anton was going to kill Yegor. Zavulon also reveals to the boy that Anton once did try to have him aborted. All Anton's efforts to reform and be a good father seem to have come to nought, for Yegor ends up believing that Anton wants him dead, and as a result the boy joins the Dark Ones in order to seek revenge. The film concludes pessimistically, suggesting that the sins of the father are not so easily repented or forgiven, that they may be visited upon and perpetuated by the son. But then there is a sequel, *Day Watch* ...

SERBIA

A Serbian Film (Srpski film) (2010)

Director: Srdjan Spasojević
Cast: Srdjan Todorovic (Miloš), Luca Mijatovic (Petar), Jelena Gavrilović (Marija), Slobodan Beśtić (Marko), Andela Nenadović (Jeca), Sergej Trifunović (Director)

Miloš is a semi-retired adult film star trying to reconcile sexuality with marriage and family. When his six-year-old son Petar watches some porn tapes and says that they give him a strange feeling down below like a 'wheel spinning' or a 'family travelling', Miloš encourages these as healthy metaphors for his son's first stirrings of desire. When his wife, Marija, after viewing a porn video of Miloš vigorously taking some actresses from behind, asks him, 'How come you've never done me like them?' he at first subjects her to some pounding rear entry, but then turns her around to kiss her face-to-face, thrusting more gently, if still vigorously, until she climaxes. Miloš seems quite different from his brother, Marko, whose question about a stuffed toy bunny, bought for Petar, is 'where's his pussy?' In addition to showing contempt for childhood innocence, Marko also lusts after Marija and envies Miloš's on-screen ability to stay 'so hard for so long', mistakenly believing that this must be the sole reason why his brother was able to marry such a beautiful woman.

And yet Miloš, despite having found some happy medium between self-abnegation and selfish desire, is drawn back into the world of porn, ostensibly to make money for his family, but when his wife asks him if he misses that life, his answer is an unconvincing no. As part of the adult video, Miloš is expected to have sex with Jeca, a virginal teenage girl. Miloš is told that her own father would have deflowered her had he not died in the Bosnian War. Although Miloš baulks at the assignment, he nevertheless has fantasies of Jeca licking a lollipop while he is being fellated by a woman. It turns out that Miloš is being injected with animal aphrodisiacs, so he may not be fully responsible for his exorbitant desires, but we should remember that Miloš's specialty as a porn star has always been rough sex in such films as *Acockalypse Now*, and his current director says that Miloš was hired for his proven 'talent' to 'humiliate' women and that he is 'the only one in this film who is not a victim'. For one porn scene, this director cries, 'Hit the whore!' and encourages Miloš to have pounding sex with Jeca's mother from behind and to beat her. Gone is the sense that a woman (like Marija) could be both desired and respected (as a wife and mother), as Miloš unleashes pure lust on a female whom he despises as a slut. When a machete is put into his hand, Miloš uses it to hack off the woman's head and continues to screw the corpse, for he himself is now nothing but a 'headless dick', selfishly stuffing any available hole.

For the climax of the porn film he is making, Miloš thrusts into a hooded person from behind while a masked man next to him does the same to another hooded figure. Miloš's carnal appetite had nearly led him to feast on Jeca's young flesh as if he were an incestuous father, and now he is made to face the consequences of such unfettered desire, for when one hood is removed, he sees to his horror that he has sodomised his own son, Petar. The masked man next to him is revealed to be his brother, Marko, who smiles in smug satisfaction that he has finally been able to take sexual possession of Miloš's wife, for it is Marija who is under the other hood. Marko thus serves as a lesson for Miloš in the pitfalls of sexual rivalry between men and its dehumanising reduction of the woman to an object. In the end, after trying but failing to rouse his wife and son from a near-comatose state following the trauma they have suffered, Miloš lies with his arm around them in bed and fires a bullet that passes through all three of them. On the one hand, this is Miloš's last act of penetrative violence, the culmination of the damage he has done to his family. On the other hand, at least by dying with them, he identifies with the victims rather than perpetuating his role as an aggressor.

SOUTH KOREA

The Host (Gwoemul) (2006)

Director: Joon-ho Bong
Cast: Kang-ho Song (Gang-du), Ah-sung Ko (Hyun-seo)

Upon its first appearance, the ferocious monster in this film – an amphibious mutant with slavering jaws and a tentacular tail – climbs out of a river and runs along a crowded embankment, swallowing people whole. The beast also slips and falls on a hillside, taking a bit of a tumble. This unexpected 'pratfall' is an early sign of director Joon-ho Bong's intention to upend the usual monster-movie conventions. 'I have a real love and hate feeling towards American genre movies,' he has said. 'I'll follow the genre conventions for a while, then I want to break out and turn them upside-down.'[101] Ostensibly, the film depicts the Korean people's battle against the beast, focusing on one family's struggle to rescue their daughter after the creature kidnaps her. However, when we see her father trip and fall the way the creature did, we begin to suspect that the film may be setting up a sly parallel between the family and the monster that runs deeper than their apparent opposition. As Bong notes, 'The system suppressing the family could really appear more monstrous than the monster itself.'[102] But what is this 'system'? The mutant monster is first created when the American military disposes of toxic chemicals by dumping them into the Han River – the same river that supplies drinking water to the people of Seoul, making them as much victims as the creature. The beast begins its life as a tadpole with more than one tail. Having no parent to provide for it, the creature must roam the riverbank, stealing away people as food, much like two little boys who, orphaned and homeless, rob an embankment snack bar to assuage their hunger. Another destitute Korean, this one a businessman bankrupted or fired during the economic recession, commits suicide by jumping off a bridge, and we see the creature hang from that same bridge before dropping into the river.

The family's father, Gang-du, is a clumsy nurturer of his schoolgirl daughter, Hyun-seo, swigging from cans of beer while offering her some, and the monster, after carrying Hyun-seo within its mouth to its lair, regurgitates her along with some beer cans. When she tries to escape, the creature grabs her with its giant tail but then gently sets her down. Gang-du has trouble convincing the authorities that his daughter has been kidnapped by the beast. In an attempt to explain, Gang-du mimes, 'I'm the creature; I ate her,' in what may also be a confession of his poor parenting. Rather than helping him, officials decide that the creature and anyone who came into contact with it are carrying a deadly virus, and so they begin chasing after Gang-du and his family, who are now feared and hunted like the beast. In the end, just as Gang-du is battling to get the beast to release his daughter from its jaws, the authorities have all three of them bombed with a toxic gas known as Agent Yellow. Referring to this mistreatment of man and beast, Bong has said, 'Maybe the climax is the struggle between victim and victim. Maybe the real monster is Agent Yellow'[103] and the various officials – government, medical and military – who deploy one toxic chemical (the gas) to cover up the disastrous results of another toxic chemical (the one they originally dumped in the river).

SPAIN

Pan's Labyrinth (El Laberinto del fauno) (2006)

Director: Guillermo del Toro
Cast: Ivana Baquero (Ofelia), Sergi López (Vidal), Doug Jones (Faun and Cannibal), Maribel Verdú (Mother)

It is Spain in 1944. Ofelia is a 13-year-old girl forced to grow up under fascist rule. Her father, a humble tailor whom she idolised, has died and been replaced by a cruel stepfather, a dictatorial military captain named Vidal who seems far from ideal. To cope with this perplexing change in paternity, Ofelia creates a fantasy world where she enters a labyrinth and encounters a faun that walks upright on its goat legs

28 Days Later (2002)

Berberian Sound Studio (2012)

Piranha 3D (2010)

The Cabin in the Woods (2012)

Byzantium (2012)

The Descent (2005)

Drag Me To Hell (2009)

Dead Snow (2009)

Open Water (2003)

Paranormal Activity (2007)

High Tension (2003)

Hostel (2005)

Pontypool (2008)

Taxidermia (2006)

The Witch (2015)

The Conjuring (2013)

Trick 'r Treat (2007)

The Babadook (2014)

Eden Lake (2008)

Sinister (2012)

Halloween (2007)

The Host (2013)

Nina Forever (2015)

Only Lovers Left Alive (2013)

The Neon Demon (2016)

Under the Skin (2013)

and cloven hooves and speaks with a man's face under its curved horns. Sometimes humane and at other times animalistic, the bearded goat-man is either offering her wise guidance or devilishly leading her astray, and Ofelia must learn to discern the difference. A father used to be someone she always trusted and listened to, but should she heed the advice of her father now that he is Vidal? The mysterious faun and the labyrinth represent Ofelia's attempt to figure out this paternal problem. Vidal has shaken her faith in fathers, and Ofelia is looking for a way to restore that belief, as when she finds a fallen stone eye and replaces it in the face of a faun statue.

The faun counsels her to complete three tasks, the first of which involves crawling through a hole in a blighted tree to confront the monstrous toad that keeps it from thriving and to take a key from the toad's belly. As Ofelia journeys through the opening at the base of the tree, it looks as though she is crawling into a womb. Ofelia's fantastic journey is her way of imagining how to face a real-life predicament. Her evil stepfather (the toad) has impregnated her mother (the tree), causing her to feel sick (the blight). Ofelia fears that the offspring implanted there is consuming her mother's life, so she pours milk and some drops of her own blood onto a mandrake root as if she herself could help nourish the baby. She also imagines delivering the child (taking the key from the belly) to save her mother.

The faun advises Ofelia to undertake a second task that has her entering the banquet room of a blood-covered monster who has fallen asleep after gorging on a tableful of fruit and meat, the latter of which probably includes the flesh of children given the paintings of cannibalism hanging on the walls. Ofelia must purloin the creature's dagger without waking him up and she must not, the faun warns, eat anything from the table. Her stepfather, Vidal (a monster), has also hoarded food and feasted on it, consuming provisions that could have fed the region's children, and Ofelia imagines stealing his knife so that he can eat no more. But she herself gives way to temptation and eats two grapes, which causes the monster, who keeps his own eyeballs in a dish on the table, to palm them and hold them up to his face so that he can see and pursue Ofelia. The two grapes in her hands are linked to the eyeballs in his palms because Ofelia has acted like a greedy monster in snatching food for herself. When the monster then comes after her, she realises that she was wrong not to have followed the faun's advice.

The third task set by the faun for Ofelia requires her to spill the blood of her innocent baby brother, who has recently been born as their mother died in childbirth. Ofelia defies the faun's final command and, rather than allow her brother to be harmed, lets her own innocent blood be shed when Vidal fires a bullet into her belly, causing crimson drops to fall into a puddle containing a reflection of the full moon. Thus Ofelia comes of age, making the mature decision to sacrifice herself to save her brother, giving up her own life to preserve his, much as her mother did. This time Ofelia is right to disobey the faun. She has learned to tell the difference between trustworthy fathers and those who must be opposed. She is killed by her stepfather, but as a reward for her selfless action, she is allowed to join her true father in heaven.

SWEDEN

Let the Right One In (Låt den rätte komma in) (2008)

Director: Tomas Alfredson
Cast: Kåre Hedebrant (Oskar), Lina Leandersson (Eli), Patrik Rydmark (Conny), Rasmus Luthander (Jimmy), Per Ragnar (Håkan)

In a working-class district of Stockholm, 12-year-old Oskar is subjected to daily torment by school bullies, who verbally demean him, soak his trousers in the urinal, and flog him with sticks. Oskar meets a mysterious young person named Eli, who encourages him to fight back: 'Hit harder than you dare. Then they'll stop.' On a school skating trip, when the bully Conny threatens to dunk him in an ice hole, Oskar whacks him across the ear with a pole. However, rather than stopping the violence, this act merely provokes Conny's older brother, Jimmy, to attempt to drown Oskar in a swimming pool, at which point Eli arrives to dismember and decapitate Jimmy and the other bullies, saving Oskar. Each instance of 'hitting back harder' just becomes another link in the chain of predation, pulling Oskar deeper into the cycle of violence. Speaking of Oskar's decision to whack Conny, director Tomas Alfredson has said, 'You really can understand him 100 per cent. Yet at the same time we can't tell our children to fight each other ... A lot of stories suggest that fighting back is the solution – I really don't believe that it works in the long run.'[104]

Although Eli means to help Oskar when he tells him to fight back, Eli is himself deeply enmeshed in a web of predators and prey. Two hundred years ago, he was castrated by a paedophile vampire who drank from the gushing wound and turned him. Now Eli is in a sadomasochistic relationship with a middle-aged man named Håkan, who preys on youths in the park and the school locker room, slitting their throats in order to bring their blood back for Eli to drink. In the relationship between Håkan and Eli, it is difficult to tell exploiter from exploited, for although Håkan is ostensibly an older man 'keeping' and 'abusing' the young Eli, this 'boy' is in fact a centuries-old vampire using Håkan to fetch him blood. Håkan himself is increasingly conscience-stricken, botching his attempts to kill the local youths and disfiguring his own face with acid out of guilt. In the end, the abusive Håkan allows Eli to drink him dry and then drop him from a window, thus putting him out of his misery.

When Eli and Oskar begin a relationship, the fear is that the vampire boy will corrupt the human one by turning him towards the commission of violence. 'Oskar, be me a little,' Eli says, encouraging him to hit the bullies. When Oskar whacks Conny, it is with the same pole that Håkan used to push another youth's victimised body into an ice hole, which makes us wonder whether Oskar will be drawn into the same kind of sadomasochistic relationship with others that Håkan and Eli had. At one point, in an effort to save Eli from a male attacker, Oskar is just about to use a knife to stab the man when Eli himself sinks his fangs into the assailant. Afterwards, Eli kisses Oskar with his blood-smeared mouth. How much will their potentially loving relationship be tainted by this penetrative violence? The film leaves us with this open question, but also with some cause for hope. The fact that Oskar and Eli are (ostensibly) the same age, a still (relatively) innocent 12 years old, suggests that they may be able to make a fresh start and establish a less exploitative relationship of greater equality. Their interest in stroking each other, hugging and holding hands evinces a tender physicality apart from the violence that otherwise surrounds them. And, after all, the vampire Eli did ask Oskar to 'be me a *little*'. Let's hope it is not too much.

UNITED KINGDOM

Eden Lake (2008)

Director: James Watkins
Cast: Kelly Reilly (Jenny), Michael Fassbender (Steve)

According to writer-director James Watkins, '*Eden Lake* is a horror movie being played out in every street, in every town in the current climate of fear that adults have toward bored and unruly teenagers.' Noting that 'newspapers are full of such "hoodie nightmare" stories', Watkins asks, 'But was our fear founded in any reality, or just a projection based on tabloid out-of-control-youth features?'[105] Rather than make just a 'hoodie horror' film, Watkins says he set out to mix 'chills and thrills with intellect', adding, 'I don't see why those have to be mutually exclusive in a genre picture.'[106] So, how does the film portray its trainer-, tracksuit- and hoodie-wearing teen characters? During the course of the movie, these youths ride their BMX bikes in front of traffic, blast hip-hop music on their boom box, stomp a boy's caterpillar, unleash a Rottweiler, ogle a woman and waggle an exposed penis at her, torment a caged bunny, joyride in a stolen car, bind a man with barbed wire to a post, stab him repeatedly with knives and box-cutters in the mouth and belly, and attempt to burn his girlfriend alive. Any nuances in the portrayals of individual teens (some of them have to be bullied or bribed into participating) tend to get lost in the overall brutality. Thus it seems fair to say that the movie demonises 'chavs' or working-class youths – to the point where a case could almost be made that it is parodying tabloid accounts of 'hoodie nightmares', were it not for the grim seriousness with which these kids' crimes are depicted.

And what about the 20-something couple who run afoul of these terrible teens? Is there any sense that they are something other than just innocent victims? Here the movie can be credited with displaying some subtlety and insight. Jenny and Steve leave their London apartments for a romantic getaway in the rural Midlands, renting a Range Rover – with luxury back massage – to get there. They seem blissfully unaware of their bourgeois privilege. He wants to show her a scenic spot on the edge of a flooded quarry, before the beachfront land is built over by developers and turned into 'Eden Lake, a secure gated community of fifty superior New England homes', according to a billboard advertisement. Even as the couple lament the impending invasion of this land, formerly a public park, which is to become a private enclave for the rich, they fail to realise that they themselves may look like well-to-do invaders to the working-class natives, who have scrawled 'fuck off yuppie cunts' on the back of the billboard. Jenny and Steve presume they are entitled to enter this community and bask on its beach, and when the local teens play their music too loud and let their dog run wild, Steve saunters over to get them under control, not seeing how this could be interpreted as arrogance. 'This is a big beach. There's room for all of us,' he says to the kids who are about to lose their land for good to wealthier, more powerful people like Steve. Returning to lie next to Jenny, Steve comments, 'We were here first.' Really? The couple were first on the beach that day, but these teens are the ones who grew up in this area and call it home. Later, after one of the teens steals Steve's sunglasses and claims they are his own shades, Steve scoffs, 'Your Ray-Ban Aviators?' Mixed in with Steve's rightful demand for his property back, there is the arrogance of class privilege. And so the film does show that the teens' violence is not mere perversity, but a reaction to the *structural* violence of economic inequality, to years of feeling exploited and excluded by more affluent urbanites such as Steve. Will the film's critique of class entitlement register as strongly with viewers as its exposé of teen brutality? Not likely.

Kill List (2011)

Director: Ben Wheatley
Cast: Neil Maskell (Jay), MyAnna Buring (Shel), Michael Smiley (Gal)

Jay is a war veteran suffering from post-traumatic stress disorder who takes pills to help prevent psychotic episodes. During the course of the film, he is repeatedly told to 'wake up', and it is never clear how much of the movie is reality or Jay's delirious dream. The film begins as a social-realist drama with Jay's wife, Shel, berating him for not seeking employment and furious that he has failed to return with the proper items on the grocery list. This list then morphs into a 'kill list' as Jay finds employment as a hit man, and kitchen-sink realism turns into crime drama. Now the concern is over assassinating the proper prescribed targets, as Jay and his ex-army buddy Gal ponder their assignment: to kill a priest. Jay figures that the priest is probably a paedophile, remarking that, as a parent himself, he would kill all such child abusers even if he weren't being paid. Just before this, Gal comments that at least their target is 'not a toddler', which implies that the two of them may have killed children before. Indeed, Jay says that killing a paedophile may help make up for 'all the terrible shit' they have done. Speaking of his wartime experiences, Jay wishes he had fought during World War Two rather than in Iraq, for the latter war lacked the moral certainties and clear-cut distinctions of the former. Before killing the priest, Jay gets angry at a religious group that is singing 'Onward, Christian soldiers, marching as to war'. 'God loves you,' a congregant tells him. 'Does He?' Jay asks. It would seem that Jay's killing of the 'paedophile' priest is a desperate assertion of his own goodness as separate from the other man's evil. Director Ben Wheatley points out that Jay's 'have-a-go-hero style' represents a 'total misunderstanding of the way that violence goes both ways. You commit these things, but they look into you as much as you look into them.'[107]

Jay's next target is a snuff-video librarian, and after watching footage of women being tortured and killed, Jay sears the librarian's ear with a lit cigarette, hammers his kneecaps, and pounds his head to a pulp, finally burning the body. As Jay watches the man's flesh go up in flames, he comments, 'They're bad people. They *should* suffer. I used to love looking at fires when I was a kid.' Earlier, Jay has roasted and eaten a rabbit the cat dragged in. Shel decides that the cat's gift of the rabbit wasn't about providing food for the family. 'I just think the cat likes killing rabbits,' she says, and the same comment could apply to Jay, who kills as much because he likes it as to bring money home. But Jay denies this truth about himself, clinging instead to the idea that *his* violence is justified to rid the world of *other* violent men. 'It's not a crusade,' Gal warns him, but Jay sees himself as a heroic knight doing battle against evil. As the film finally morphs from crime drama to full-on horror, Jay engages in a kind of jousting match with what he thinks is a member of a satanic cult in a scene lit by flaming torches. As the victorious Christian Jay fatally stabs the disguised figure, its mask and cloak come off to reveal that Jay has in fact killed his own wife and son. Blinded by self-righteousness, Jay has become the very villain he sought to defeat. His violence has rebounded on his own family, making him a murderer of the woman and child he wanted to protect.

UNITED STATES

Red State (2011)

Director: Kevin Smith
Cast: Michael Parks (Cooper), Michael Angarano (Travis), Kyle Gallner (Jarod)

Viewers who go to a Kevin Smith film would normally expect it to be funny rather than frightening, so *Red State*, which he has called his first horror movie but which also contains elements of a teen sex comedy, provides an opportunity to explore the differences between the world of humour and the world of horror. Somewhere in Middle America, a far-right fringe of religious extremists lures three horny teen boys with an online ad promising group sex. The cult plans to tie each boy to a cross in the church, bind him with plastic wrap, and shoot him in the head as punishment for being gay. This world of horror is created by divisive rhetoric and exclusionary violence. Cult leader Cooper's jeremiad against homosexuality blames gays for everything that is wrong with the world, including 'rampant fornication', 'adultery' and 'abortion'. Cooper's dehumanising rhetoric reduces gays to 'insects' or 'germs', so the Lord's 'commandment ... against killing your fellow man' supposedly does not apply to them. This crazed preacher's hate speech is designed to whip his congregation into a killing frenzy. Cooper's God is not one who 'forgives your sins', but one who 'abhors the wicked', as seen when a cult member pulls a gun from a bible to kill the infidels. Cooper and his congregation feel so threatened by the spread of 'wickedness' that they must forcibly contain and eliminate it. 'Watch that gay saliva ... it can turn ya,' Cooper warns, which is why their victims are covered in plastic wrap before being executed. The thought that any of the congregants themselves might have gay desires must be ruthlessly repressed and expelled by being projected onto others, who are then killed.

The teen boys (lured by the congregation) are also subject to gay panic, but like comedian Kevin Smith, they deal with their homophobia by using humour to defuse the fear and establish empathy for their fellow human beings. 'I've always said I'm one cock in the mouth shy of being gay myself,' Smith jokes, acknowledging his discomfort by making inclusive humour out of it. (Smith has also frequently noted that he has a gay brother whom he loves.) The horny teens in *Red State* clown around as a way of managing their fear of their own immoderate desires. Travis, who has wondered whether the three of them having group sex with the same woman is not 'a little faggoty', has earlier been told jokingly by Jarod, 'You're not gay. You're just curious.' Because these guys discharge their fears through humour, they avoid violence. The three boys talk constantly about sex, bragging about their sexual prowess and desirability ('This bitch wants my dick, don't she?'), but they seem to be virgins using macho words in an attempt to overcome performance anxiety and work up the courage to even approach a woman. The boys' language may be homophobic and sexist, but their joking provides a peaceful way for them to express their anxieties – until their sex comedy is ended by the cult's horror.

Lost River (2014)

Director: Ryan Gosling
Cast: Christina Hendricks (Billy), Iain De Caestecker (Bones), Saoirse Ronan (Rat), Barbara Steele (Grandmother), Matt Smith (Bully)

In bankrupt Detroit, single mother Billy is sold a subprime mortgage. Desperate to make the payments so that she and her two sons can remain in their home, Billy takes a job at a Grand Guignol cabaret where audience members are titillated by watching women 'bleed' from staged stabbings and other gruesome modes of mock murder. Billy wows the crowd with an act where she slices into and then removes the skin from her own face. With such horrific scenes, the movie finds a physically affecting metaphor for something otherwise abstract: predatory lending practices and their vicious impact on female victims like Billy, who are bled dry by capitalism. (Note that the Grand Guignol club is run by a bank manager.) Billy's self-flaying is also a metaphor for her masochistic attachment to her house. No matter what the terrible cost to herself, she clings to this last remnant of the American Dream, long after it has turned into a nightmare.

Billy's son, Bones, has a girlfriend, Rat, whose grandmother is also a prisoner of the past, for all she does is watch home movies of her honeymoon. These date from the time before her husband was drowned by reservoir water while working on a dam construction project. Once again, the film finds a horrifically concrete symbol for capitalism's betrayal of the American Dream: the promise of abundant water for everyone actually meant the flooding of an entire town and the loss of those people's homes. In her mute suffering, the grandmother remains obsessed with that broken promise, the life she could have had with her husband. Like a gothic heroine, she is haunted by the past, and in the end, her house goes up in flames as she succumbs to suicidal despair.

By contrast, gang leader Bully chooses a more active way to deal with economic deprivation. Emitting howls of rage, he engages in a vicious competition for the few remaining scraps left to the people, fighting with Bones over the copper scavenged from abandoned buildings. In an effort to comprehend and contain the threat posed by Bully, Bones likens the gang leader to a dragon that must be slain, an act which would also break the spell placed on the people when the town was flooded. This 'spell' has kept people attached to the past, in a sense underwater with the drowned and thus vulnerable to scavenging predators like the bank manager and Bully. In the end, Bones defeats the 'dragon' Bully by turning his own violence against him, and he rescues Rat and his mother, the 'damsels in distress', which is to say that Bones gets beyond sadistic aggression and masochistic self-mutilation as responses to the economic crisis, freeing his family to leave this devastated region and start afresh somewhere else. As writer-director Ryan Gosling explained, 'These kids had created this idea of what's happening to them as being like a fairy tale' – a dark narrative fantasy that eventually enabled them to find the light.[108]

INNOVATIONS

3D HORROR

My Bloody Valentine 3D (2009)

Director: Patrick Lussier
Cast: Jaime King (Sarah), Michael Roberts McKee (Jason)

Saw 3D (aka *Saw: The Final Chapter*) (aka *Saw VII*) (2010)

Director: Kevin Greutert
Cast: Sebastian Pigott (Brad), Jon Cor (Ryan), Anne Greene (Dina)

Final Destination 5 3D (2011)

Director: Steven Quale
Cast: Jacqueline MacInnes Wood (Olivia)

In *Saw 3D*, two men and a woman are trapped inside a storefront window. Each is strapped to a circular saw, with Brad and Ryan facing each other and with Dina suspended above them. Either man could save himself and Dina by pushing the saw so that it will cut through and kill his opponent, as she encourages each in turn to do. However, when the men realise Dina has slept with both of them, they decide she isn't worth saving. Taking their seemingly justified revenge against the 'lying bitch', they allow the saw to slice through

Dina. Indeed, the punishment Dina receives appears apt for a two-timing woman. Instead of being an innocent angel above them, she has used her sexual wiles to manipulate them into thinking she loves them. The emergence effect of 3D emphasises her breasts pushing out of her pink top as the men look up at her from below, and the saw cuts through her bare midriff as a fitting punishment for this female double-crosser, as if to divide her between the two men she has cheated on. 'I think we're *breaking up* with you, Dina,' Ryan quips sardonically. And yet, despite the moral condemnation of Dina, the 3D also makes us feel physical compassion for her. As the saw draws nearer and nearer to her, we see its spinning blade jutting out at her from her point of view, just as we also see the saw blades approaching Brad and Ryan from their perspectives. Thus the scene has us share Dina's fear of bodily injury as well as Brad and Ryan's. As the saw cuts into Dina's stomach, blood splatters on the two men's faces and into ours, as the arterial spray seems to shoot out of the screen and into our laps. We may think that Dina deserves to be judged and executed, but the 3D forces us to face the fact that, in feeling that way, we, too, have blood on our hands.

The sight of that approaching saw makes a lacerating impression, reminding us of how often 3D horror is an ophthalmologist's nightmare of assaults on our vision. Later in *Saw 3D*, a woman is clamped to a metal platform that gradually rotates so that her eyes are brought closer and closer to the pointed ends of two steel rods. We view these sharp spikes projecting outwards towards us as seen from her point of view. Eventually, a shot of the woman in profile shows the spikes piercing her eyeballs and penetrating her skull through her eye sockets. This is the scene that garnered the film a Golden Raspberry Award nomination for the 'Worst Eye-Gouging Misuse of 3D', but by horror-movie standards, the scene is effective in its slow build-up of fear and its squishy and splatterrific climax. 'In eye-popping 3D' was the tagline for this *Saw* movie.

It is no accident that 3D horror films often include assaults on characters' eyes, which are stand-ins for our own ocular orbs. Cartoon characters are sometimes shown with eyes extending outwards on their stalks – a figurative way of depicting their shock and surprise at something they've just seen. And the startle effect in 3D horror is typically created by objects jumping out at us from the screen, as if in mirror image of our own distended eyeballs. In *My Bloody Valentine 3D*, teens are being terrorised by a pickaxe-wielding killer wearing a gas mask and miner's helmet. Sarah's eyes bug out in fright when she sees a man in a gas mask, but as he removes it, his laughing face reveals him to be merely a boy named Jason who was throwing a scare into her. However, this brief comic relief is then disrupted when a pickaxe, having been swung and sunk into the back of Jason's head, pushes his eye out of its socket towards the viewer, with his eyeball stuck on the pick's point. This literally eye-popping moment displays the shock felt by Jason, Sarah and us as we suddenly realise that the real killer is standing behind Jason, having put out his eye and darkened his vision for good, intending to come for us next. The killer smashes a light bulb with his pickaxe and then shines the headlamp on his miner's helmet directly into Sarah's eyes and ours, creating a blinding effect with the bright beam of light. 'You can't get closer than this' – the movie's tagline – suggests that these attacks on characters' eyes are a way of doubling 3D horror's assault on our own gaze, of bringing us nearer to ocular injury and destruction.

In regular '2D' films, the screen acts as an invisible 'fourth wall' separating spectators from the action, securing us in our position as mere onlookers. The jump scares of 3D are often achieved by breaking the fourth wall, with the shattering of glass as one way of having objects seem to burst out at us through the screen. In *My Bloody Valentine 3D*, the killer hurls his pickaxe at the windshield of a truck in which a terrified Sarah is seated. The axe embeds itself in the fractured glass, with the point of the pick poking through at us in an emergence effect, just inches from Sarah's eye. By appearing to break forth from the screen and invade our viewing space, the 3D projectile targets us as part of the onslaught, inducing bodily fear for our safety. In another scene, a car with two teens in it crashes in the woods. The pointed end of a large tree branch breaks through the front windshield, causing them to duck, and then it smashes through the rear window glass, causing us to duck. As noted by *Boxoffice*, 'Horror is a perfect genre for 3D because it amplifies the terror by allowing audiences to be fully immersed in the environment.'[109]

By breaking the frame and thrusting pointy objects at our eyes, 3D pop-outs work to physically involve us, but at the same time they distance us, too, by reminding us that we are only watching a movie. After wincing at the sight of characters being pierced and impaled, we can laugh in relief at the realisation that our eyes and bodies are still intact, that we are apart from – and not a part of – the mayhem on screen. Viewing 3D horror, we are alternately absorbed by and disconnected from the fear and suffering we witness. During the laser eye surgery of a young woman named Olivia in *Final Destination 5 3D*, she is so nervous that she twists the head of the teddy bear she is holding until one eye pops out. Our laughter fades quickly as we watch from her point of view as the laser gun above malfunctions, sending a searing beam of red light down to slice into her eye. Half blinded and reeling in panic, Olivia staggers around the room, and in a 'banana peel' moment of high comedy, her shoe slips on the teddy bear's fallen eye. Less humorously, this causes her to fall out of the window and smash into the windshield of a car below, the impact of which leads her own eyeball to pop out and roll towards us into the street, where it stares at us, pupil dilating, before being crushed by a passing vehicle. Looking destruction in the eye, we may feel that 'Death has never been closer' (as the film's tagline puts it), but we can also say that death seems further away from us than ever, something we can watch and laugh at, for her eye is not 'I'.[110]

Piranha 3D (2010)

Director: Alexandre Aja
Cast: Steven R McQueen (Jake), Kelly Brook and Riley Steele (Nude Swimmers), Gianna Michaels (Parasailing Woman), Jerry O'Connell (Derrick)

Lecherous leering and punishing guilt go together as surely as teens and horror, and 3D films are no exception. In this film, teenage Jake watches through the window of a glass-bottomed boat as two nude women perform an undulating ballet together underwater. But while he enjoys the eye-popping sight of curvaceous flanks and bodacious ta-tas, his ears receive a phone call from his mother, who is also the town sheriff. His head is thus divided between bulging video of jiggling flesh and intrusive audio which interrupts his visual pleasure. What Jake would love to do is dive in and ogle these 'naked honeys' up-close, but another diver who does plunge in ends up being attacked by piranhas. As we see his severed eye float towards us in a pop-out effect, a passing piranha gobbles it up – no more leering looks at women for him!

In another scene, an excited Jake uses a phallic camcorder to film the 'flying ta-tas' of a woman parasailing. Feeling guilty, he misses the moment when her breasts pop out of her bikini top and then protrude below the surface of the water, as seen from below by ravenous piranhas. Here the film asks us to consider whether the male craving for mammaries – the reduction of women to meat – might not be that different from the piranhas' predatory hunger. Now that we have seen her topless, why not bottomless as well? As if in sardonic answer to our voracious sexual appetite, when the parasailing woman is again lifted out of the water, she is bottomless in the sense that her lower half has been eaten away by piranhas. Unlike the guilt-ridden Jake, wannabe pornographer Derrick has no qualms about his sexploitative lust for female flesh. It seems fitting, then, that when the piranhas devour *his* lower half, one of the razor-toothed fish spits out his severed penis at us in the viewing audience, as if to castrate our ogling eyes.

Piranha 3DD (2012)

Director: John Gulager
Cast: Danielle Panabaker (Maddy), Katrina Bowden (Shelby), Jean-Luc
Bilodeau (Josh), Meagan Tandy (Ashley), Paul James Jordan (Travis)

In the classic slasher films, teens are often killed just before,
during or after sex, as if their deaths are provoked by a fear of
parental punishment, internalised guilt or adolescent anxiety
about each other's unfamiliar bodies. *Piranha 3DD* deals with the
latter, prompting us to consider what difference 3D makes when
it comes to the female fear of penetration and the male dread of
dismemberment. While female friends Maddy and Shelby are
sitting on a jetty with their spread legs dangling in the water, they
are frightened by piranhas swimming up towards them. As the girls
flee, two of the wooden boards on the pier begin to separate, leaving
Shelby with her legs straddling an open expanse of water. From her
terrified point of view, we look down to see one of the phallic fish
leaping out of the water towards her crotch in a 'cominatcha' effect.
In another scene that has Shelby and her boyfriend, Josh, skinny-
dipping together in the lake, she says, 'I just felt something against
me. Is that you? … Ow! What are you doing?' Underwater, we see
piranhas thrusting themselves forward towards us and between
her legs, accompanied by a noise that sounds like a baseball going
into a catcher's mitt. By representing intercourse as penetration
by a piranha, the film both acknowledges female fears of the male
sex and defuses those fears by making them seem absurd. 3D
exaggerates the terror, augmenting it only to diminish it.

The piranha turns out to be an equal opportunity symbol when it
comes to anxiety over erotic activity. In a scene where Shelby and
Josh make love, ripples in her belly indicate a piranha swimming
around inside her as if it were a deadly sperm deposited there by
him. Then a crunching sound, followed by an 'in-yer-face' view of
the piranha attached to the end of Josh's erection, shows *his* fear
of Shelby's sex as a *vagina dentata*. After this shot of the protruding

piranha, we see Josh grab a knife and swing it downwards in a self-castration with blood spatter coming at his face and ours, confronting us with the deadly consequences of sex with Shelby. 'What the hell did you do to me?' he accuses her. And yet the dismemberment of Josh is so over the top that it discredits the very fear it depicts. By literalising the female sex as a mah-eating piranha, the film pokes fun at gynophobia, as in the later scene where Shelby quite blatantly says, 'Josh cut off his penis because something came out of my vagina.'

In another scene, kinky Ashley handcuffs her boyfriend, Travis, and then uses her teeth to undo the drawstring of his shorts prior to having sex. When the van they are in begins to sink into the lake, he is trapped by the cuffs and subjected to attack by sharp-toothed piranhas, resulting in a 3D 'out-of-the-screen' shot where he thrusts the bloody stump of his flesh-eaten arm out at Ashley and at us. The scene brings into sharp relief the male fear of women as the devouring and castrating sex while also making ghoulish fun of this fear.

The Hole 3D (2009)

Director: Joe Dante
Cast: Chris Massoglia (Dane), Nathan Gamble (Lucas)

Dracula 3D (2012)

Director: Dario Argento
Cast: Unax Ugalde (Harker)

Nurse 3D (2013)

Director: Douglas Aarniokoski
Cast: Katrina Bowden (Danni), Melanie Scrofano (Rachel), Paz de la Huerta (Abby)

Poltergeist 3D (2015)

Director: Gil Kenan
Cast: Kyle Catlett (Griffin)

While most stereoscopic scares involve sudden protuberances jutting out from the screen, a more subtle use of 3D can induce a deeper sense of creeping dread. In *Poltergeist 3D*, when a boy named Griffin backs slowly away from a mysteriously rolling baseball, a supernaturally stacked house of cards looms in the extreme foreground just behind his shoulders, making us feel that some evil entity has crept up on him and is about to topple his happy home. In another scene, Griffin looks down to see a red ball on a string being drawn between his legs and behind him, where it is revealed to be a retractable nose that snaps back into place on the face of a spooky clown. As the terrified boy bends down to watch the 'ball drop' between his spread legs, leading to an inverted shot of his world turned upside-down, the 3D emphasises the physicality of his experience, positioning us to share his pubertal fear of bodily changes.

3D can heighten our proprioceptive awareness of our bodies in an eerie or perilous space. When Griffin peers into a dark closet, it seems to recede into the far depths as if trying to suck him into the unknown. In *The Hole 3D*, brothers Dane and Lucas enter a closet and discover a ladder whose rungs seem to stretch upwards into endless night, figuring the fears they must face and surmount. In *Dracula 3D*, following an attack by the vampire, a weakened Jonathan Harker struggles to descend a spiral staircase, as the additional spatial amplitude of the steps twisting away below him helps to convey his disorientation within this unfamiliar and hostile place. Unlike the intrusive images of negative parallax (objects that appear to pop out in front of the screen), these 'extensive' effects deploy 3D in a more subtle way, using stereoscopic vision to convey a sense of sinister space opening up behind the screen and pulling the viewer in. According to the creators of *The Hole 3D*, their goal was to 'think how far in to the picture can we go':[111] 'If this is a scary [place] with fear all around, you want the fear to be all around the theatre – and the best way to do that is to make [viewers] feel like they're in the picture. So most of the 3D is not the "throwing things out of the screen" 3D – it's a "drawing you into the picture" kind of feel.'[112]

The dual capability of 3D – to bulge in your face or to extend into depth of space – can be disturbingly ambiguous, for it is not always clear what is near and what is far or where the threat is coming from. In *Poltergeist 3D*, when a tree branch breaks through a window into Griffin's bedroom, the boy runs out of the room, closing the door behind him. The mirror on the back of the door shows us the tree's claw-like hand reaching out for him, and it appears to be simultaneously protruding from the screen to grab us *and* extending into the space beyond the closed door to grasp Griffin. The tree's reach knows no bounds; its menace is everywhere. When Lucas in *The Hole 3D* peers out of his bedroom window at night, his abusive father appears to be standing outside in the dark – or is it his father's reflection in the window that the boy sees, which means the menacing man is standing right behind Lucas in his bedroom? Further depth is added to this scene when we realise that Lucas could grow up to become a violent man like his father, as figured by the stereoscopic overlay of his father's reflection upon his own in the window. Finally, in *Nurse 3D*, as Danni is Skyping with her friend Rachel, the laptop monitor shows Abby, a crazed nurse with a hypodermic needle, creep up behind Rachel's back. 'Rachel, look behind you!' Danni warns, frantically motioning with her hands as if she could somehow reach behind her friend to ward off the threat. But despite the three-dimensionality of the image that makes Rachel and Abby seem present in the flesh, they are far removed from Danni, as the camera shows by arcing around to a side view of the laptop screen to reveal the empty space behind it. This confusion between surface and depth becomes even worse when we realise that Abby is really stalking Danni, so as Danni peers at her laptop monitor, she might as well be looking into a mirror and warning herself about the crazed nurse coming up behind *her* with that needle. Threatening objects on the screen are actually closer than they appear.

ASIAN HORROR AND AMERICAN REMAKES

Dark Water (Honogurai mizu no soko kara) (2002)

Director: Hideo Nakata
Cast: Hitomi Kuroki (Yoshimi), Rio Kanno (Ikuko), Mirei Oguchi (Mitsuko)

Dark Water (2005)

Director: Walter Salles
Cast: Jennifer Connelly (Dahlia), Ariel Gade (Ceci), John C Reilly (Estate Agent), Pete Postlethwaite (Superintendent), Matt Lemche and Edward Kennington (Boys), Dougray Scott (Kyle), Tim Roth (Lawyer)

Yoshimi is a single mother whose recent divorce has required her to return to work. When she is repeatedly late to pick up her five-year-old daughter, Ikuko, after school, Yoshimi's dereliction triggers memories of her own neglectful mother, which she herself is afraid of becoming. This fear begins to haunt her, taking form as the ghost of a girl, Mitsuko, who used to live in the apartment above Yoshimi and Ikuko. When Mitsuko's mother abandoned her, the unsupervised girl ended up drowning in the building's rooftop water tank. Now, as Yoshimi spends less and less time with her daughter due to work, a damp stain on their apartment ceiling begins to leak, with water drops gradually building to a virtual downpour. The warm baths Ikuko used to take with her mother turn into cold tears as the child feels increasingly abandoned, and the ghostly arms of Mitsuko reach out in an attempt to drown Ikuko in the bathtub. Yoshimi believes that the only way to save her daughter, Ikuko, is to become a full-time mother to Mitsuko, and so Yoshimi dies in the flooding waters so that she can spend eternity as a ghost caring for the ghost girl. Needing and possibly wanting to work but unable to do so without feeling that she is a neglectful mother, Yoshimi fails to find balance in her life. To avoid becoming like her often-absent mother, Yoshimi swings to the opposite extreme, sacrificing her entire life to motherhood. To make up for the past maternal neglect suffered by Mitsuko and by Yoshimi herself when she was a child, Yoshimi becomes the spiritual ideal of a mother – a woman always there for her child, but in a sense never there for herself, for any aspect of life beyond motherhood, and thus a kind of ghost self.

However, the film's epilogue suggests that the future may hold something different for women, a way beyond the two extremes of negligence or self-sacrifice. When Yoshimi gives up her life to become a mother to Mitsuko, Ikuko is ostensibly left without maternal care. And yet when Ikuko grows up to be a teenager with desires for a life that includes but also exceeds motherhood, she begins to understand the dilemma her own mother faced. Even though her deceased mother has not been physically present in her life, Ikuko comes to believe that she has always spiritually been there, watching over her – much as working mothers are still a presence in their children's lives, even when those women are at work. In this way, the film gestures towards a time when children of working mothers will not feel so abandoned, and when those mothers themselves will not feel such self-mortifying guilt.

Beyond the challenge of balancing work obligations with single motherhood, newly divorced women may also have to contend with the fear that they and their daughters have been rendered more vulnerable to predatory males. This additional dread is explored in the Hollywood remake of *Dark Water*, where mother, Dahlia, and daughter, Ceci, encounter a series of men who may or may not pose a sexual threat. An unctuous real estate agent is suspiciously positive about the building and overly avuncular with Ceci. The building superintendent says that some 'pervert' must have snatched the girl who used to live in the apartment above Dahlia and Ceci's, but he himself can't wait to watch porn videos on his lunch break. Some teenage boys, who leer at Dahlia in the laundromat, have broken into that girl's upstairs apartment and are doing mysterious things in the dark. Later, Dahlia thinks she sees her ex-husband Kyle paying these boys, who are perhaps part of a plan to drive her crazy so that she will be declared an unfit mother and he can have custody of their daughter. Their acrimonious divorce has left Kyle angry and vengeful, and he seems to be stalking Dahlia, having stubbed out his phallic cigarette on the elevator button for her floor. At the custody hearing, Kyle claims that Dahlia's father was 'physically abusive' and that she is 'mentally unstable' and subject to 'paranoid delusions'. Dahlia does not deny the history of abuse, and her anxieties about men could be due to paranoia, especially given that, in the end, Kyle appears to be benevolent enough, and Dahlia's kindly lawyer seems to help her learn to trust males again. However, the fact that we find out that the lawyer lied to her (about spending time with his family) makes us suspect that her fear of men is not entirely unfounded …

A Tale of Two Sisters (Janghwa, Hongryeon) (2003)

Director: Jee-woon Kim
Cast: Su-jeong Lim (Su-mi), Geun-young Moon (Su-yeon), Jung-ah Yum (Eun-joo), Mi-hyun Park (Mother), Kap-su Kim (Father)

The Uninvited (2009)

Directors: Guard Brothers (Charles and Thomas Guard)
Cast: Maya Massar (Mother), Emily Browning (Anna), Arielle Kebbel (Alex), Elizabeth Banks (Rachel), David Strathairn (Father), Jesse Moss (Matt)

In *The Uninvited*, after some time spent in a mental care facility following the trauma of her mother's death in a fire, teenage Anna returns home. She and her sister Alex are appalled to find that their mother's former nurse, Rachel, is about to marry their father. This woman, who is acting as though she is essentially already their stepmother, is the one they suspect of having murdered their mother. Anna is haunted by the sound of her invalid mother's bell ringing for help that never came, and Anna later remembers that on the night of the fire she spied her father and Rachel having sex. It seems to Anna that her mother's illness was basically caused by Rachel's usurpation of her role as wife and mother, and when the sickly mother returns as a charred ghost to point an accusing finger, the sisters are convinced Rachel set the fire that finally killed her. On the night of the fire, Anna had been with her boyfriend, Matt, about to have sex for the first time, but she went home when she sensed there was something wrong with her mother, only to find the wicked Rachel in lascivious congress with her father while her mother burned. When the sisters later discover a vibrator in Rachel's room, they are disgusted by this evidence of their wicked stepmother's inordinate desire, so excessive that it extended to their father. And when Rachel has Anna try on a pearl necklace which her stepmother claims she inherited from a former invalid client, Anna fears that Rachel wants to choke her with it, to get rid of the daughter just as she eliminated the mother in order to take total possession of the father. To confirm Rachel's culpability in the mother's death, Anna makes a date with Matt so that he can tell her what he saw that night, but when he comes to her in her bedroom, he is only a broken-backed ghost. The next day, he is discovered to have died from a fall – one that Anna suspects was caused by Rachel to prevent him from revealing her guilt. Fearing for their own lives, the sisters become distraught. Rachel jabs Anna with a needle, causing her to black out, and when she comes to, she finds her stepmother's bloody body in a dumpster, with her sister standing nearby, holding a knife. Anna explains to her father that Alex had to do it because their stepmother was trying to kill them. Her father says that Alex is dead – she died in the fire that killed their mother – and Anna sees that in fact she herself is the one holding the knife.

This revelation prompts us to revisit the film's events from a different perspective. Anna leaves the party before her boyfriend can have sex with her so that she can go home to her father, to whom she is overly attached. It is Anna, not her mother, who is jealous of Rachel's being with her father – a jealousy inflamed when she spies the two of them making love on that night in the main house. When Anna walks to the nearby boathouse where her mother lies in her sickbed, it is not to answer her mother's bell, but to fill a can with gasoline so that she can burn down the main house with Rachel in it. When she is interrupted by her sister Alex's arrival on the scene, Anna 'inadvertently' leaves the gas tank dripping and a candle lantern precariously placed on a table's edge. When the lantern falls and the gas catches fire, the resulting explosion kills both her mother and her sister. It is not Rachel who failed to nurse the mother that night, but Anna who didn't answer the call for help. Rachel isn't the one who wanted the mother and sister out of the way; it is Anna who killed them so that she could have her father all to herself. Anna's lust is exorbitant, desiring her own father. Anna covets the maternal necklace, wanting to be in her mother's place. Anna is accused by her mother's ghost, who is conjured up because the daughter is haunted by her own guilt. Repressing the terrible truth, Anna causes Matt's fatal fall so that he will not tell her what she doesn't want to know. Finally, even though her stepmother was just injecting her with a sedative to calm her down, Anna knifes her to death, not in self-defence but to remove the final obstacle separating her from her father. 'I finished the job I started' are Anna's words as she is taken back to the mental hospital.

Instead of admitting her own unacceptable desires, Anna denies them by projecting them onto a 'wicked' stepmother, whom she blames for them while unconsciously acting them out herself. Anna's sense of guilt gives her glimpses into the reality of the crimes she is actually committing, but ultimately her conscience is too weak for her to move much beyond solipsism and psychosis. If reality finally disturbs her fantasy, this is due less to internal promptings than to external factors such as her father's intervention. By contrast, in the original version of this family tragedy – the Korean film known as *A Tale of Two Sisters* – there is more reason to hope that the surviving sister will recover her sanity.

Like its American remake, the K-horror original has two sisters, Su-mi and Su-yeon, who blame their stepmother, Eun-joo, for their mother's death and who fear that this woman will be coming after them next. When Su-mi discovers blood on her sister's bed, she fears the worst, but it turns out to be the younger girl's first menses. The stepmother and Su-mi also get their periods at this same time. After the chirping of Eun-joo's pet bird interrupts the sisters as they attempt to whistle their mother's favourite song and the bird is then found dead in Su-yeon's bed, the enraged stepmother locks the younger sister up in a wardrobe, where Su-mi finds her and lets her out. Later, when Su-mi sees Eun-joo beating a blood-soaked sack, she believes that her stepmother has closed Su-yeon up inside it and is now brutally punishing the girl. As Su-mi works frantically to free her sister, Eun-joo attacks. Su-mi defends herself by grabbing a nearby pair of scissors and impaling Eun-joo's hand with them, but her stepmother then attempts to crush her with a statue of a figure that has its hands covering its eyes. At this point, the father intervenes to save Su-mi – from herself.

For this film contains a double reveal: not only is Su-yeon a figment of Su-mi's imagination (her sister is actually dead), but Eun-joo is imaginary as well (the stepmother is alive, but in another location). Afflicted with dissociative identity disorder, Su-mi has fantasised these two other personalities, bringing her sister back as an innocent victim so that she herself can save her, and conjuring up a wicked stepmother to battle and blame for her sister's suffering. Like the statue with its hand-covered eyes, Su-mi has wilfully blinded herself to certain harsh truths she would rather not see. What really happened is that their mother hanged herself in the wardrobe, and when Su-yeon found her and tried to take her down, the girl pulled the wardrobe over on top of herself. Eun-joo was just about to help the suffocating child when Su-mi, not knowing about her mother's death or her sister's peril, began to berate the stepmother about taking the mother's place, leading Eun-joo to decide not to save Su-yeon, who ended up perishing under the weight of the wardrobe. When Su-mi found out about the role she herself played in her sister's death, she could not bear the truth. And so she replaced it with a more comforting fantasy where she is the rescuer, freeing her sister from the wardrobe and the sack, and where her stepmother alone is the guilty aggressor, confining Su-yeon within those suffocating enclosures and trying to crush Su-mi with a statue.

But with her father's help, along with the proddings of her own conscience, Su-mi gradually begins to see through the fantasy and face the truths hidden behind it. There were not three simultaneous periods but only one – Su-mi's. Su-mi killed the bird found under Su-yeon's bedcovers, just as Su-mi was partially responsible for her sister's death by smothering. Not only does she feel implicated in her sister's demise, but Su-mi also suffers from survivor's guilt. It is she herself, not some wicked stepmother, who threatened to bring the statue down onto her own body as if she could thereby be crushed the way her sister was under the wardrobe. And it is Su-mi, not Eun-joo, who stabbed her own hand with the knife, lacerating herself in remorse over her sister. These truths about herself are painful to confront, but by acknowledging them, Su-mi has the chance to overcome her paranoid schizophrenia, to stop blaming imaginary others and deal with her own guilt. According to writer-director Jee-woon Kim, 'I wanted to say that if you examine all the unknowable misfortune that comes upon you, it's all within yourself. You look for all of these things generated by your own deficiency and ambiguity, certain desires, [falsely finding them] in the outside world and in others, and [you] even come to hold a feeling of hostility [towards other people], but when you look back it's all inside of you.'[113] At the film's end, after some time spent in a mental hospital, Su-mi still grabs the real Eun-joo's wrist in a hate-filled grip, but then she lets her go, as if realising she can no longer lay all the blame on a wicked stepmother. Su-mi must leave comforting fairy tales behind and enter real life.

BODY HORROR

The Human Centipede (2009)
and *The Human Centipede 2* (2011)

Director: Tom Six
Cast: Dieter Laser (Heiter), Laurence R Harvey (Martin)

A human centipede is composed of people surgically sewn together, lips to anuses, so that they form one gastrointestinal system, with the excrement passed by one person becoming food for the next and so on down the line. After giving a very brief explanation of why anyone would want to 'commit this atrocity' of bringing to life such a monstrous idea ('He is insane'),[114] reviewer Roger Ebert famously called the films 'reprehensible, dismaying, artless, and an affront to any notion, however remote, of human decency'.[115] According to writer-director Tom Six, 'I came up with the idea when I was watching television with some friends. I saw one time a very nasty child molester, and I told my friends they should stitch his mouth to the ass of a very fat truck driver as a punishment for him.'[116] *The Human Centipede* begins when a mad surgeon named Heiter abducts a truck driver just as the man is about to defecate in the woods, but if being on the receiving end of excrement is intended as a punishment, why does the doctor then choose two naïve young women to serve as the rear of his centipede? They are closer to being innocent children than they are to resembling a child molester. Is the centipede about punishing the guilty or torturing the innocent? In his DVD audiocommentary, Six often expresses sympathy for the suffering of the young women ('Imagine being in a situation like this where this sadistic, maniacal doctor chases you'; 'Imagine waking up like this, attached to someone's asshole'),[117] yet Six himself came up with this fiendish idea and he is the one making the characters, the actresses and the audience suffer.

In *The Human Centipede 2*, a middle-aged man named Martin soils his bed after having a nightmarish memory of his father molesting him when he was a child ('Stop them tears; you're just making Daddy's willy harder'). It's not clear whether this abuse consisted of enforced fellatio, rimming or anal rape, but the trauma of the experience seems to have arrested Martin's sexuality at the oral and anal stages of development. A chubby man with a baby face who often wears only white underpants that look like a diaper, Martin masturbates, sucks his finger and defecates while watching a video of *The Human Centipede*, for the abuse has linked his sexuality to oral and anal violence. Martin keeps a pet centipede, whose 'phallic' bite he associates with the 'sexual abuse by his father', as a psychiatrist explains. Identifying with his aggressive father in order to feel less like a helpless victim, Martin tries to construct his own human centipede in imitation of Dr Heiter in the video. The project also gives Martin the chance to take revenge on his father by victimising others in ways that he himself was hurt. Thus Martin kidnaps a man with a centipede tattoo who had called him a 'little cocksucker', breaks the man's teeth with a hammer and staple-guns his lips to an anus to form part of a human centipede. No longer crying tears like a baby, Martin aspires to achieve the detachment and control exhibited by Dr Heiter, whose experiments can be compared to those of the pitiless Dr Mengele in the Nazi death camps. 'I have a very dark vision on humanity,' Tom Six has said. 'When wars happen … we turn into monsters. Human beings kill out of pleasure. People are very sadistic.'[118] To differentiate his vision from the more sentimental and redemptive view of humanity presented in a movie like *Schindler's List*, Six brings colour into *The Human Centipede 2* – a movie which is otherwise in black and white – only in the scenes of coprophagia: 'While Spielberg uses the little red dress and the girl, I use the brown diarrhoea.'[119]

In the end, Martin fails to attain the hardheartedness of a stone-cold sadist. Unlike Dr Heiter's surgical cutting and careful suturing in a clinical setting, Martin's more frantic and frenzied approach to constructing his human centipede involves hacking away at his victims with kitchen knives and duct-taping their front and hind parts together in a filthy warehouse. When Martin then wraps his own erection in barbed wire and rapes the rear end of the human centipede, he may be trying for a sadistic superiority and detachment, but he also inflicts torment and degradation on himself, in effect sharing his victims' suffering and becoming one with the pain-wracked centipede. In a sense, Martin has never stopped being that traumatised child abused by his father, and no amount of agony inflicted on others has lessened his own, or blocked him from feeling at least some empathy for their suffering. To Martin's (and Six's) moral credit, the last thing we hear in the movie is the sound of an infant crying. *The Human Centipede 2* is a film of vicious depravity – and of tears.[120]

The Skin I Live In (La piel que habito) (2011)

Director: Pedro Almodóvar
Cast: Antonio Banderas (Robert), Elena Anaya (Vera), Jan Cornet (Vicente), Susi Sánchez (Vicente's Mother), Bárbara Lennie (Cristina)

Robert has been practising illegal and unethical surgery on Vera, performing transgenetic grafts of pig cells onto human DNA. Thus, she is literally the guinea pig for this horror-movie mad scientist. But what if Robert's operations *improve* Vera, making her skin tough enough to withstand terrible burns (and emotional rejections) while also still allowing her to feel the gentlest caresses? Is being half-human and part-pig too high a price to pay for what could be physical (and psychological) evolution? Robert's skin transplants also change her face into that of his deceased wife, so Vera is cut to fit his desire to 'reanimate' a dead woman. He keeps Vera captive in his house and watches her on closed-circuit monitors, making her a prisoner of the way he sees her. Yet Vera also seems to enjoy being looked at, as if she finds pleasure in being the admired object of his gaze at her as a beautiful woman. This, however, could be a ruse on her part, playing into his fantasy of her until she can seize the opportunity to escape its trap.

It turns out that Vera was once a young man called Vicente, who was given unwanted sexual reassignment surgery by Robert. Vicente wakes up one morning to find himself castrated and the recipient of a vaginoplasty, along with a woman's face and breasts. Is this the ultimate horror for a man? Certainly, Robert intends the forced sex change as revenge. Flashbacks reveal that Vicente was a womaniser who even offered drugs to a lesbian co-worker to get her in the mood when she rejected his advances. Then, after meeting Robert's daughter at a party, Vicente ignored her fragile psyche and pressed himself upon her in what amounted to a rape. In retaliation, Robert surgically removed the offending organ from Vicente so that he could never take advantage of another woman in that way again. Furthermore, Vicente, who now has the female body of Vera, is himself raped by Robert's brutish brother and thus experiences what it is like to be on the receiving end of such violence.

Fighting against his enforced feminisation, Vera/Vicente at first rips up the dresses given to him and kisses a newspaper photo of his former male self, nostalgic for that state of being. But then he starts to don high heels and women's attire. Is he merely acting the part in order to seduce Robert and make an escape from that man's fantasy of Vicente as a female, or is Vicente beginning to live the fantasy himself and enjoy being part woman? When Vicente eventually shoots Robert, the violent use of a gun could be interpreted as Vicente's reassertion of his masculinity, and the last line of dialogue in the film has him saying 'I'm Vicente' to his mother, apparently hoping that she will recognise *him* inside his female body and attire. And yet, having walked in their shoes and having felt in his own body what women have suffered, Vicente seems to look with new understanding at his mother and his female co-worker, Cristina. Moreover, Vicente's way of reclaiming his male identity is peculiar. 'Do you remember this dress?' he asks Cristina, referring to the female outfit he is wearing. 'Six years ago, I said I'd give it to you … You said if I liked it so much, I should wear it myself.' So Vicente reaffirms his masculinity by reminding Cristina how much she thought he liked dresses? Vicente's former occupation was as a women's clothing designer in his mother's shop. Could all his past womanising have been a defence against being thought an effeminate mama's boy? Perhaps in the end he has moved beyond raping women as a macho defence, beyond his horror at castration, to embrace the female within himself. Rather than living a transgender nightmare, he might find happiness in being between genders – neither wholly male nor completely female, but some of both.

American Mary (2012)

Directors: Soska Sisters (Jen and Sylvia Soska)
Cast: Katharine Isabelle (Mary), David Lovgren (Dr Grant), Jen and Sylvia Soska (Demon Twins), Paula Lindberg (Ruby), Travis Watters (Husband)

Mary is a medical student who wants to become a surgeon and be accepted into that patriarchal profession. Hoping to please her professor, Dr Grant, she agrees to meet him at a party, but there he drugs and then rapes her on a bed in a back room. On operating tables, women who receive cosmetic surgery are also anaesthetised and penetrated by men like Dr Grant, their female bodies made over to conform to male-defined norms of feminine beauty, so Mary's rape can be seen as further extending patriarchal control over and violation of women. Unwilling to play the passive victim, Mary has Dr Grant kidnapped. After penetrating *him* with a syringe, she proceeds to mutilate his genitals, to amputate his arms below the elbows and his legs below the knees, and to hang his torso from suspension hooks stuck through the skin on his back. By these means, Mary seeks to launch a physical strike at his psyche, for Dr Grant's body no longer fits the image he has of himself as a phallically dominant male. By being repeatedly 'castrated' or 'feminised', he now fails to match the masculine ideal; his body projects the very opposite of what he intended it to mean.

By contrast, Mary begins to practise *voluntary* body modification on women who come to her for help in expressing themselves, such as the 'Demon Twins from Berlin' who want her to put phallic horns on their foreheads and to remove and then reattach their left arms after they have exchanged them with each other. The twins want their bodies to show their sisterly solidarity and devilish defiance of patriarchy. (The twins are played by the film's writer-directors, the Soska Sisters, whose compassion for outsiders comes from personal experience: 'Being identical twins, we've always been looked at as a walking punch line – we're freaks, so something we have in common with the body mod community is that people look at us and jump to conclusions,' says Jen Soska.)[121] Another woman, Ruby, has her nipples and labia removed and her vagina sewn up. 'No one looks at dolls in a sexual manner,' she explains, and when Mary guesses that this is 'because they don't have all their parts', Ruby affirms, 'A doll can be naked and never feel shy or sexualised or degraded. That's what I want.' Mary practises genital mutilation on both Dr Grant and Ruby, but in his case the operation is nonconsensual and takes him away from the image he wants to project, whereas she desires the surgery as a form of self-expression. Certainly, women have had quite enough of being told what they should and shouldn't want, but it is hard not to wonder whether Ruby's extreme body modification might be an overreaction to the male gaze. She may no longer be sexually objectified, but what about her own female pleasure? The nullification of her own erogenous zones seems like a high price to pay for freedom from demeaning and intrusive men's eyes.

Similarly, when Mary takes Dr Grant's scalpel and uses it on him, has she not stooped to the level of her patriarchal oppressor and become a rapist herself? At the end of the film, after the operation she performs on Ruby, Mary is herself confronted by someone else seeking revenge: Ruby's husband. Furious at the discovery of his wife's sealed vagina, he attempts to reassert phallic control by stabbing Mary in the belly, near her female sex. Mary manages to sew up the wound, closing herself off against further male attacks, but she dies in the process. Whatever may be the proper answer to male dominance and control, the film suggests that it is not to become as hardened and desensitised, as alienated and violent, as the oppressor.

Antiviral (2012)

Director: Brandon Cronenberg
Cast: Caleb Landry Jones (Syd), Sarah Gadon (Hannah), Nicholas Campbell (Boss)

Thirty-seven years after David Cronenberg practically defined body horror with *Shivers* (aka *They Came from Within*, 1975), his son Brandon makes his own directorial debut with this innovative entry in the genre. In a near future where celebrity worship has run amok, fans are no longer satisfied with visual images of their idols, so they pay to eat meat steaks grown from the human cells of their adored stars. In this way, the film critiques celebrity culture as a form of cannibalistic consumption, the reduction of spiritual significance to mere flesh devoured by fans whose insecurity amounts to a hollowness that they are forever trying to fill with fresh meat. Other fans pay to be injected with celebrity viruses so that they can share the same afflictions suffered by the famous, engaging in a 'bodily communion' with the stars they would otherwise only see on the screen and worship from afar. 'She's perfect somehow, isn't she? More than perfect, more than human' – this is the way salesman Syd pitches a viral sample from star Hannah Geist, showing a client photos of the fair-skinned blonde beauty. But the Hannah herpes virus that Syd offers to sell and inject into one side of the client's mouth mars the very idea of perfection that this star is supposed to embody. Furthermore, when Syd approaches a sleeping Hannah with a syringe to draw a sample of another virus from her veins, the needle he sticks into her arm and the funereal flowers around her suggest a rape/murder, as if 'the penetration shots in this indirect eroticism that exists in the fan-celebrity relationship' are destroying the very idol he worships.[122] Syd then injects himself with this new Hannah virus in the hope of achieving immortality by means of her transcendent beauty, but instead finds himself connected to her in a way he never intended, coughing up blood and dying of the same disease.

Syd could learn from this joint affliction to stop idolising and exploiting celebrities. His corporate boss, who says that 'celebrities are not people; they're group hallucinations', is wrong. As Syd discovers through his corporeal connection with Hannah, behind the stars 'as social constructs, as deities who exist purely in the cultural consciousness', there are 'flesh and blood human beings' like himself,[123] with a 'frail, decaying body that dies',[124] as Brandon Cronenberg puts it. But rather than recognising their shared vulnerability and mortality, Syd devises an Afterlife Capsule resembling an iron lung to keep Hannah's remaining tissues alive. While the visual image of her flawless beauty continues to inspire worshippers worldwide, her tissues will be injected and infected with viruses to be sold to her foolish fans. In the last we see of Syd, he penetrates Hannah's cell-cloned arm with a scalpel, putting his mouth to the wound to drink the death he still believes will give him immortal life.

ECO-HORROR

The Last Winter (2006)

Director: Larry Fessenden
Cast: Ron Perlman (Ed), Zach Gilford (Maxwell), James Le Gros (James)

Ed works as team leader for North Industries, an oil company with plans to drill in the Alaskan wildlife refuge. Ed's godson, Maxwell, is a young man new to the team. Out in a blizzard of snowflakes, he is frightened to see spectral shapes like a ghostly herd of caribou charging at him. Maxwell tries to convince his godfather that the drill site is 'haunted' by 'something out there that's trying to drive us out of here', but Ed won't listen. Increasingly distraught and disoriented, Maxwell ends up walking naked onto the tundra and dying of fright and hypothermia, his frozen body found near the drill site. Maxwell's nakedness is his desperate attempt to re-establish a rapport with the land which, though once his home, now seems foreign to him 'like a familiar friend acting strangely'.[125] What Maxwell sees as spooky and supernatural is really just the natural world from which he has become alienated, fearing it as a vengeful 'other' because he no longer feels at one with it. As writer-director Larry Fessenden explains, 'People crack up and come up against their own limits, which are the limits of their own imagination to integrate with the natural system.'[126] Maxwell's vaporous visions of vengeful caribou are entirely natural in origin. A piece of wood and some caribou antlers lying on the tundra remind us that oil consists of fossilised flora and fauna, once-living creatures that have been crushed. Now, due to human-caused global warming, the tundra's permafrost is melting, emitting 'sour gas' or toxic fumes from its fossil-fuel deposits. The ghosts of the caribou haunting Maxwell are thus literally there, the vapours from their dead bodies rising from the tundra to poison the humans who have been destroying the environment.

But Ed, despite being disturbed by the death of his godson, writes it off to cabin fever, much as he dismisses the thawing permafrost and atmospheric vapours as fluke abnormalities. Even when the ice literally melts under Ed and he falls into freezing water, he still denies that it is due to climate change. The worse things get for the drill team and the more exposed they become to nature's wrath, the more Ed doubles down on his old beliefs and tries to force a path to start the drilling anyway. 'What's needed out here is a pipeline and a base camp and a couple of wells. That's what God wants,' Ed says. Yet, as Fessenden notes, Ed's 'sort of gung-ho, stick-to-it, all-American attitude is not sufficient'[127] when nature itself has turned against humanity, punishing us for having ruined our own homeland. According to James, the movie's despairing environmentalist, 'There is no way home … This is the last winter – total collapse. Hope dies.' *The Last Winter* imagines a worst-case scenario – it ends in apocalypse – to scare us into doing something about climate change before it *is* too late. As Fessenden comments, 'We don't want to wake up in horrible super storms … We don't want to have wars over the last drop of water … We don't want to live in a horror film. We want to go to them at the movies – and come out, and have a sweet and beautiful life.'[128]

The Happening (2008)

Director: M Night Shyamalan
Cast: Mark Wahlberg (Elliot), Zooey Deschanel (Alma), Frank Collison (Nursery Owner), Betty Buckley (Lady Hermit)

In defensive reaction against humanity's heedless destruction of the planet's natural resources, trees and plants begin to fight back by emitting a neurotoxin that causes people to commit suicide. Science teacher Elliot, his wife, Alma, and some friends flee from Philadelphia to the Pennsylvania countryside in an attempt to find a safe haven from ecological disaster. Here are seven environmental messages – or inconvenient truths – told by this eco-horror film:

1. What goes around comes around. Construction workers who build over the natural environment are led to jump off skyscrapers; men who prune trees hang themselves from them; and those who cut grass with lawnmowers end up lying beneath the blades.

2. It is foolish to think that natural forces can be easily confined, tamed or domesticated. A lion in a zoo rips off the arms of a human keeper. Trees in a park prompt strolling visitors to freeze as if suddenly confined and then fall to the ground like dead leaves. Parks are like zoos for trees. By placing such severe limits on the green world, we put ourselves in peril.

3. Environmental crises are not like enemy invaders, so the answer is not for humans to band together and launch a counterattack against nature. The more damage we do to the planet, the more we destroy our own habitat, like the soldier in this film who fires his gun and ends up shooting himself.

4. A human world too removed from nature is not a home, as Elliot finds out when he cannot eat the plastic food or drink the fake wine that has been laid out for show on the dining table of a model home that is part of a new housing development. His attempts to establish a more respectful relationship with nature also fail when he realises that the indoor tree he is talking to is artificial. There is no substitute for healthy interaction with the real thing.

5. Humans can live in harmony with nature and each other, carefully husbanding natural resources so that there is enough for everyone to share, or these resources can be irresponsibly depleted and we can fight to the death over them. A nursery owner and his wife nurture plants and save the lives of Elliot and Alma, who respectfully request a ride to safety. By contrast, when two teenagers try to kick in the door to a house, its inhabitants, who are holed up inside and denying anyone entrance, shoot the boys dead. A lady hermit initially allows travellers to take refuge in her house, but is eventually overcome by fear that they will steal from her. In refusing them hospitality, she denies her own humanity and ends up beating her head bloody

against the walls of her house. Just like the destruction of nature, the abrogation of the social contract is a kind of suicide.

6. Survival may well depend on recognising that there are no 'other' people and no world of nature 'outside' of our own. When Elliot tries to interest his science class in the disappearance of honeybees, one self-absorbed teenager can't see past an obsession with his own good looks. (He perhaps reminds the teacher of his own younger self, especially considering that Elliot is played by Mark Wahlberg, who was formerly known as underwear model Marky Mark.) But 'no bees' means no more pollination of plants, which means no more food for animals or humans, so the bees are us. Elliot and Alma survive because they commit to the larger human family, caring for an orphaned girl as if she were their flesh-and-blood daughter. They also survive because, instead of communicating via cell phones and hiding in houses, they walk outside to physically embrace each other under the trees, thus acknowledging their interdependence with the natural world.

7. Whether it be the collapse of bee colonies, the depletion of the ozone layer, or some airborne neurotoxin, there is much we don't know about the cause of environmental disasters. But just as science offers hypotheses, so eco-horror films provide possible models for understanding and responding to ecological threats which seem beyond our ability to explain. In one of the movie's last images, after nature's wrath has ended (for now) and humans have returned to happier living, we see a sign on a restaurant saying 'OPEN – PINE DELI'. Imagine a world where trees and people coexisted in peace …

Nature's Grave (aka *Long Weekend*) (2008)

Director: Jamie Blanks
Cast: Jim Caviezel (Peter), Claudia Karvan (Carla)

Peter and Carla are a wealthy urban couple who drive their SUV on a camping trip to a forest near a beach in an isolated part of Australia. *Nature's Grave* can be seen as an 'animals attack' film where the local fauna fight back against the humans' invasion of their territory. The film could also be viewed as an extended example of the pathetic fallacy where the surrounding environment expresses human emotions, such as lightning representing the vacationing couple's anger at each other, or dawn depicting a moment of hope for their marriage. But a reading of *Nature's Grave* as an eco-horror film sees all of its relationships – man and wife, human and animal, creature and environment – as interdependent biosystems, with damage or pollution in any one part negatively affecting the whole. Prior to their trip, Carla has responded to Peter's sexual interest in another woman by having an affair, followed by an abortion of the foetus that may or may not have been Peter's. The trip is an attempt to 'revitalise' their relationship, but when Peter puts his hand between her legs as they are lying on the beach, Carla rejects his advances, still angry at him over his adulterous impulses. Her subsequent attempt to masturbate alone in their tent is interrupted by sounds of a manatee pup wailing for its mother – cries which haunt Carla throughout the film and which are related to her own guilt over the abortion. Here the film suggests an ecological connection between disturbances in the life cycles of humanity and the manatee, a spooky 'supernatural' affinity which is actually just the natural bond all creatures share as parts of the earth's ecosystem.

Earlier in the film, Peter carelessly discards a plastic bag, and the couple finds a dead manatee pup washed up on the beach, wrapped in a similar, non-biodegradable plastic. While swimming, Peter is shadowed by a dark shape in the water, which he then shoots at, discovering it to be a mother manatee. Though apparently dead, this creature will haunt Peter for the rest of the film, seeming to creep up on him when he is not looking, the way guilt over the damage he has caused to Mother Nature and to Carla gradually overcomes him. Feeling rejected by his adulterous wife and unmanned by her abortion, Peter tries to reclaim his masculinity through phallic domination of nature: flicking away a lit cigarette onto the forest floor, chopping at a tree with an axe, and shooting ducks with a rifle. But rather than impressing his wife, these macho antics only alienate her further, which in turn increases his anger at her. These marital tensions culminate in a night-time scene where Peter, feeling threatened by what he fears is the mother manatee, fires a harpoon into the dark and accidentally spears his wife through the throat. Thus, Peter's previous shooting of the manatee rebounds on him and his own, for an attack on nature is an attack on humanity. Weeping in remorse at the sight of what he has done, Peter takes panicked flight from his wife's dead body, but as he attempts to drive away, the SUV keeps going in circles, returning him to the site of his crime, forcing him to face the fact that what goes around comes around. At the start of the film, when he first drives into the forest, Peter ignores the posted signs and heedlessly runs over a kangaroo. At the movie's end, while attempting to flag down a truck, Peter is crushed by the oncoming vehicle, himself becoming roadkill.

The Ruins (2008)

Director: Carter Smith
Cast: Jonathan Tucker (Jeff), Jena Malone (Amy), Shawn Ashmore (Eric), Laura Ramsey (Stacy)

Two vacationing American couples – Jeff and Amy, Eric and Stacy – take some time off from partying at their luxurious Yucatán resort to do some sightseeing in this exotic locale, trekking into the depths of a dense rainforest to find 'an ancient Mayan temple off the beaten path'. Blithely ignoring the warnings of the local tribes, whose language and customs these tourists haven't bothered to learn, the group walks all over the indigenous vines like a mini-onslaught of deforestation. Unlike the natives who built the temple, the group fails to show respect for nature as something sacred. Since their destructive invasion has disturbed the equilibrium of the ecosystem, the balance must be righted, and so the natives 'quarantine' the Americans by forcing them to remain at the temple site until they either self-destruct or learn their lesson and no longer pose a threat to nature. The group is ill-equipped to survive their eco-educational ordeal. Despite their contempt for the native water supply, which they consider to be 'contaminated with human faeces', the group has brought very little bottled water to supplement their plentiful tequila. Prior to their arrival, a team of European archaeologists have been excavating the site, violating the land, and one of their corpses is found penetrated by and overgrown with vines, having been reclaimed by nature. But rather than learning from this example of the violator violated, the Americans just want a way out and so they look for the man's cell phone, which they think they hear ringing. Yet this turns out to be the plants mimicking the phone's sound, as if mocking the tourists' belief that they could use their sophisticated technology to 'conquer the wilderness' and escape from the ecological trap they have put themselves in.

Alienated from nature, the group is also at odds with each other, failing to achieve an external or internal harmony. The tourists bring with them all the fears and doubts bred by civilisation, and rather than using their time in nature to resolve the tensions threatening group cohesion and psychological integrity, they split apart even further under the stress. Back at the resort, Amy has been somewhat aloof from Jeff, happy to have him go off sightseeing without her. When they end up trapped at the temple, the rift between them grows greater. On the morning after a night in which Stacy at least tries to comfort Eric by masturbating him, Amy sits apart from Jeff, who stands with his back to her and with his organ in his own hand as he urinates on the vines. At odds with nature, they are also estranged from each other. While at the resort, Stacy has proposed playing a card game of war, and has engaged in a bet with Eric – the winner to give the other oral sex – over whether or not Amy will 'cheat' on Jeff by kissing another man. Now, at the temple, Stacy's competitiveness grows into paranoid jealousy that Amy will pursue Eric, Stacy's boyfriend. As the three of them are going to sleep in the tent, Stacy takes manual possession of Eric, masturbating him in Amy's presence. On another night, Stacy thinks she hears Amy's moans of passion and accuses her and Eric of betrayal. Amy has actually been weeping, and the noises of her crying are mimicked by the vines to sound like moans, which is to say that Stacy's own jealousy has caused her to hear them this way, because there are no vines. There is only Stacy at war with herself, divided from her better nature. 'It's just everywhere. It's in my head,' she says about the threat of the vines, not realising that they are outside and inside because nature is a part of her. Stacy's discordant relation to nature is also shown when her fears of sex and pregnancy get the better of her. Imagining that she sees a vine snaking under the skin of her leg ('I can feel it moving'), Stacy yells for her boyfriend to 'get it out!' Then, as Amy holds her and tells her to 'keep breathing', Stacy hears the vine shriek like a crying baby as it is pulled out of her.

Estranged from Mother Nature and from her own nature as a mother, Stacy begins cutting into herself with a knife, and when Eric tries to stop her, she stabs him in the fury of her madness. And yet, just when it seems that the group will break apart and self-destruct rather than learn the lesson of interdependency, their suffering brings a new awareness. Too far gone to recover, Stacy begs to be put out of her misery, with her cries of 'Kill me!' echoed by the vines, as if nature itself agrees with this course of action. In pleading with Amy to kill her, Stacy offers herself up to death so that her friend may live, and as Amy puts an end to Stacy's discordant cries, the Mayan natives standing outside the temple seem to accept this human sacrifice. It is as though, in dying, Stacy takes all the antagonism with her, leaving Amy free to establish a more harmonious relation to nature. Similarly, Amy's boyfriend, Jeff, lets himself be killed in order to ensure Amy's escape, thereby proving the strength of his love for her. They have progressed from being a group of arrogant, self-centred tourists to becoming people with some humility and natural compassion. By showing these tourists that *they* are the invaders, the consumers and the parasites, the vines have taught their lesson.

Upstream Color (2013)

Director: Shane Carruth
Cast: Amy Seimetz (Kris), Shane Carruth (Jeff)

Far from being a typical horror film, *Upstream Color* is long on vague dread, supplying numerous potential reasons for fear, but short on definite explanations. A young woman named Kris undergoes a traumatic experience with elements of kidnapping and extortion, alien abduction, cult indoctrination, sex slavery, involuntary surrogate motherhood, invasive organ harvesting, and genetic experimentation. By not clarifying which – if any – of these events has occurred, the film maintains a pervasive doubt. This results in a free-floating anxiety and a paranoid dread that something terrible could happen at any moment, but it also creates the hope that what has happened to Kris may be more psychological than real and thus might be mentally surmountable, even ultimately positive, rather than permanently crippling.

Admittedly, there are aspects of her peculiar experience that seem horrific. At one point, Kris sees a worm crawling under her skin and tries to cut it out with a knife. After her ordeal, Kris awakens with no memory of what happened and finds that she no longer has a job or any money. Moreover, she thinks she's pregnant, but a doctor tells her she is not and that internal damage means she can never have a child. Fortunately, Kris then meets Jeff, a young man who appears to have suffered the same kind of eerily inexplicable experience, also depriving him of his job and former social identity. As traumatic as these losses are, they also force the young couple to let go of preconceived notions and see the world anew. As writer-director Shane Carruth explains, he wanted to 'strip' away these characters' 'understanding of who they were' and 'what they thought of the world' so that they would have to 'adopt a new narrative' and 'try to rebuild and follow through on that no matter how foreign it seemed'.[129]

And it is fair to say that their life after the ordeal often does seem quite foreign. For example, when two pigs nuzzle nose to nose in a corral, Kris and Jeff get the urge to pair-bond. After the sow is impregnated, Kris feels as though she herself is with child, and when the sow's piglets are later taken from her and drowned, Kris starts diving to the bottom of a pool to pick up pebbles and deliver them to the surface, as if trying to rescue the piglets. As the boar and sow, bereft of their offspring, huddle together in sadness and fear, Jeff and Kris curl up in an empty bathtub, holding each other close against an outside world which they, too, find hard to understand. Thus, there appear to be strange affinities linking humans and animals, as if the characters are being affected by things at a distance from them.

This sense of inexplicable influences upon our behaviour can be frightening since it suggests something more than just our individual wills controlling our destiny. The film implies that there are unseen forces forging ecological connections beyond our current comprehension. Saying that he wanted his movie to 'put us sort of in the mind of biological processes',[130] Carruth notes the real-life existence of 'parasites that burrow into the heads of wasps and ants and make them fly erratically or climb to the top of trees and throw themselves off in order to benefit from something else, maybe a fungus on the forest floor. And then that fungus maybe benefits from the parasite.'[131] *Upstream Color* begins with some worm-like parasites being scraped off a plant. These are then implanted in Kris, where they gestate until being transplanted into a sow that gives birth. The piglets are drowned in a river, where their decomposing bodies emit a substance that leaches into the root systems of plants, which grow more worm-like parasites. The three-stage life cycle of this parasite, moving it through people, pigs and plants, is one explanation for the strange symbiosis between the human couple and the swine. It is terrifying to think that some mysterious force could so drastically alter one's life, but when childless Kris takes an adopted piglet into her arms at the end, the smile on their faces suggests that life may offer equally unexpected compensations.

FOUND FOOTAGE

The Blair Witch Project (1999)

Directors: Daniel Myrick and Eduardo Sánchez
Cast: Heather Donahue (Heather), Joshua Leonard (Josh), Michael Williams (Mike)

Heather, Josh and Mike are three student filmmakers who go off to make a documentary about a local legend involving a murderous witch. From their sarcastic comments, it's clear that these kids don't take any of this seriously. They just want fame from the movie, and maybe to be safely spooked while having some fun on a Halloween adventure. Their condescending attitude towards superstitious people suggests that they also see themselves as investigative reporters debunking silly myths. But as they shine the light of their camera on various strange occurrences, they are disturbed to find things becoming less and less clear. One interviewee describes the witch as a vaporous mist rising from the river, while in another account she is covered in hair that is half human and half horse. The witch's unsettling ambiguity extends to her victims as well. Late in the film, Heather finds a small lump of torn flesh wrapped in some of Josh's bloody clothing, but it's not clear what bit of the body this is or whether it was ever part of Josh.

Heather is the documentary's director and she also helms one of the two handheld cameras. As Mike tells her, 'It's like looking through the lens gives you some sort of protection from what's on the other side' – the night forest and the supernatural. But in fact the camera's light, like their flashlight beams, barely penetrates the dark woods around them, revealing piled-up rocks and stick men hanging in trees that remain mysterious in their meaning. Moreover, sounds of inexplicably snapping twigs and strange cries in the night create the fearful impression of terrible events occurring off-screen, just beyond the camera's view. Rather than gaining knowledge and control through the camera, Heather is trapped behind it, squinting to see what its light only half-reveals and shrinking in fright at what might be coming at her from the edges of the frame. In the end, it seems that Heather is attacked, for the camera she was holding is knocked to the ground and, as if through its viewfinder, we see it struggling – perhaps like Heather's dying eyes – to refocus the image in its sights. A cut to black then plunges her and us into final obscurity.

Part of the mystery of *The Blair Witch Project* is that we never see the Blair Witch or any ghostly projection of her. We *hear* about people possessed by her, like Rustin Carr who would take two kids to his house in the woods and have one of them face a corner while he killed the other one so that Rustin would not have to feel 'the eyes watching him'. Could it be that the real horror of this film involves three naïve young people who venture into the wilderness and who, spooked by their unfamiliar surroundings, become increasingly paranoid and possessed by their own fears, turning on each other? Heather is in charge of reading the map, but when the group gets lost, the guys begin to suspect her of deliberately keeping them in the woods in order to do more filmmaking. Josh hears a strange cackling in the night, as if it were Heather laughing at them. The next day, he films Heather in the forest and 'jokes' that she might be the Blair Witch. Disgusted by Heather and her map, Mike kicks it into a creek and starts laughing at *her*. More and more disoriented, the three find themselves going in circles, chasing their own tails. When Heather hears an eerie groan, it sounds like her own fearful moaning, and the children they hear crying in the night might as well be themselves. Later, Mike warns Heather to stop filming Josh while he is crying, and an angry Josh shoves a camera in Heather's face, causing her to weep in distress. At the end, prompted by Josh's calls for help ('Please, follow my voice!'), Heather and Mike enter an abandoned house, where Mike turns to face a corner while Heather is attacked by an assailant we never see. Were all three of them victims of the Blair Witch? Were Josh and Mike possessed by the witch into luring Heather to her doom? Or were the two guys angry at Heather and just pulling a trick on her, playing on her sympathy (for Josh) and her fear (why is Mike facing the corner?) in order to throw a Blair Witch-inspired scare into her? Finally, it could be that all three of them are playing a trick on us, leaving us with this frightening found footage of their apparent demise in order to make money off this movie.

Paranormal Activity (2007)

Director: Oren Peli
Cast: Micah Sloat (Micah), Katie Featherston (Katie), Mark Fredrichs (Psychic)

Micah and his girlfriend, Katie, live in a two-storey tract home in suburban San Diego. 'Kiss the camera,' Micah says, pointing his camcorder at Katie; despite her protestations, he wants to film her performing a striptease and the two of them having sex. Katie begins to feel stalked by an eerie presence, but it's not clear whether what is haunting her is a voyeuristic demon or Micah's spying camera. 'It's looking at me,' she says about the camera when Micah sets it up on a tripod to film them while they sleep at night, and she later comments fearfully about the nocturnal demon, 'I can feel it watching me.' Reviewing the overnight footage on the morning after, Katie sees her bedsheet billow as if an invisible shape is getting under the covers with her, and she recalls that she 'felt him breathing'. Katie recounts a 'horrifying' memory of when she was an eight-year-old girl and a 'breathing' demon used to visit her in bed at night. This buried memory of sexual abuse by her father seems to come back to her now that she is being psychologically abused by her boyfriend, Micah.

Ironically (given that Micah with his intrusive camera is the leering demon haunting Katie), he tries to capture the evil spirit on film. Disturbed by sounds of rumbling, rattling and creaking that could be coming from the ceiling, floor or walls, Micah attempts to gather ocular evidence that will pinpoint the source. He pours talcum powder on the floorboards in order to make thudding footsteps visible, but the results are not clearly discernible. Like the white noise on his television screen, whatever is haunting them cannot be observed and mastered by his gaze. It cannot be captured by his camcorder because, as Katie tells him, 'You and your stupid camera are the problem.' Instead, like Katie herself, the haunting presence must be *listened to* and understood. In one scene, Micah's camera zooms in on Katie, attempting to bring her into focus and to record what she is whispering, but the microphone fails to register her words, so intent is he on visual mastery. The banging on the walls and the sound of fingernails being dragged down them could be heard as Katie's unconscious attempt to communicate how caged she feels by Micah, but he doesn't hear her. Her car keys that mysteriously drop on the floor are a sign of her desire to leave him. The glass that breaks over his face in the photo of them as a couple shows her growing anger at him. The Ouija board, which Micah has insisted on getting despite Katie's objection that it frightens her, bursts into flames just like the house that burned down when she was a girl. In both cases, the fires are Katie's surreptitious way of fighting back against an abusive father and boyfriend.

'These hauntings, they feed off of negative energy,' a psychic warns them, 'so if there is something negative going on here, it will help spur on the haunting.' But Micah is in denial about the part he has played in the couple's domestic discord. Asked what their relationship is like, he answers with an oblivious 'It's good.' Because Micah refuses to temper his controlling and domineering gaze, Katie eludes and strikes back against it, eventually becoming so furious at him that she is entirely 'possessed' by her anger. His camera has watched her at night, so now she stands and gazes down at him while he is vulnerable and sleeping in the bed. Then her screams draw him out of the bedroom and into the hallway where he does battle with something unseen. We hear thudding footsteps – like those of the demon on previous nights – approach the bedroom, and as Micah's corpse is thrown at the camera, Katie is revealed standing in the doorway. She crawls over to Micah's body, smiles, and then lunges at the camera with a demonic expression on her face. He didn't listen, and now he'll never see her again.

Cloverfield (2008)

Director: Matt Reeves

As Manhattan is attacked by a giant monster, a woman witnesses her brother die. 'Will somebody please, please tell me what just happened?' she begs. 'I mean, it came from nowhere! And he was there and then he was gone!' As a result of the rampaging creature, 'one of the skyscrapers collapses' and 'we see the wall of debris from the collapse start to radiate outward – right toward us'.[132] As this moment from the screenplay makes clear, the monster is a metaphor for the 9/11 terrorist attack, and this movie, for better or worse, represents one way for America to deal with the trauma. As heinous and indefensible as the terrorists' actions were, these men were human beings like us with faces and families, motives and histories. We are less likely to understand or prevent such attacks if we dehumanise the perpetrators and view them merely as murderous monsters, like this film's creature, which could be an invading alien, a marauding dinosaur, a predatory insect or a raging sea beast. The monster also sometimes resembles an old man staggering around, trying to hold himself up with canes, but this caricature of Osama bin Laden as decrepit does not help us understand the anger or the intelligence of a chief terrorist. Flakes fall from the giant monster's back and turn into spider-like assailants that bite human beings, infecting them with a virus that eventually causes them to explode. This narrative of falling flakes, spider bites and viral contagion tells us nothing about what motivated the men who followed bin Laden's orders or about how people become radicalised into serving as suicide bombers. 'It was eating people! It was eating everyone!' a woman exclaims about the monster, but whatever the terrorists were, they were not cannibals. When the creature decapitates the Statue of Liberty, leaving the headless body standing in New York Harbor, we are reminded of the beheadings on the jihadist videos. Yes, the terrorists may 'hate our freedom', but to tar them as evil tyrants and to whitewash ourselves as freedom-loving innocents does not help us see what they believe we have done to them to provoke their attacks.

And yet, while *Cloverfield* may be politically problematic, it does speak to certain emotional needs in the aftermath of 9/11. While most of us saw the attack on the news videos that were ceaselessly replayed on television, we do not know what it was like to actually be there. As a film that purports to be home-movie footage shot by persons as they experienced the attack, *Cloverfield* bridges that gap between video and reality. (We have a similar desire to know about the subsequent Iraq War, which only a small minority of soldiers lived first-hand. As director Matt Reeves notes, *Cloverfield* was in part inspired by 'footage online of troops in Iraq', where 'you could hear the bombs getting closer and these guys were screaming in the tent, and you actually saw the leg of this table they were hiding under, and it was very visceral and really frightening'.[133]) The events of 9/11 were felt as a loss of innocence for America, which had never before been invaded from outside in this way. *Cloverfield* marks this loss by having video of the monster's attack overwrite previously shot footage of an idyllic day at Coney Island – a carefree time that, following the devastation in New York, may never be lived in the same way again. Yet, despite the deaths of almost all the main characters, the film also shows New Yorkers acting courageously and attempting to save each other out of love, as we'd like to think we would have done. Portions of the old footage representing past happiness can still be glimpsed in the gaps between scenes of carnage wrought by the attack, suggesting that some foundation for hope may not be entirely inaccessible.

NEO-GIALLO

Amer (2009)

Directors: Hélène Cattet and Bruno Forzani
Cast: Cassandra Forêt (Child Ana), Bianca Maria D'Amato (Mother), Bernard Marbaix (Grandfather), Delphine Brual (Housekeeper), Charlotte Eugène Guibeau (Adolescent Ana), Marie Bos (Adult Ana), Harry Cleven (Taxi Driver)

The Strange Colour of Your Body's Tears
(L'étrange couleur des larmes de ton corps) (2013)

Directors: Hélène Cattet and Bruno Forzani
Cast: Klaus Tange (Dan), Ursula Bedena (Edwige), Jean-Michel Vovk (Detective), Hans De Munter (Doctor), Sam Louwyck (Dermont), Birgit Yew (Dora), Anna D'Annunzio (Barbara)

Featuring bold colours, gloved killers and sensual women in peril, these two films pay homage to the 1970s' Italian *giallo* genre and form a diptych, with the first focused on the sexual maturation of a troubled female, and the second on a male's sexual anxiety stemming from his childhood trauma. In *Amer*, a child named Ana peers into forbidden rooms and, too young to understand what she is seeing, ends up shocked by her premature discovery of the facts of life and death. Looking into her parents' bedroom, she spies them having sex and misinterprets their passion as a violent encounter, for her mother's moans and writhing seem like suffering. In another room, Ana views the corpse of her age-wrinkled grandfather laid out on a bed, while behind a third door she sees the elderly housekeeper veiled in the black of mourning and lying on her bed, as if mortified by the old man's demise. Ana pries a pocket watch from the dead fingers of her grandfather, who seems to clutch it as though holding on to the last precious minutes of life. Her foot then gets caught in the watch chain, which has become wrapped around a bedpost as she is trying to escape the grip of the black-gloved housekeeper's hand, and she also imagines her grandfather's bony hand reaching out as if to drag her into the grave with him.

The sight of these shocking bedroom scenes – one of sex that looks like violence, another of death that seems to threaten the living – causes confusion in Ana's mind, which forms a disturbing link between desire and dying. As she matures into an adolescent, Ana finds herself attracted to and yet fearful of men, such as some sweaty, muscular bikers with their outthrust motorcycles. As she sneaks peeks at them, she is reminded that certain sights are still forbidden when she is slapped in the face by her mother, who is either protective or jealous (of her daughter's youthful appeal). Her mother's prohibition adds to Ana's sense that sex is something dangerous and frightening.

Some years later, Ana returns as an adult to her childhood home, where she must finally face the fears first instilled in her there. An ambiguous ending leaves it unclear whether she ultimately conquers or succumbs to them. The leather-gloved and leering taxi driver who takes her to her home possesses a knife. That night, the driver comes back, and when gloved hands unsheathe a straight razor and threaten her with it, Ana is afraid of being penetrated by the blade, so she kills the man. But once the driver is dead, another man – a phantom figure in black – appears to menace Ana, who strikes out in self-defence at him, only to reveal that the gloved hands are in fact her own and that she has cut her own wrists with the blade. In the film's last shot of Ana's dead body laid out on a bed in the morgue, we see that, unable to vanquish her fear of her grandfather's corpse, she has become one. Unable to dissociate sex from violence, she has ended up a victim. Her fear has not only led her to murder the driver, a guiltless man; it also proves suicidal. And yet, just before the film cuts to black, Ana's pallid face is infused with living colour again and her eyes begin to open. Instead of actually committing homicide and suicide, Ana may have been playing out a fantasy that brings her to a moment of self-realisation freeing her from her fear. By imagining the innocent driver's stabbed body and her own slashed wrists, Ana may have come to see that hers are the hands filled with menace, that all she really has to dread is her own fear. With this eye-opening recognition, she can now go on to live her life.

Whereas *Amer* begins with its female protagonist's childhood trauma, *The Strange Colour of Your Body's Tears* only gradually works its way around to revealing what shocked its male protagonist when he was a boy. Adult Dan returns from a business trip to find that his wife, Edwige, has disappeared from their apartment. Eventually, her decapitated head is discovered with a gaping wound within the hair on its top. As Dan investigates to determine who did it, he encounters other male characters – the Detective, the Doctor, and a landlord named Dermont – who all seem to be versions of Dan himself. The Detective tells Dan about a previous case involving a husband's search for a vanished wife, but in that case 'it wasn't she who disappeared; it was he who was afraid of disappearing'. Could the murder of Dan's wife also have something to do with Dan's own fears? Dan hears about the Doctor, who interrupted intercourse with his wife, Dora, because he was afraid someone was watching him from above. There was a mural of a woman painted on the ceiling, and the Doctor drilled a hole through her head hair. The Doctor then went to the apartment above and peered down at Dora through the hole, as one drop of blood also fell on her face. As she reports, 'I saw an eye staring at me, filled with hatred, madness, fear.' Dan's last clue comes when the Detective tells him about a lovemaking scene involving the landlord, Dermont, and a woman named Barbara. As she is moving on top of Dermont, her body grinds broken glass into his, cutting him open. Then, as she is straddling him during sex, she removes her spiky hair-pin and is just about to stab it down into the top of Dermont's head when the Detective shoots her with his gun.

The mystery is solved when we realise that all these exaggerated fears regarding threatening women stem from a trauma that occurred in Dan's (and these other men's?) past. As suggested by the film's title, *The Strange Colour of Your Body's Tears*, which presents the perspective of an uncomprehending boy, the young Dan did not know much about the facts of life. The sight of a girl bleeding between her legs shocked him because he did not understand menstruation or the difference between boys and girls. Misinterpreting the blood as a sign that the girl had lost her penis, Dan began to fear that he might lose his own, and the female sex became connected in his mind with castration anxiety. When the boy saw a model spreading her vulva in a pornographic magazine, it looked like a red eye staring balefully at him, threatening to turn his own sex into a 'bloody hole'. Scared by this prospect, Dan has grown into an adult afraid of contact with the female sex. It seems that, in defence against this fear of castration, he has raised his knife erect and used it to stab his wife within the hair on her head, as if he can thereby prove his own potency and also, with the phallic knife sticking out of her gash, return her 'lost penis' to her. For his wife's sake, it's too bad Dan hasn't been able to face his own fears earlier. If he had realised sooner that his gynophobia was rooted in nothing more than a misunderstanding about a menstruating girl, he might have moved beyond a violent defensiveness, resulting in the stabbing of his wife, to see that he was never really in danger from her. Just as the Detective needs to investigate his own fears, and the Doctor needs to heal himself, so husband Dan must overcome a feeling of traumatised masculinity in order to love his wife.

Berberian Sound Studio (2012)

Director: Peter Strickland
Cast: Toby Jones (Gilderoy), Cosimo Fusco (Francesco), Antonio Mancino (Santini), Jozef Cseres (Massimo), Pál Tóth (Massimo), Fatma Mohamed (Silvia), Chiara D'Anna (Elisa)

Gilderoy lives a peaceful life in pastoral Dorking, Surrey, with his mother. His normal employment is as a sound engineer on nature documentaries, but when he travels to Italy to mix sounds for a movie called *The Equestrian Vortex*, the film turns out to be a gothic horror production like Dario Argento's *Suspiria* or Mario Bava's *Black Sunday*. Not only that, but Francesco, the film's producer, is verbally abusing the actresses who are dubbing the characters' voices, and the film's director, Santini, is sexually molesting them. Francesco's and Santini's assaults are strikingly similar to those by inquisitorial priests within the film, who vilify as 'whores' and sexually torture women they accuse of being witches. Although Gilderoy sympathises with the women both on- and off-screen, he is gradually drawn into the vortex of male sadism surrounding him. He starts off in a rather removed position behind the mixing board, criticising his male colleagues for their misogynistic movie, but when the Foley artists are sick, Gilderoy takes their place, creating such customised sound effects as plucking stems out of radishes to represent a witch's hair being pulled from its roots, and hacking at watermelons with knives and smashing them with mallets to aurally simulate the stabbing and crushing of female flesh. Although he baulks at squirting water into a sizzling pan to sound like a witch's vagina being penetrated with a red-hot poker, by the end of the film he, too, has become cruelly invasive: he hikes up the volume on a female dubber's headphones to an unbearable level so that she will be forced to emit a convincingly terrified scream.

But is Gilderoy really the innocent abroad, corrupted by foreign misogynists? There is reason to believe that the evil has its roots closer to home. After persistent attempts to get reimbursed for his plane fare to Italy, Gilderoy is finally told that there was no such flight. 'Did he ever leave his garden shed in Dorking?' asks writer-director Peter Strickland,[134] as we begin to wonder whether this entire Italian trip is a fantasy concocted by Gilderoy, who is actually still in the English garden shed which he uses as a makeshift sound studio. The fantasy is a cover for a terrible truth about himself that Gilderoy has avoided facing. 'You English, always hiding,' Santini tells him – or, rather, it is Gilderoy half-realising this fact about himself, since there is no Santini. The Gilderoy who goes to Italy is actually a false double for the real Gilderoy in England, which is something that his unconscious tries to tell him by creating so many 'mirror' characters in his fantasy. There are two Foley artists, both of them named Massimo. There are two actresses, Silvia and Elisa, playing the same movie character, Teresa, and Gilderoy keeps getting them confused with each other and with the character they portray. Gilderoy himself is duplicated, sometimes speaking English while unable to understand Italian, and at other times speaking fluent Italian, as if he were in the movie (which movie? the horror film or the fantasy about the Italian dubbing studio?).

At one point in the film, Gilderoy listens to a woman's screaming voice on tape from one of the dubbing sessions, while he (and we) are looking at a photo of the garden shed near his mother's house. There appears to be a mismatch between sound and image – but is there? Later, a shot of a woman's screaming mouth cuts to tomatoes in a whirring mixture, and some of the red liquid splatters out onto

Gilderoy, who turns to look at his 'bloody' face in a mirror. Later still, there is female screaming on the audio track as Gilderoy is plunging a knife into a cabbage to simulate the sound of a witch being stabbed in the horror film. Thus, the film implies that Gilderoy stabbed his mother in the shed and then developed an elaborate fantasy that conceals the truth from himself but also gradually allows him to reveal it. Stabbing a cabbage is silly and harmless, and Gilderoy focuses on the sound of the act to distract himself from the horrible sight of a woman being knifed. He tries to separate audio from video, so the woman's scream floats free of any anchor in an actual female. It could be Silvia or Elisa or Teresa getting stabbed – anyone but his own mother, just as the knife could be wielded by Francesco or Santini or Massimo – anyone but himself. But because Gilderoy has a conscience that plagues him with guilt, he keeps replaying the scream in search of its true source, his mother, and the sound of the stabbing repeats until it loops around as linked to the image of his own hand on the knife. As Strickland says, 'The whole film itself is based on the loop structure and eating its own tail.'[135] In the end, the film loops around to its beginning as frames of the Italian horror film burn up during projection, revealing through the hole Gilderoy's own English country home, the site of the actual horror he committed.

REMAKES OF 1970s HORROR

Halloween (1978)

Director: John Carpenter
Cast: Will Sandin (Boy Michael), Sandy Johnson (Sister), Tony Moran and Nick Castle (Adult Michaels), Jamie Lee Curtis (Laurie), Donald Pleasence (Psychiatrist)

Halloween (2007)

Director: Rob Zombie
Cast: Daeg Faerch (Boy Michael), Hanna Hall (Sister), Malcolm McDowell (Psychiatrist), Tyler Mane (Adult Michael), Scout Taylor-Compton (Laurie)

At the beginning of the original *Halloween*, six-year-old Michael puts on a clown mask and stabs his teenage sister to death in her bedroom after she has had sex with her boyfriend. Fifteen years later, he escapes from a mental institution and begins stalking and slashing other teen girls and their boyfriends. If Michael has a motive for his killings, the characters do not speculate about what it is. This leaves open an extremely wide range of possibilities as to what the threat of Michael represents – in his own mind and in that of others. Does he begin as a naïve child just playing a Halloween prank, dressing up as a clown and not realising that the knife he stabs his sister with can really kill? When the boy is unmasked after the murder, his face looks innocent. Does his eventual shock at what he has done so traumatise him that he becomes obsessed with repeating it, acting it out again and again without ever being able to deal with it so that he can stop? Note that, when he returns as an adult murderer, he steals his sister's headstone from her grave and puts it on the bed above the dead body of another teen girl he has just killed, and then he begins to stalk a third girl named Laurie. Laurie is a virgin and seems quite leery of boys, despite the fact that all her female friends appear to be engaging in carefree sex with their dates. For the more conservative and repressed Laurie, Michael's knife attacks on fornicators could represent her fear of penetration as violent and deadly, or her fear of punishment for premarital sex. Due to his boyhood stabbing of his sister, sex and violence have become confused for Michael as well, and it could be that his knife thrusts at women are his perverse way of expressing desire. Sexual feelings that have been disturbed by trauma (in Michael's case) or repressed by guilt (in Laurie's case and possibly Michael's, too) can come out as violence. 'She and the killer have a certain link: sexual repression,' says director John Carpenter.[136] Referring to the scene where Michael, who has been trying to stab Laurie, drops his knife and she picks it up to counterattack, Carpenter states that 'the one girl who is the most sexually uptight just keeps stabbing this guy with a long knife. She's the most sexually frustrated' and 'all that repressed sexual energy starts coming out'.[137]

As informative as such musings may be, the characters *within* the film don't achieve these insights. Rather than viewing Michael as a psychologically damaged human being in need of help, they tend to depersonalise and demonise him. Perhaps it's understandable that a young boy would refer to him as 'the boogeyman', but even Michael's psychiatrist – in what has to be a low point for the profession – diagnoses him as 'purely and simply evil'. 'This is not a man,' the doctor says, but something that has 'the Devil's eyes'. Michael's expressionless white mask, his relentless stalking and his superhuman strength all make him seem inhumanly evil. (Even his otherwise ordinary name, Michael Myers, comes to seem eerily resonant through the strange doubling of its initial syllables.) Someone who kills without cause is someone beyond cure – indefinable and thus unstoppable. The psychiatrist fires six bullets at point-blank range into Michael, causing him to fall from a balcony, but later 'the boogeyman' has disappeared from the spot where he landed. The film concludes by showing us a series of places where Michael did his stalking and killing – all empty now but still haunted by the sound of his breathing. As an indestructible force of supernatural evil, he could be anywhere – or everywhere.

For those who believe that human monsters are made and not born bad, the *Halloween* reboot will come as a welcome change. A prequel as well as a remake, this film devotes almost an hour to delving into Michael's backstory, revealing the environmental factors that influence him to become a killer. On the Halloween night when his sister is supposed to babysit him, she leaves ten-year-old Michael alone to go upstairs and have sex with her date. When the boy later dons the mask her date had been wearing and enters his sister's bedroom, it is clear that he feels neglected and starved of attention. Michael has been disturbed at school by bullies making lewd comments about his stripper mother – comments which both shame and excite him. When he sees the scantily clad body of his sister lying in bed, he is confused between incipient lust and a desire to punish her for 'promiscuous' behaviour, which reminds him of his mother's. Michael's stepfather has also been belittling him as a 'faggot', giving rise to an urge in him to prove his manhood. All these influences help to explain why, when his sister slaps him for staring at her body, Michael stabs her with his phallic knife.

The film then gives considerable screen time to the months Michael spends in therapy, but his apparently well-meaning psychiatrist must be strikingly incompetent for he never seems to explore the root causes of his patient's mental illness, nor does he appear to prescribe any particular course of treatment. Instead, like the psychiatrist in the original film, this 'doctor' begins to talk about how 'Evil is here. It's walking amongst us.' He calls Michael 'a soulless killing machine' and even implies that he may be 'the Antichrist'. However, by having the psychiatrist get rich off a book called *The Devil's Eyes* that he writes about Michael, this film tends to discredit the doctor's religious and supernatural explanations, suggesting that he is more interested in fame than in helping his patient.

Psychological insight returns when the remake departs from the ending of the original. Instead of having Michael continue his violent acting out with no understanding of the reasons for his knife attacks and thus little hope of ever stopping them, the new film suggests that all of Michael's repeated stabbings have actually been an attempt by him to achieve self-knowledge and gain mastery over his own behaviour. As he realises when he sees the teenage Laurie, it is not a desire to kill that has been driving him, but rather a need to connect, to receive love. Michael does not stab Laurie. Instead, because he recognises her as his own baby sister now grown up, he takes off his killer's mask and shows her a photo of the two of them when they were young, appealing to *her* to recognise *him*. Tragically, Laurie has been told nothing about the brother she once had, and so, viewing him merely as a threat, she picks up his knife and stabs him with it. In the end, feeling rejected by his own sister, Michael steadies her hand so that she can fire a bullet into his brain. He doesn't want to live any longer without his sister's love, which is all he really wanted from his older sister when he entered her bedroom many years ago. People may see him as the embodiment of evil, but soulless monsters don't commit suicide.

I Spit on Your Grave (1978)

Director: Meir Zarchi
Cast: Camille Keaton (Jennifer), Anthony Nichols (Stanley), Gunter Kleemann (Andy), Richard Pace (Matthew), Eron Tabor (Johnny)

I Spit on Your Grave (2010)

Director: Steven R Monroe
Cast: Sarah Butler (Jennifer), Jeff Branson (Johnny), Andrew Howard (Storch), Chad Lindberg (Matthew), Daniel Franzese (Stanley)

A combination of rape-revenge and hillbilly horror, *I Spit on Your Grave* has caused controversy in both its versions. Each tells the same basic tale: a young woman from the city rents a cabin in the country, where she is gang-raped by local men; she then turns the tables on them and wreaks vengeance. But the versions differ in a number of significant ways.

There is negative stereotyping of rural natives as redneck hillbillies in both films, but the men in the original movie are ignorant in an almost childlike sense and seem less aware of the immorality of their actions. Stanley and Andy make whooping sounds, throwing a rope to lasso Jennifer's canoe as if they were children playing a game of cowboys and Indians. They laugh while chasing Jennifer through the woods before proceeding to rape her – an act they commit gleefully, as though it were equally unserious. In their stupidity, they appear to have convinced themselves that, as a 'loose' 'city' woman, Jennifer will welcome the rape. Although Matthew is the only one among them who is truly mentally challenged, he seems to stand for the rest of them, for they are all in a sense developmentally disabled. 'You want to be a man, don't you?' they say, encouraging Matthew to have intercourse with her, and indeed they all seem to be boys whose sex with her occurs in front of their buddies because they feel the need to prove to the others and themselves that they are men. Matthew, wearing boys' tube socks and smiling in self-satisfaction while he rapes her, exemplifies their arrested development.

By contrast, the men in the 2010 remake are more conscious of their own evil. Before forcing her to fellate his gun, Johnny debases Jennifer by having her show him her teeth, knowing full well that she is not a horse. As evidenced by his calling her a 'stuck-up city bitch' and a 'big-city, cock-teasing whore', Johnny's rape of her is motivated by class resentment and covetous desire, not by childish ignorance. Moreover, the remake adds a new character, Storch, who is the rapists' ringleader. As an older man and a sheriff, Storch should and does know better. Frisking her as an excuse to feel her up, offering her help as a pretext to assaulting her himself, and raping her anally because he enjoys her pain, Storch is a corrupt and perverted adult, not a boy.

The depiction of Jennifer, the rape victim turned avenger, is also different in the two films, particularly after the assault. The 1978 version has Jennifer go to church and ask God for forgiveness in advance of her revenge, as she feels guilty, knowing the sinfulness of what she is about to do. Jennifer then uses her sex appeal to seduce each of the men, luring them all to a violent demise. While there is a certain poetic justice to this (they treated her like a whore and so she whores herself to get back at them), it is disturbing to see her adopt their degrading view of her as a sexual plaything – and to see her continue to link sex and violence as they did. 'Come on, killer,' Johnny encourages Matthew during the rape when he is unable to ejaculate. Afterwards, Johnny equips Matthew with a phallic knife and sends him off to actually kill her, but he can't do that either. 'I was chosen to kill you and I didn't,' Matthew laments to Jennifer, holding up his knife. 'You will this time,' she assures him, and draws him into having intercourse with her. At the moment of his climax, she strangles him to death with a noose around his neck. This disabled young man, whose 'friends' have led him to confuse coming and killing, penis and knife, is further taken advantage of by Jennifer, who plays on his ignorance to bring him to an eroticised end. And, for her revenge on Johnny, Jennifer gets naked with him into a bathtub where she gives him a sensual massage ('God bless your hands,' he says), masturbates him to climax, then severs his sex organ with a knife, afterwards sitting in a chair near the red carpet she was raped on while he bleeds out. Once again, despite the poetic justice (the violator is violated, red for red), the film implies that Jennifer has descended to the level of her rapists. Her bloody revenge indicates that she continues to 'see red' and has not overcome the trauma of being assaulted. They forced her into a confusion of sex and violence, and revenge only mires her deeper in it rather than helping her to find a way out. The half-smile she gives at the end of the movie may suggest she's achieved some satisfaction through her castrating vengeance, but she guiltily knows that God has not blessed those hands. They are damned.

If the original Jennifer's revenge is realistic and guilt-ridden, the remake presents it as fantastic and conscience-free. After escaping from her rapists by falling – martyr-like with arms spread – backwards into a river, Jennifer rises again as an almost supernaturally divine avenger. To Matthew, she appears as a kind of ghost. 'Are you sure you're not dreaming?' she asks. In this version, Matthew is so stricken with remorse over his part in the rape, which is greater than in the original film, that even he seems to think he deserves to die for what he has done, so her vengeance on him appears divinely justified. As for her killings of the other assailants – voyeuristic Stanley has his eyelids dragged open with fishhooks so that crows can peck out his eyes; oral rapist Johnny has his teeth broken with a metal bridle and is castrated by equine-emasculating shears; and anal rapist Storch is violated with his own shotgun, which is then triggered to explode in his ass – these executions are so elaborately contrived that they seem to be the work of some avenging higher power and not the acts of a real woman. It is as though some righteous deity were acting through Jennifer to bring poetically just retribution to these rapists. Certainly, there is little sense that Jennifer's moral character is being further damaged by these actions or that she has any reason to feel guilty about them. When Storch tells her, 'I'll see you in hell,' we may wonder for a moment if the movie wants us to consider whether she belongs there, too, given the terrible things she has now done, but when he then adds 'I'll rape you in hell' and 'you're just a piece of meat', we realise that we're expected to cheer his demise. In this version, when Jennifer gives her half-smile at the end, we are not supposed to worry about the decline in her morality or mental health. We're expected to share her smirk of satisfaction at a violent job well done.

Carrie (2013)

Director: Kimberly Peirce
Cast: Chloë Grace Moretz (Carrie), Portia Doubleday (Chris)

When Stephen King, author of the novel *Carrie*, heard there was going to be a remake of the iconic 1976 film, he asked what was on everyone's mind: 'The real question is why, when the original was so good?'[138] Director Kimberly Peirce decided to make her version both more realistic and more mythic – two interesting goals that sometimes end up working at cross purposes. To make the story more realistic and contemporary, the teenage Carrie is now a victim of cyberbullying. When she gets her first period in the shower and fears she is bleeding to death, the other high-school girls not only pelt her with tampons while shouting 'Plug it up!', they also film her humiliation with a smartphone and post the video on YouTube. On the night of the senior prom, when bully Chris and her posse of mean girls arrange to have pig's blood dumped on Carrie, the video of her bleeding in the shower is played on giant screens in the gymnasium, adding to her shame and abasement. Given that news reports have familiarised us with the pain endured by misfits and outcasts who are persecuted via social media, Carrie's suffering feels real to us and we empathise with her. But ours is also a world of mass shootings like the one at Columbine where two high-school seniors murdered fellow students, so when Carrie begins to deploy her killing powers in the prom massacre, she risks losing our sympathy. To retain it, the film attempts to portray Carrie as having been so victimised by bullying that she snaps, striking back at her tormentors with a mad fury. 'I wanted to make sure she doesn't have actual control,' Peirce has said, 'because I thought that if she had actual control, then she could be more liable for what she does at the prom', particularly 'in a post-Columbine world'.[139]

And yet the Carrie we see at the prom, telekinetically lifting a kindly gym teacher to safety while crushing, burning and electrocuting her specific student enemies, often seems very much in control, and this could be because the film also wants to present her as a mythic superhero. Co-scripted by Marvel Comics writer Roberto Aguirre-Sacasa (of Fantastic Four and Spider-Man fame), the movie has been described by Peirce as 'a superhero origin story'.[140] Speaking of Carrie's prom massacre, Peirce has said that 'the audience is meant to get behind these kills and want to cheer for them. By and large that happened, and I think that's because you love Carrie and you feel a sense of justice to the revenge that she's taking.'[141] While it's easy to applaud movie superheroes who use their mythic powers to defeat the dastardly villains, it is much harder to cheer the sight of a high-school girl deliberately killing many of her classmates, even if they did bully her. In real life, the escalation of violence by a vigilante avenger is unlikely to solve the problem of bullying – and may even exacerbate it by perpetuating a cycle of viciousness and revenge. By making Carrie a more realistic character, the movie makes it hard for us to enjoy the violence she commits, and that's a good thing.

SELF-CONSCIOUS SLASHER

High Tension (Haute tension) (aka *Switchblade Romance*) (2003)

Director: Alexandre Aja
Cast: Cécile de France (Marie), Maïwenn (Alex), Philippe Nahon (Trucker), Andrei Finti (Father), Oana Pellea (Mother), Marco Claudiu Pascu (Brother)

Everyone knows that, at the end of a slasher film, the Final Girl defeats the killer. But what if the Final Girl is the killer? In her own mind, 20-something Marie spends most of the movie trying to save her girlfriend, Alex, from a murderous male trucker, only to have it revealed near the end that Marie has a split personality: the killer she has been fighting is really herself.

That trucker is both Marie's worst nightmare and a strange wish-fulfilment fantasy, for even though he threatens Alex, he also removes the obstacles separating Marie from the woman she secretly desires. The two friends are staying at the home of Alex's parents in the French countryside. As night falls, Marie, who has gone outside for a smoke, glances at an upstairs window and catches sight of Alex naked in the shower. Once back inside, Marie pleasures herself in bed, a scene that is cross-cut with shots of the menacing trucker pulling up outside the house. 'In a way, she's calling – in her fantasy – the killer,' says director Alexandre Aja. 'She's masturbating and, at the same time, the killer arrives.'[142] The killer strikes down the family dog and decapitates Alex's father. Earlier that day, when Marie first arrived at the door with her friend, Alex had assured her, 'Don't worry – he doesn't bite,' and her father had said, 'Are you talking about me or the dog?' Now the killer violently removes both watchdogs that might keep Marie from Alex. The killer then cuts Alex's mother's throat and shoots her brother. Earlier that night, Alex, who is rooming on the same floor as the rest of her family, has shown her maternal instinct by putting her little brother to bed, while Marie is left alone in an attic room. Now the killer puts an end to heterosexual marriage and mother-son bonding so that Marie can have Alex to herself. Alex is interested in a guy who already has another girlfriend, so Marie conjures up a serial murderer who will scare her friend into her arms by showing her what men are 'really like'. The trucker cuts Alex's face out of a family photo and puts her picture up next to those of all the other women he has had his way with. The trucker also takes the severed head of a woman who looks like Alex and uses it to perform fellatio.

These frightening images of a man sexually objectifying and fragmenting women should, Marie figures, draw Alex to her in female solidarity, except for one thing: Marie is the one doing these terrible things. So intent is Marie on attaining the object of her desire that she has unwittingly become as possessive and violently penetrative as the patriarchal villain she conjured up. Thus, we see Marie-as-the-killer pursuing Alex with a power saw while saying, 'I'm gonna take care of you, Alex.' 'Take care' in what sense? Marie's kind of covetous love is more menacing than protective. In the last we see of Marie, she is in an insane asylum, repeatedly saying to Alex, 'I won't let anyone come between us any more.' Marie never realises that the key obstacle between her and her beloved was herself.

Hellbent (2004)

Director: Paul Etheredge-Ouzts
Cast: Andrew Levitas (Chaz), Matt Phillips (Tobey), Hank Harris (Joey), Dylan Fergus (Eddie), Bryan Kirkwood (Jake)

Hellbent is one of the first slasher films to feature overtly gay characters. Despite the disclaimer by writer-director Paul Etheredge-Ouzts that 'the sexuality of these characters is wholly incidental',[143] the fears and desires of the gay community can be seen as a central concern of the film. In the opening scene, two men meet in a cruising park and then hook up in a car. One man brings coloured balloons, suggesting his interest in a playful encounter. The other man, while receiving oral sex, looks up at the moon, implying a desire for romance. However, the scene ends with the second man being decapitated during fellatio by a killer, as if the fear of being 'castrated' by a stranger picked up in the park overwhelms any hopes of fun or love. The rest of the film rings changes on this central conflict between desire and dread, as played out through the lead characters, four young friends named Chaz, Tobey, Joey and Eddie.

Pill-popping, hard-drinking and bisexual Chaz is all about the joys of promiscuity. He'll swallow anything or anyone. Chaz is the life of the party, and the film celebrates his joyous abandon while also being afraid of where his openness to all comers might lead. As Chaz, high on Ecstasy, is dancing with multiple partners in a club, he does not even notice when the killer begins slashing his torso, eventually cutting his throat. The gyrating clubbers dance on, heedless of his headless corpse on the floor – a nightmare of partying with everyone, but being connected to no one, as Chaz himself used to be.

Fit and buff Tobey, an underwear model, is tired of being wanted for his body alone, so he dresses up in drag to see if he can get someone interested in his wit and intelligence. But after being dismissed all night long, a desperate Tobey eventually reveals his chiselled chest to a man, who turns out to be the killer. The horns on top of the killer's devil mask and the sickle he wields reveal his arousal at the sight of male flesh, and the blade's penetration of Tobey's body indicates Tobey's despair at the thought that he will never be more than a sex object, a piece of meat for the taking.

Virginal Joey, garbed in S/M fetish gear, is snubbed by a varsity football player, who follows him into a restroom for what Joey fears will be a gay bashing. When the guy instead gives him his phone number, Joey is overjoyed at having met the man of his dreams – only to have the killer take the guy's place, manhandle Joey, and penetrate him with his blade. Joey finds that his attraction to a tough guy, his flirtation with being the bottom in an S/M scenario, has turned from masochistic delight to a victim's dead-end.

Will nice-guy Eddie's cruising of a tattooed biker lead him to a similar fate? The biker, Jake, pushes Eddie down and handcuffs him to the bed – signs of dominance that could be delicious or dangerous. Eddie's desire to keep risk within safe limits (Jake agrees to use condoms) gives way to fear of anal rape, which is figured when the killer sticks his blade up to Eddie's eye and then pokes it out (the eye is artificial, due to a prior accident). In the end, care and commitment conquer fear when Jake and Eddie join together to defeat the killer and tend to each other's wounds. But the film leaves us with one last image of castration anxiety – the killer, still alive, holds Eddie's eye between his teeth – as a haunting reminder that fear never really dies.

The Cabin in the Woods (2012)

Director: Drew Goddard
Cast: Richard Jenkins and Bradley Whitford (Engineers), Anna Hutchison (Jules), Chris Hemsworth (Curt), Kristen Connolly (Dana), Fran Kranz (Marty)

Five college kids go to an *Evil Dead* cabin near a *Friday the 13th* lake where they get attacked by a *Texas Chain Saw*-like family. Seeming to fit the formula of a '70s or '80s slasher film ('You think you know the story' is the movie's tagline), *The Cabin in the Woods* is actually a meta-horror film that critiques the genre. The unsuspecting youths are being electronically monitored by engineers in a control room, who deploy subtle means, such as pheromone mists and slight rises in temperature, to influence their behaviour. Thus Jules, despite being a brainy female pre-med student, is overcome with whorish lust for Curt, who starts to assert his dominance like an alpha-male athlete, even though he is on an academic scholarship. Pressured to conform to the stereotypes of 'slut' and 'dumb jock', Jules and Curt proceed to have sex, while the leering engineers watch them voyeuristically on monitors. A zombie then appears to skewer Jules's hand with a blade (a symbolic rape) and then to cut Curt's throat (a kind of castration). Soon afterwards, the engineers cheer and party while a zombie is torturing and trying to kill another woman, Dana (the 'virgin'), for it turns out that this entire scenario is a recurrent ritual whereby young blood is spilled to appease the Ancient Ones – old gods who demand the sacrifice of youth.

These old gods and the ageing engineers are like the audiences at slasher films who first peep at and then punish the randy teen characters. As co-writer Joss Whedon has said, 'It's so ingrained in our society that this is the normal course of horror entertainment and that there is this weird obsession with youth and sex, and at the same time this very puritanical desire to punish it that I think is unseemly and really, really creepy.'[144] The engineers with their video voyeurism are not so different from the zombie father who watches girls undress through a one-way mirror. As the engineers (and horror-movie audiences) spy on teen sex, they are filled with frustrated lust and envious rage. The old take delight in punishing the young for enjoying the sex they themselves can no longer have. Because watching 'the cutting of the flesh' makes them get a trouser 'bulge', the engineers (and slasher-film viewers) are no better than the 'zombified, pain-worshipping, backwoods idiots' who are the movie's monsters. When Dana hits the 'purge' button and turns these monsters on their masters so that the zombies kill the engineers, she is really only hastening the ancient system's own self-destruction, for if the old feed off their young, none can survive. Another youth, Marty (the 'fool'), is told that he and Dana must die or the Ancient Ones will destroy all of humanity. But Marty is no fool. Realising that only a monstrously immoral world would make such an inhumane demand, he refuses to shoot Dana. If that means the end of everything, so be it. It is better to die making a decision his conscience can live with. As director Drew Goddard says, 'If, to save the world, you have to execute your friend, you should say no.'[145]

TECHNO-HORROR

Ringu (1998)

Director: Hideo Nakata
Cast: Rie Ino'o (Ghost Girl), Nanako Matsushima (Mother)

The Ring (2002)

Director: Gore Verbinski
Cast: Daveigh Chase (Ghost Girl), Naomi Watts (Mother)

Both the original Japanese *Ringu* and its American remake, *The Ring*, begin with teenage gossip about the urban legend of a cursed video, which, once seen, leads viewers to die of fright within one week. As one teen girl tells another this story, she says that she herself saw the video a week ago and then she pretends to die, taking advantage of her worried friend's sympathy in order to throw a scare into her. However, the girl who plays this 'campfire tale' prank really does die, which suggests a connection between the curse and people who lack compassion for others. Indeed, the video has been created by the vengeful ghost of a girl rejected by her adoptive parents and left to die at the bottom of a well. In *Ringu*, characters call this girl 'a monster' and speculate that she may have been the spawn of a sea-demon father who 'wasn't human'. To most watchers of the video, the ghost girl also appears as a vision of supernatural evil, climbing out of the well with her long, damp hair covering her face, except for one creepily staring eye. Because we do not see her whole face, she looks dehumanised, an object of fear rather than a person worthy of sympathy. Interestingly, in the week before they die, those who see the girl with the obscured face in the video begin to view their own faces as blurred or distorted in photos, and (in *The Ring*) they begin to scribble out other people's faces. Before she died, the girl at the bottom of the well saw its cover closing above her, obscuring the sun and effectively effacing her life. Now the video's victims seem to see what she saw as their eyes stare at a frightening vision of encroaching darkness, their own self-effacement. Much as recounting an urban legend spreads fear through the rumour mill, so watching the cursed video seems to spread people's fear of dying, as if seeing the horror of what happened to the abandoned girl leaves people fatally traumatised. In the film's scariest scene, the ghost girl in the video crawls out of the well and then *through the television screen* to attack a viewer, as if images themselves can take on corporeal form and literally kill.

But instead of scaring each other to death with televisual 'chain letters' of fear, what if we watched with some empathy? What if seeing what the girl saw became an opportunity to feel what she felt? This is what a female journalist and mother tries to do, investigating the images in the video as clues to understanding the girl's suffering, then overcoming her own fear of death (she has seen the video, too) by going down into the well and clasping the girl's corpse to her bosom. By recovering this abandoned child and showing sympathy for her as a person (and not some demon-spawn), the mother seems to lift the curse, for she does not die within a week of having seen the video.

To believe that a vengeful spirit can be appeased by human understanding is a hopeful view, but these films ultimately refuse such optimism. Rather than including the ghost girl within the community of suffering humanity, they demonise her as irredeemably evil. After the mother cradles the girl's body, her own son tells her, 'You weren't supposed to help her. Don't you understand...? She never sleeps' – she is supernatural and relentlessly malevolent. When the girl's ghost tries to take possession of the son in *The Ring Two*, the mother repudiates her – 'I'm not your fucking mommy!' – and then pushes her back down the same well from which she had earlier recovered her body. The mother's action thus repeats the girl's parents' original rejection of her and implies that they were right. It turns out that the mother's earlier compassion for the girl did not lift the curse. Instead, the only way to avoid death after viewing the cursed video is to make someone else watch it before the week is up. This implies that, in order not to become the victim of a trauma, one should become a victimiser, identifying with the aggressor and inflicting that same trauma on somebody else. It is hard to imagine a more pessimistic ending – or one more despairing and destructive of humanity.

Kairo (2001)

Director: Kiyoshi Kurosawa
Cast: Kenji Mizuhashi (Taguchi), Kumiko Aso (Michi), Kurume Arisaka (Junko), Koyuki (Harue)

Pulse (2006)

Director: Jim Sonzero
Cast: Jonathan Tucker (Josh), Rick Gonzalez (Stone), Kristen Bell (Mattie)

Taguchi works in a greenhouse with other 20-something friends, but he leaves behind their companionship and loses his link to nature when he shuts himself away in his darkened apartment, spending all day on his computer. *Kairo* means 'circuit', as in the human circulatory system or Internet connectivity, and Taguchi is lured by the promise that if he 'plugs in' to the Web, he will overcome loneliness and be connected with other people. However, what he finds, after the on-screen greeting of 'Would you like to meet a ghost?', are webcam images of other online users, sitting alone in front of their monitors and looking lethargic and depressed, drained of life. Taguchi's monitor also shows him images of himself looking at a computer screen of himself looking at a computer screen of himself, as if his life were receding into the Internet, making him a mere ghost of his former self, now trapped in virtual reality. When his friend Michi visits him, she sees Taguchi standing behind a hanging plastic curtain, a virtual presence, there but not there, cut off from her and the real world. Michi sees another computer-enthralled friend, Junko, lose her identity to the machine and become a black smudge of her former self, eventually breaking up into bits and bytes that float away into the ether. And a computer expert named Harue finds herself flickering between actual views and pixelated images of herself to the point where 'real' life and 'reel' life become indistinguishable. Lured by the false promise of connectivity, Harue exclaims, 'I'm not alone,' and then shoots herself in the head, after watching an online user kill himself in the same way on her computer screen. With these scenes, the film refers to the phenomenon of *hikikomori* where adolescents withdraw from society by taping out the light from their rooms and spending their lives hunched over computers. Youths have also engaged in suicide pacts, live-streaming their deaths via webcam to other online users who are thereby invited to join them in the cyberworld beyond.

Although they are both techno-horror films, *Pulse*, the Hollywood remake of *Kairo*, differs from the Japanese original in a number of revealing respects. The youths in *Kairo* grow increasingly isolated and eventually fade away into their cyberworlds. The 20-somethings in *Pulse* are a gregarious bunch, so it is hard to view them as threatened by loneliness. When one of them texts another while they are sitting at the same table, the telecommunication does not make us fear that the friends are growing apart. Rather, the gap between them seems humorous and easily surmountable, if they just put down their cell phones and talked. Rather than gradually dispersing into the ether, the youths in *Pulse* die sudden, spectacular deaths, less out of suicidal despair and more because they are attacked by aggressively evil ghosts. Josh is assaulted by a grotesque spectre with an elongated face that literally sucks the life's breath out of him. Stone is infected with a disease that manifests as an ugly rash spreading over his body. Mattie is menaced by a writhing mass of arms that threaten to pull her into the virtual world, which resembles a hell full of tormented souls. It is rarely clear what, if anything, links these ghosts or what they have to do with the particular threat represented by the Internet. 'We took it up a few notches,' director Jim Sonzero said in comparing his amped-up version with the original, noting that he also wanted to give the story 'more structure' so that it would not be so 'lethargic' or 'glacial'.[146] Effects designer Gary Tunnicliffe added that each of the deaths in *Pulse* has 'a different tone' so that 'it wasn't the same thing over and over again'.[147] It's a long way from the original where all the youths die essentially the same quiet death, their anomie and disconnection from society leading them to fade away into the Internet. For *Kairo* director Kiyoshi Kurosawa, 'Ghosts are beings that lack human emotion and personality. They're human-like, but all the emotional elements of a normal person are missing. They're empty shells. That's what scares me when it comes to ghosts.'[148] In *Kairo*, ghosts are us after we have been drawn into the Web, whereas in *Pulse*, ghosts are evil techno-spirits trying to invade our human world. Unlike the in-your-face attacks and killings by the ghosts in *Pulse*, the closest *Kairo* gets to a spectacular death is a view of a woman, positioned way off in the distance, who dies by leaping from a water tower, with the camera showing her entire fall to the ground. With this scene, Kurosawa makes a point about how many suicides are barely even noticed, with people just dropping away from society and perishing in despair. By holding the woman's body in frame all the way down and showing her hit the ground, he emphasises the fact that this is a loss of life, the presence of a real person who is no more.

FearDotCom (2002)

Director: William Malone
Cast: Stephen Rea (Pratt), Gesine Cukrowski (Jeannie)

Pratt is a serial killer who live-streams his slayings on a website where viewers can choose the tools of torture he will use to penetrate female flesh. Those watching thus become accessories to murder, their sadistic desires enacted by the killer's hands, their eyes as cold as the camera's. But one of Pratt's victims, a young woman named Jeannie, begins to haunt the Web, appearing as a seductive avatar to ask PC users, 'Do you like to watch?' and 'Do you want to hurt me?' Users who answer 'yes' then have the tables turned on them, for instead of getting to identify with an aggressive serial killer, they find themselves being tortured by whatever it is they most fear. For the haemophiliac Jeannie, this was being made to bleed, so Pratt's knives were especially terrifying to her. Much as her protective skin was ruptured, so the interface shielding users from the violence they are watching on-screen is breached when this vengeful ghost punishes them for their snuff-movie voyeurism.[149] One female viewer, who has a fear of insects, is made to watch in horror as her own computer gets a bug, with cockroaches crawling out of her hard drive and all over her helpless flesh. Another user becomes so immersed in her viewing of violence that her worst fear is realised: she drowns. The mind of a third watcher is overwhelmed by the torture he's seeing and his system crashes, leaving him dead from a collision in an out-of-control car. In each case, before dying, users see their own faces reflected back at them from the computer screen as if in a distorting mirror, revealing their true moral ugliness.

Before taking a scalpel to one victim, Pratt, who calls himself the Doctor, tells her, 'I'd like to say I can feel your pain, but I can't

... I know what I should feel. I just can't.' It could be that the self-diagnosis here is accurate and that underlying Pratt's sadism is a desire to feel empathy for his victims, but his fear of vulnerability gets in the way, prompting him to become an aggressor instead. Whatever the reasons for this physician's inability to heal himself, Jeannie's avenging ghost does get him to suffer some of the pain he has inflicted on others. 'Time to feel' and 'Time to die' she tells him with her screaming, violated mouth, and her ghost becomes a train barrelling out of the video screen towards Pratt's now-vulnerable eye.

TEEN ROMANCE

The Twilight Saga (2008–12)

Directors: Catherine Hardwicke, Chris Weitz, David Slade, Bill Condon
Cast: Kristen Stewart (Bella), Taylor Lautner (Jacob), Robert Pattinson (Edward)

When a werewolf and a vampire are rivals for your love, which do you choose? There are aspects of male sexuality which appear during adolescence that can seem monstrous and frightening (yet strangely sexy) to girls. The growth of body hair, increased muscle mass, a voracious appetite and a tendency to hunt in packs can liken some teen boys to lycanthropes. Others have bushy eyebrows, mesmerising eyes, full lips and penetrating teeth that make them resemble vampires. Seventeen-year-old Bella must decide between lupine Jacob and vampiric Edward, who are competing for her affection.

Jacob is associated with the physical realm. His body heat warms her on a freezing night. 'Let's face it: I *am* hotter than you,' he tells the undead Edward. Jacob's musky odour attracts Bella, and his powerful physique protects her as he runs through the forest, carrying her in his muscular arms. Noting how often Jacob's bare torso is exposed, Edward wonders, 'Doesn't he have a shirt?' 'I can sense how I make you feel, physically,' Jacob tells Bella, and she straddles the back of his motorcycle as if in anticipation of riding this hunky heartthrob. A Native American, Jacob is often backgrounded by green mountains and blue lakes, offering Bella a connection to the land and its natural freedom, an opportunity to run with the wolves. In marrying him, she would get to join the Quileute clan, becoming part of their tribal family and experiencing the joys of being a wife and mother. Yet Jacob's physicality is also something she feels as a potential threat. In his passion, he presses her with unwanted kisses, making her fear that his carnivorous desire for her will lead to rape. Is he a savage who will ravage her? 'The wolves have no control,' Edward says disdainfully, and Jacob himself apologises for the 'inner animal thing' that he has unleashed.

In contrast to Jacob and his carnal appetite, Edward maintains an almost spiritual self-restraint. Whereas brawny Jacob has tan skin and dark hair, Edward is slim, blond and pale-faced – more angelically beautiful than handsomely masculine. His body is so pure that it sparkles in the sunlight. A 'vegetarian' vampire, Edward controls his bloodlust and abstains from penetrating Bella before marriage. By preserving her virginity in this way, he offers her a soulful communion unsullied by lust, an idealised pleasure with no physical pain. By becoming this spiritual kind of vampire with Edward, Bella would be able to remain young for ever, living out the girlish fantasy of a never-ending fairy-tale romance. But this absence of attention to her body disturbs Bella, for she is a woman of flesh and blood who desires sexual fulfilment. She chafes against the bonds of enforced chastity, finding anaemic Edward to be too 'pure' and withholding, whereas Jacob is too hot-blooded and hungry. Edward, speaking of having penetrated multiple women in the past before learning the value of abstinence, tells Bella, 'It might be too late for my soul, but I will protect *yours.*' Yet Bella doesn't accept the argument that premarital penetration would mean that, once having experienced such physical pleasure, she would no longer be able to control her bloodlust and would consequently thirst for other men besides Edward. 'Everyone says that once I'm changed, all I'm going to want is to slaughter the whole town!' Bella scoffs. 'When we first taste human blood, a sort of frenzy begins and it's almost impossible to stop,' Edward warns, but Bella wants a man 'body and soul', not just body (Jacob) or soul (Edward). She is looking for a balance between vegetarian and vampire, between were- and wolf.

In one scene where Bella and Edward are in close physical proximity, she thinks she sees him 'leaning away' from her and 'averting his face like he smelled something bad'.[150] But Edward later tells her that, rather than being disgusted by the odour of her human flesh, he found it so powerfully alluring that, in order to avoid taking her then and there, he had to leave the room and slake his thirst elsewhere as a way of relieving himself. However, whether Edward is so refined as to be above fleshly temptation, or so repressed that his barely contained desires threaten to erupt as violence, he is a problem for Bella, who wants neither an ascetic angel nor a vicious vampire, but someone who will pierce her with love.

Warm Bodies (2013)

Director: Jonathan Levine
Cast: Nicholas Hoult (R), Dave Franco (Perry), Teresa Palmer (Julie)

As a zombie, R is one of the undead, but he is also an emo/goth teen boy who, despite having adopted the dark hair, pale face and heavy eyeliner of his ghoulish brethren, suffers deeply in his alienation from regular human society. Neither a ghoul nor a regular guy, R is an awkward adolescent who wanders aimlessly with no clear orientation, in contrast to Perry, a square-jawed, GI Joe-type who knows how to use a gun and to please his girlfriend, Julie. When R satisfies his hunger for Perry by consuming his brains, it's not clear whether sexually ambivalent R desires the other boy or wishes to identify with him – to desire Julie in the way Perry does. 'I just want to feel what you felt,' R says to Perry while eating him, before smearing some of Perry's blood and grey matter on Julie's face as if that could help R transfer his desire from the boy to the girl. Like a stuttering Romeo who can't get past the first letter of his name, R keeps stumbling on his first date with Julie, trying to walk and talk the part of a typical boyfriend. Taking her for a ride in a red convertible (the 'cool guy'), playing her vinyl records (the 'hipster') and shaking a snow globe with figures of a couple holding hands inside (the 'romantic'), R tries on different roles, but he never quite seems to fit any one of them. 'Stop shrugging,' Julie tells him, frustrated at times by his indeterminate nature; 'it's a very noncommittal gesture'. 'You can be whatever you want,' she assures him. But when he asks, '*We* can, right? You and me?', R hears the ghost of Perry saying, 'It's not gonna happen, lover boy – not after you tell her you ate her ex,' as if reminding R that his desires will always be too queer to settle for one straight part.

And yet Julie also seems to like the fact that R is so different from the resolutely macho Perry. She appreciates that he is sensitive and sentimental as well as protective of her. In one complexly gendered scene, Julie and another girl give R a makeover as if he were one of their female friends on a sleepover, but their goal in applying foundation and blush is to help him pass as a regular guy when he goes to meet Julie's father. R ends up looking feminine and manly, sensitive and virile, and the girls like his queer undecidability, telling him, 'You look hot!'

TORTURE PORN

Saw (2004)

Director: James Wan
Cast: Tobin Bell (Jigsaw), Leigh Whannell (Adam), Cary Elwes (Lawrence), Mike Butters (Paul), Paul Gutrecht (Mark), Shawnee Smith (Amanda)

This film's Jigsaw killer cuts puzzle-shaped pieces of skin from the bodies of his victims. The film itself is a fragmented narrative of puzzle pieces that fit together to connect different meanings of 'saw': to see and to cut. Two men, Adam and Lawrence, have each been chained by the ankle at opposite ends of a room, in the middle of which lies a gun. Watched by a camera in the wall,

Lawrence must use a hacksaw to sever his own foot, crawl to grab the gun, and shoot Adam, or else Lawrence's wife and daughter will be killed. Jigsaw's stated aim is to get Lawrence to prove how much he values his family, but in fact Jigsaw is looking forward to watching Lawrence fail, for that will justify the killer's cynical view of humanity's faults and his cruel desire to mete out punishment for them. Jigsaw *wants* to see that hacksaw slicing through flesh. His is a sadistic kind of seeing that enjoys others' suffering, the cuts inflicted upon them. As one detective comments after noticing a peephole through which the killer spies on his victims, 'Looks like our friend Jigsaw likes to book himself front-row seats to his own sick little games.' Although most sports fans root for their team to win, perverted Jigsaw gets excited over the prospect of people losing his games, as he is turned on by death and destruction.

After a man named Paul makes a half-hearted suicide attempt using a straight razor, Jigsaw creates a game where Paul has to escape from a roomful of razor wire. Ostensibly, this is Paul's chance to prove how much he really wants to live, but his most strenuous efforts lead only to a fatally lacerated stomach, so the game seems rigged, as if designed to confirm that people are basically self-destructive. Another man, Mark, has been feigning illness to receive benefit cheques, so Jigsaw devises a game where Mark has to take sickness seriously. In order to obtain the antidote to a slow-acting poison in his system, Mark, whose body has been smeared with a flammable substance, must open a safe before a candle sets him on fire. But rather than cheering Mark on to success, Jigsaw wants him to go up in flames so that all the people he 'burned' with his fakery will have their vengeance. Jigsaw isn't out to rescue or reform people; he seeks retribution and revenge. A drug addict named Amanda is locked in a 'reverse bear-trap' that will rip her head apart if she doesn't slice open the belly of her drug dealer to obtain a key to the lock. While this game may seem designed to force her to overcome her dependency on the dealer, Jigsaw fully expects to see Amanda cut open the man, choosing her own survival over the other's life – and she does.

Thus, while outwardly civil and altruistic, politely explaining how his games are for people's betterment, Jigsaw is actually sadistic, punitive and vengeful. Jigsaw's hypocritical duality can be seen in his avatar, Billy, the ventriloquist's doll through whom he speaks. The dapperly dressed Billy, who wears a tuxedo and bow tie, also has glaringly judgemental red eyes and lunatic spirals on his cheeks. It could be argued that all the victims who play Jigsaw's games become his ventriloquist's dummies, for they serve as the means by which he commits his acts of homicide or self-destruction. Jigsaw himself kills no one; he induces others to do that for him.

But *Saw* ends with a character who finds the ingenuity and courage not to play entirely by Jigsaw's rules. Lawrence is being punished for desiring a woman other than his wife and for working so much he neglects his daughter. As we noted above, in order to save his family from being killed, Lawrence must saw off his chained foot so that he can reach a gun and shoot his chained cellmate, Adam – these are the rules of Jigsaw's game. But unlike the guilt-ridden and self-mortifying Paul, Lawrence does not commit suicide. He severs his foot at the ankle, but is careful to use his shirt as a tourniquet to tie off his leg so that he will not bleed to death. Lawrence picks up the gun and shoots Adam, but unlike the homicidal Amanda, Lawrence (who is a doctor) avoids killing his victim, for he is careful to aim at non-vital organs. By finding a middle way between homicidal anger and suicidal despair, Lawrence plays along with Jigsaw's game but makes his own terms, refusing to accept that murder and self-mortification are the only allowable outcomes. Whereas Jigsaw sees others sadistically, enjoying the cut, Lawrence views Adam with sympathy, feeling his suffering as being similar to his own and wanting to alleviate their shared pain. 'Your aim in this game is to kill Adam,' Jigsaw tells him, but Lawrence wins the game by rewriting the rules.

Hostel (2005)

Director: Eli Roth
Cast: Derek Richardson (Josh), Jay Hernandez (Paxton), Barbara Nedeljáková and Jana Kadeřábkova (Slovakian Women), Jan Vlasák (Josh's Tormentor), Petr Janis (Paxton's Tormentor)

What fuels the horror in *Hostel* is a never-ending cycle of victimisation and revenge. US college students Josh and Paxton are backpacking through Europe, alienating locals by displaying an arrogant sense of entitlement ('Kiss my American ass') and reducing local women to flesh in a meat market ('I hope bestiality is legal in Amsterdam because that girl is a fucking hog'). At a brothel, Paxton fist-bumps another male friend as the two of them are simultaneously serviced by a prostitute, and after Josh and Paxton both score with two Slovakian women in adjoining beds, Paxton congratulates him on his sexual conquest by stating, 'Mission accomplished.' However, as with President Bush's declaration of victory in Iraq, this claim of phallic triumph over the female sex proves premature, for the two women sell the American guys to an organisation called Elite Hunting, which caters to rich people who pay to torture and kill captured victims. These two domineering males are now forced to submit to violation by others, as the women turn the tables on them. Relishing her revenge, one woman taunts Paxton by saying, 'I get a lot of money for you, and that make you *my* bitch.' Like the women displayed for male consumption at the brothel, Josh and Paxton join other men being marketed to rich sadists who pay to abuse their flesh. 'These guys' who were 'making fun of the hookers in the window' now 'become the meat', comments writer-director Eli Roth.[151] As their flesh is penetrated by scalpels and drills, Josh and Paxton are given the opportunity to feel what it is like to be on the receiving end of phallic violence, to experience something similar to the pain they themselves inflicted on the females. And yet a sense of shared suffering does not lead to sympathy, for when Paxton escapes from the torture house, he in turn takes revenge on the two Slovakian women who sent him there by deliberately running them over with a car. 'This gets the biggest applause in the movie,' Roth notes,[152] as viewers gain vicarious enjoyment from Paxton's act of vengeance.

In the scene where Josh is tortured by a client of Elite Hunting, he protests to his tormentor, 'I didn't fucking do shit to you!' But Josh has been chosen because he is American. The fact that those of his nationality fetch the highest price on the torture market suggests that some see Americans as the worst offenders on the world stage, worthy of the most terrible punishment. Thus, Josh is illegally abducted and taken to a secret prison in an Eastern European country, as if in retaliation for the US government's 'extraordinary rendition' of people to 'black sites'. Josh is stripped of his clothes, hooded, and shackled to a chair, where he is dominated, dehumanised and sexually humiliated like the Abu Ghraib captives who were subjected to 'enhanced interrogation' techniques by US military personnel and the CIA.

When Paxton is in the torture chair, he appeals to his tormentor's common humanity ('I know you don't want to do this') and even tries to forge a bond with the man by speaking his native tongue, but the other's vindictive hatred overcomes any sense of compassion and he charges at Paxton with a chainsaw, severing two of his fingers. After escaping and finding his way back to civilisation, Paxton has the chance to end the cycle of violation and vengeance. Yet when he catches sight of the man who tortured and killed Josh, he follows him to a restroom stall where he 'waterboards' him in the toilet and slices off two of his fingers, taking revenge for the loss of his own (and for the loss of the Twin Towers on 9/11?). As Paxton lifts the man's head out of the toilet, he sees his own face reflected in a chrome fixture right next to the man's, giving Paxton the opportunity to recognise that he himself is becoming the torturer who subjects the other to terrible suffering. But Paxton proceeds to slit the man's throat, in retaliation for the earlier cutting of Josh's.

After he is killed, Josh's body is burned, resulting in smoke and ashes that pour from a chimney, and Eli Roth has compared the Elite Hunting torture facility to Auschwitz and its crematorium.

Within the movie, attention is called to the fact that Josh is Jewish, and Paxton's tormentor is, pointedly, German. When Paxton kills Josh's torturer – an execution that occurs in a restroom marked 'Herren' (German for 'men') – he is taking revenge for all the Jews exterminated by the Nazis. (In the World War Two film *Inglourious Basterds*, Roth himself plays a Jewish soldier who beats Nazis to death with an American baseball bat.) The Iraq War, 9/11, World War Two – the reasons for revenge recede ever backwards in time, just as they seem to reach forever into the future.

Martyrs (2008)

Director: Pascal Laugier
Cast: Morjana Alaoui (Anna), Catherine Bégin (Mademoiselle), Mylène Jampanoï (Lucie)

A young woman named Anna is held captive in an underground torture chamber. There she is force-fed gruel while shackled to a chair with a hole in the seat and a pail below for her waste matter. At other times, she is repeatedly slapped, punched and knocked to the floor, and then lifted to her feet for it to happen all over again. Finally, she is clamped to a metal contraption and skinned alive, resulting in the excruciating exposure of her muscles and veins. Anna's torment is ordered and funded by a secret society of wealthy and elderly people who subject her to 'pain' and 'total deprivation' in the hope that she will 'transcend' this world and be granted a martyr's vision of heaven, which would prove that there is an afterlife. The society's leader, a grande dame known as Mademoiselle, hears Anna's dying testimony about what she saw that 'lay beyond death'. Mademoiselle then tells a fellow member of the sect to 'keep doubting' and proceeds to shoot herself in the head.

It seems likely that Mademoiselle shoots herself in despair because Anna has told her that she saw nothing: she did not witness any life beyond this one. But this does not mean that no heaven exists. It merely shows that Mademoiselle was unable to obtain empirical proof of it. A thoroughgoing materialist, Mademoiselle places value on the things of this world – her luxury car, fine clothes and physical existence – and her longing for an afterlife is fuelled by a desire to extend these things. She has no spiritual values and so she fails to see that belief in an afterlife is not a matter of empirical evidence but of faith. Although she is old enough to be a grandmother, Mademoiselle does not nurture or guide young women into adulthood for, in her view, ageing is just one more step towards death. Instead, she selfishly sacrifices girls like Anna in a futile attempt to extract a vision from them of how Mademoiselle herself can attain eternal life beyond death.

Before Anna was captured, she had tried but failed to save her beloved Lucie, another victim whose physical and mental wounds Anna had soothed and tended for years. As Anna dies, the vision she is granted is of Lucie. Anna's compassion for Lucie's suffering, her belief in the enduring strength of their relationship, has given her faith in an afterlife where the two of them will be reunited.

The Angels' Melancholy (Melancholie der Engel) (2009)

Director: Marian Dora
Cast: Zenza Raggi (Brauth), Frank Oliver (Katze), Pietro Martellanza (Heinrich), Janette Weller (Melanie), Patrizia Johann (Anja), Margarethe von Stern (Clarissa)

The question of 'why?' hovers over this film of characters committing a depraved litany of atrocious acts – scatological, sacrilegious, penetrative, eviscerating – to frequently emetic effect. Brauth, Katze and Heinrich are three middle-aged men who torture women – Melanie, Anja and Clarissa – at an old house in a secluded valley far removed from civilisation. Some indication of the men's motives can be gleaned from an early montage linking shots of dolls, animatronic puppets and real people, such as when we cut from a guy in a wheelchair shaking his head to an animatronic boy moving 'his' mechanical head. We then see the half-destroyed head of a female doll attached to the bones of an animal carcass. These shots convey the men's shocked realisation that human bodies are made of matter that decays and becomes inanimate in death. Ranting about how, these days, 'cripples' have more rights than a 'normal' person, Brauth walks up to the wheelchair-bound Clarissa, rips out her colostomy bag, and then sticks his finger in the excremental hole, causing her to scream in pain. Brauth's goal is to deny her human dignity, to show that she, like everyone else, amounts to nothing more than waste matter. But it is he who is reducing her to such, acting as a degrading force to keep her from claiming her dignity, which her disability has never before stopped her from doing. Later, Brauth tells the women that, nearby, there is a slaughterhouse where 'brute men' work. His violent rape of shrieking Anja is then cross-cut with shots of a squealing pig being stuck with a knife by a butcher, as if to imply that brutal forces rule the world and that a woman is nothing more than meat. However, it seems as wrong to assume that the workman who kills the pig is a brute and a sadist (who knows what he's feeling about the pig?) as it does to equate sexual desire with violent predation. Only in Brauth's mind does it appear so.

The men actually seem afraid of forming an amorous connection with a woman because they would feel *too much* the pain of its loss were it to end. 'Your kiss is as poisonous as a spider's bite,' Brauth tells Melanie when she tries to show him a little affection, and the melancholy Katze thinks, 'Do not entice me with gifts of love,' as these will only be taken away, since he believes that 'forever through tears will I see the sun's light'. Indeed, much of the men's extreme violence can be understood as a desperate defence against empathy of the kind that Katze shows when, seeing a snail's erect eye-stalks sliced off, he feels himself suddenly struck with blindness. The men cannot love when they are so overwhelmed by fear of losing their beloved's body or their own physical ability to make love – a fear seen in a series of shots linking Brauth's penis to a worm, followed by a worm-ridden skull touched by Melanie.

In the end, Brauth stabs his friend Heinrich in the gut and Katze eviscerates him. As Heinrich is thrown onto a bonfire to be burned alive, Katze has Anja masturbate him to orgasm while he enjoys the sight of his friend's head as it is charred to a skull. Director Marian Dora has described his film as one of 'violence, hatred, madness, and depravity'.[153] The men commit violence in an effort to avoid feeling empathy or loss, so strong is their hatred of death. But the men's violence is a kind of confused madness, for it brings on the very death they fear, as in the killing of their friend Heinrich. Finally, the men try to find a depraved enjoyment in watching others suffer and die, but every perverse climax only brings them closer to their own denouement and demise. They end up in love with death, whereas if they weren't in such dread of the body's eventual disintegration, they could see it as a reason to live and love every moment of being.

TRAVESTIES AND PARODIES

Shaun of the Dead (2004)

Director: Edgar Wright
Cast: Simon Pegg (Shaun), Nick Frost (Ed), Kate Ashfield (Liz)

Underachiever Shaun and his slacker buddy Ed must somehow summon the energy to fight the 'slow and shambolic' zombies that are attacking North London. Here are four funny moments from this film and how their humour adds meaning to the movie:

1. Shaun picks up a cricket bat, swings it to make a few tentative hits against a zombie, and then bashes the creature to the ground with a frenzied series of blows as he ends up covered in blood spatter. Quintessentially British, cricket is a civilised game played by genteel people – here repurposed to devastating effect. It is a proud moment for a nation sometimes disparaged for its effete politeness and weak civility. Brits can play by the rules or, if necessary, turn savage in their own defence.

2. To head off an onslaught of the flesh-eating ghouls, Ed reaches for whatever is at hand, including wanting to hurl Shaun's vinyl records at them. But even under threat of death, Shaun is hesitant to part with any albums from his prized collection and insists that Ed select carefully among them, weaponising only Shaun's least

favourite records. The overvaluing of pop albums is ridiculous – until we pause to consider that music is part of what makes life worth living, that it is one aspect of the humanity we are fighting for. Whether or not the songs saved by Shaun – New Order's 'Blue Monday' and Prince's 'Sign o' the Times' – are necessary for the survival of civilisation is perhaps debatable.

3. When one character accuses Shaun of endangering others by having a pointless argument with his 'boyfriend' Ed, Shaun replies indignantly, 'He's not my boyfriend.' Immediately afterwards, Ed slides Shaun a beer, and Shaun tells him, 'Thanks, babe,' and gives him a wink. The fact is that Shaun's guy time with Ed *has* been a problem for Shaun's girlfriend, Liz. Although Shaun finds his bromance with Ed fulfilling on its own terms, which involve playing video games, smoking dope, and downing pints at the pub, these laddish activities do tend to detract from other things he could be doing, like having sex with his girlfriend.

4. As Ed is playing a video game, Shaun encourages him to reload. 'I'm on it,' Ed says, and fires at enemies on the video screen. 'Ooh, nice shot,' Shaun compliments him. Later, as the two of them are facing the zombie apocalypse, Ed hands Shaun some shells so that he can reload his rifle. 'I'm on it,' Shaun says and fires, hitting a zombie in the head. 'Ooh, nice shot,' says Ed. Having been told that their gaming is a pointless slacker pastime, Shaun and Ed can now boast that all that sofa loafing actually prepared them to save the world. Before, the time they spent together was considered a waste and a distraction from their social responsibility to others. Now the two of them can stay leagued as best friends while simultaneously serving the needs of society. If only the real world were a first-person shooter game and its problems could be solved by two bros firing at them ...

Zombieland (2009)

Director: Ruben Fleischer
Cast: Jesse Eisenberg (Columbus), Woody Harrelson (Tallahassee)

In this film, the apocalypse is caused by a mutant strain of mad cow disease that spreads to humans, turning them into zombies. This funny-horrible scenario extrapolates from an existing threat, viral contagion, and hysterically imagines that it has led to the end of the world. It is the kind of fear a child might have, one whose expectation that cows are there to provide us with sweet milk and fresh meat has been brutally dashed. At one point in the film, the human survivors begin smashing all the items in a shop. As co-screenwriter Rhett Reese explains, 'Part of the joy of the post-apocalyptic landscape … is that there are no rules. You can do things like walk into a store and break everything, which is something we always wanted to do as kids.'[154] Throwing a tantrum of destruction becomes an outlet for grief and anger over the loss of loved ones turned zombies. In another scene, the survivors find actor Bill Murray still alive and he re-enacts for them a hilarious scene from his 1984 movie *Ghostbusters* – until he is accidentally mistaken for a zombie and shot dead. While nostalgic for a time when fighting the undead was funny, the survivors increasingly fear that everything now is deadly serious, that there is no return to humour or hope. One member of the group, Columbus, who has always had a fear of clowns, ends up smashing an attacking zombie-clown with a sledgehammer as if to prove that his sneaking suspicion was right all along: there never was anything to laugh about because the world is really a hostile place. Another survivor, Tallahassee, is gleeful when he finds a cache of big guns with which to mow down the zombie hordes, implying a teenager's view that the best way to deal with the world's threats is to shoot them as callously as targets in a video game. Tallahassee does retain a love of Twinkies, and his fond memory of this childhood treat suggests that he may still have a soft spot open to forming a human connection with someone. However, it could be that his sentimentality is merely the flipside of his violence. Can a person really gun down hundreds of beings who still resemble people and then turn with love towards another human being?

Pride and Prejudice and Zombies (2016)

Director: Burr Steers
Cast: Lily James (Elizabeth), Matt Smith (Collins), Sam Riley (Darcy), Bella Heathcote (Jane), Jack Huston (Wickham)

A mash-up of Regency-era romance and zombie action/horror, this film works to deconstruct the traditional opposition between the sexes, showing that women can have masculine traits. Elizabeth Bennet is both a society lady trained in ballroom dancing *and* a master at musketry and swordsmanship. Under her dainty dress, she wears an ankle dagger. While the conventional Pastor Collins, when he proposes to Elizabeth, expects her to 'retire [her] warrior skills as part of the marital submission', more open-minded men find themselves strangely drawn to her unusual combination of genteel refinement and zombie-smiting ability. Darcy, for example, is 'oddly attracted' to her. 'He doesn't want to like Liz Bennet, but there's something there. And when he sees how much she's kicking ass, it really does something to Darcy's insides,' according to Sam Riley, the actor who plays him.[155] Elizabeth holds her own against Darcy both in verbal sparring and in crossing swords, and she even saves *him* on the zombie battlefield, a gender reversal that has him swooning with desire as much as he is rising to conquer her. By making Elizabeth into a skilled warrior as well as a refined lady, *Pride and Prejudice and Zombies* depolarises the genders to provide a twenty first century take on Jane Austen's nineteenth-century novel (or perhaps it brings out the latent feminism already in the original work).

Unfortunately, the film retains the book's class stratification and even exacerbates it. Rather than deconstruct the opposition between rich and poor by showing the potential nobility of the latter (and the not-infrequent venality of the former), the movie champions aristocrats as the representatives of humanity against the lower classes as subhuman zombie hordes. The most threatening zombies we see are from the lower orders – a hulking field labourer, a creepy group of hungry orphans, and grasping ghouls reaching up from graves in a potter's field (a burial site for the anonymous poor). In one scene, where an undead tradeswoman attacks Elizabeth and her sister Jane, the aristocratic ladies shoot the woman's head off and then Jane kicks the decapitated corpse back down into a ravine. In this way, a working-class uprising is decisively put down. The sisters get to be masculine, but the poor don't get to be rich. Elsewhere, Jane is particularly disturbed by the sight of a working-class zombie mother holding a zombie baby, and in a statement recalling paranoid attitudes to the procreative activities of poor people, we are told that 'the undead will always multiply faster than the living'.

There is one aristocrat, Wickham, who tries to bridge the gap between the zombie masses and the haughty humans. Rather than human brains, he has been trying to pacify the ghouls with pig's brains, which suggests that if the hungry poor were only given at least something to eat, they might not feel so driven to gobble up every aspect of high society like a mob out to destroy all art and intellect. Wickham even has the poor zombies going to church and learning to exercise some moral restraint over their appetites. But the aristocrats brand Wickham a traitor to his own kind, and they fear him as an Antichrist leading hordes of the risen undead to swarm their great estates and destroy their humanity. What 'humanity'?

BIBLIOGRAPHY

Books

Abley, Sean, *Out in the Dark: Interviews with Gay Horror Filmmakers, Actors and Authors*, Lethe Press, 2013.

Allmer, Patricia, Emily Beck, and David Huxley (eds), *European Nightmares: Horror Cinema in Europe Since 1945*, Wallflower Press, 2012.

Arnold, Sarah, *Maternal Horror Film: Melodrama and Motherhood*, Palgrave Macmillan, 2013.

Aston, James, and John Walliss (eds), *To See the Saw Movies: Essays on Torture Porn and Post-9/11 Horror*, McFarland, 2013.

Bacon, Simon, and Katarzyna Bronk (eds), *Undead Memory: Vampires and Human Memory in Popular Culture*, Peter Lang, 2013.

Balaji, Murali (ed), *Thinking Dead: What the Zombie Apocalypse Means*, Lexington Books, 2013.

Balmain, Collete, *Introduction to Japanese Horror Film*, Edinburgh University Press, 2008.

Bell, James (ed), *Gothic: The Dark Heart of Film*, BFI, 2013.

Benshoff, Harry M (ed), *A Companion to the Horror Film*, Wiley-Blackwell, 2014.

Benson-Allott, Caetlin, *Killer Tapes and Shattered Screens: Video Spectatorship from VHS to File Sharing*, University of California Press, 2013.

Bernard, Mark, *Selling the Splat Pack: The DVD Revolution and the American Horror Film*, Edinburgh University Press, 2014.

Bishop, Kyle William, *How Zombies Conquered Popular Culture*, McFarland, 2015.

Blake, Linnie, *The Wounds of Nations: Horror Cinema, Historical Trauma and National Identity*, Manchester University Press, 2012.

Blake, Marc, and Sara Bailey, *Writing the Horror Movie*, Bloomsbury Academic, 2013.

Bohlmann, Markus P J, and Sean Moreland (eds), *Monstrous Children and Childish Monsters: Essays on Cinema's Holy Terrors*, McFarland, 2015.

Botting, Fred, and Catherine Spooner (eds), *Monstrous Media/Spectral Subjects: Imagining Gothic Fictions from the Nineteenth Century to the Present*, Manchester University Press, 2015.

Briefel, Aviva, and Sam J Miller (eds), *Horror after 9/11: World of Fear, Cinema of Terror*, University of Texas Press, 2011.

Brodman, Barbara, and James E Doan (eds), *Images of the Modern Vampire: The Hip and the Atavistic*, Fairleigh Dickinson Press, 2015.

Burrell, James, *Horrorwood North: The Extraordinary History and Art of Canadian Genre Cinema*, Marrs Media, 2015.

Calafell, Marie Bernadette, *Monstrosity, Performance, and Race in Contemporary Culture*, Peter Lang, 2015.

Cherry, Brigid, *Horror*, Routledge, 2009.

Choi, Jinhee, and Mitsuyo Wada-Marciano (eds), *Horror to the Extreme: Changing Boundaries in Asian Cinema*, Hong Kong University Press, 2009.

Christensen, Aaron (ed), *Hidden Horror: A Celebration of 101 Underrated and Overlooked Fright Flicks*, Kitley's Krypt, 2013.

Clayton, Wickham (ed), *Style and Form in the Hollywood Slasher Film*, Palgrave Macmillan, 2015.

Comentale, Edward P, and Aaron Jaffe (eds), *The Year's Work at the Zombie Research Center*, Indiana University Press, 2014.

Cooper, Ian, *Frightmares: A History of British Horror Cinema*, Auteur, 2016.

Curtis, Barry, *Dark Places: The Haunted House in Film*, Reaktion Books, 2009.

Dendle, Peter, *The Zombie Movie Encyclopedia Volume 2: 2000–2010*, McFarland, 2012.

Derry, Charles, *Dark Dreams 2.0: A Psychological History of the Modern Horror Film from the 1950s to the 21st Century*, McFarland, 2009.

Dixon, Wheeler Winston, *A History of Horror*, Rutgers University Press, 2010.

Draven, Danny, *Horror Mavericks: Filmmaking Advice from the Creators*, CreateSpace, 2012.

Dudenhoeffer, Larrie, *Embodiment and Horror Cinema*, Palgrave Macmillan, 2014.

Earnshaw, Tony (ed), *Fantastique: Interviews with Horror, Sci-Fi & Fantasy Filmmakers*, BearManor Media, 2016.

Francis, James, Jr, *Remaking Horror: Hollywood's New Reliance on Scares of Old*, McFarland, 2013.

Freitag, Gina, and André Loiselle (eds), *The Canadian Horror Film: Terror of the Soul*, University of Toronto Press, 2015.

Gelder, Ken, *New Vampire Cinema*, British Film Institute, 2012.

Gore, Killian H (ed), *What's Your Favorite Scary Movie?*, CreateSpace, 2015.

Grahame-Smith, Seth, *How to Survive a Horror Movie*, Quirk Books, 2007.

Grant, Barry Keith (ed), *The Dread of Difference: Gender and the Horror Film*, 2nd edition, University of Texas Press, 2015.

Greven, David, *Ghost Faces: Hollywood and Post-Millennial Masculinity*, SUNY Press, 2016.

Gudiño, Rodrigo, and Dave Alexander, *200 Alternative Horror Films You Need to See*, Marrs Media, 2012.

Hallenbeck, Bruce G, *Comedy-Horror Films: A Chronological History, 1914–2008*, McFarland, 2009.

Hanich, Julian, *Cinematic Emotion in Horror Films and Thrillers: The Aesthetic Paradox of Pleasurable Fear*, Routledge, 2010.

Hantke, Steffen (ed), *American Horror Film: The Genre at the Turn of the Millennium*, University Press of Mississippi, 2010.

Harper, Jim, *Flowers from Hell: The Modern Japanese Horror Film*, Noir Publishing, 2008.

Hayward, Philip (ed), *Terror Tracks: Music, Sound and Horror Cinema*, Equinox, 2009.

Heller-Nicholas, Alexandra, *Found Footage Horror Films: Fear and the Appearance of Reality*, McFarland, 2014.

Heller-Nicholas, Alexandra, *Rape-Revenge Films: A Critical Study*, McFarland, 2011.

Henry, Claire, *Revisionist Rape-Revenge: Redefining a Film Genre*, Palgrave Macmillan, 2014.

Hoover, Stephen, *Cheap Scares: The Essential Found Footage Horror Films*, Stephen Hoover, 2013.

Hunt, Leon, Sharon Lockyer, and Milly Williamson (eds), *Screening the Undead: Vampires and Zombies in Film and Television*, IB Tauris, 2014.

Inguanzo, Ozzy, *Zombies on Film: The Definitive Study of Undead Cinema*, Rizzoli, 2014.

Jackson, Kimberly, *Gender and the Nuclear Family in Twenty First Century Horror*, Palgrave Macmillan, 2015.

Jackson, Kimberly, *Technology, Monstrosity and Reproduction in Twenty First Century Horror*, Palgrave Macmillan, 2013.

Janisse, Kier-La, *House of Psychotic Women: An Autobiographical Topography of Female Neurosis in Horror and Exploitation Films*, FAB Press, 2012.

Jones, Alan, *The Rough Guide to Horror Movies*, Rough Guides, 2005.

Jones, Steve, *Torture Porn: Popular Horror after Saw*, Palgrave Macmillan, 2013.

Kaay, Chris Vander, and Kathleen Fernandez-Vander Kaay, *Horror Films by Subgenre: A Viewer's Guide*, McFarland, 2015.

Kalat, David, *J-Horror: The Definitive Guide to The Ring, The Grudge and Beyond*, Vertical, 2007.

Kawin, Bruce F, *Horror and the Horror Film*, Anthem Press, 2012.

Kay, Glenn, *Zombie Movies: The Ultimate Guide*, 2nd edition, Chicago Review Press, 2012.

Kerner, Aaron Michael, *Torture Porn in the Wake of 9/11: Horror, Exploitation, and the Cinema of Sensation*, Rutgers University Press, 2015.

Kimber, Shaun, and Craig Batty, *Writing & Selling Horror Screenplays*, Kamera Books, 2016.

Lazáro-Reboll, Antonio, *Spanish Horror Film*, Edinburgh University Press, 2014.

Leeder, Murray (ed), *Cinematic Ghosts: Haunting and Spectrality from Silent Cinema to the Digital Era*, Bloomsbury Academic, 2015.

Lennard, Dominic, *Bad Seeds and Holy Terrors: The Child Villains of Horror Film*, State University of New York Press, 2014.

Levina, Marina, and Diem-My T Bui (eds), *Monster Culture in the 21st Century: A Reader*, Bloomsbury Academic, 2013.

Lombardo, Christopher, and Jeff Kirschner, *Death by Umbrella!: The 100 Weirdest Horror Movie Weapons*, BearManor Media, 2016.

Luckhurst, Roger, *Zombies: A Cultural History*, Reaktion Books, 2015.

Lukas, Scott A, and John Marmysz (eds), *Fear, Cultural Anxiety, and Transformation: Horror, Science Fiction, and Fantasy Films Remade*, Lexington Books, 2010.

Marak, Katarzyna, *Japanese and American Horror: A Comparative Study of Film, Fiction, Graphic Novels and Video Games*, McFarland, 2014.

Marriott, James, and Kim Newman, *Horror!: 333 Films to Scare You to Death*, Carlton Books, 2010.

McCollum, Victoria, *Post-9/11 Heartland Horror: Rural Horror Films in an Era of Urban Terrorism*, Routledge, 2016.

McGlotten, Shaka, and Steve Jones (eds), *Zombies and Sexuality: Essays on Desire and the Living Dead*, McFarland, 2014.

McIntosh, Shawn, and Marc Leverette (eds), *Zombie Culture: Autopsies of the Living Dead*, Scarecrow Press, 2008.

McMahon-Coleman, Kimberley, and Roslyn Weaver, *Werewolves and Other Shapeshifters in Popular Culture: A Thematic Analysis of Recent Depictions*, McFarland, 2012.

McRoy, Jay (ed), *Japanese Horror Cinema*, Edinburgh University Press, 2005.

McRoy, Jay, *Nightmare Japan: Contemporary Japanese Horror Cinema*, Rodopi, 2007.

Meehan, Paul, *The Vampire in Science Fiction Film and Literature*, McFarland, 2014.

Miller, Cynthia J, and A Bowdoin Van Riper (eds), *Horrors of War: The Undead on the Battlefield*, Rowman & Littlefield, 2015.

Miller, Cynthia J, and A Bowdoin Van Riper (eds), *The Laughing Dead: The Horror-Comedy Film from Bride of Frankenstein to Zombieland*, Rowman & Littlefield, 2016.

Miller, Cynthia J, and A Bowdoin Van Riper (eds), *Undead in the West: Vampires, Zombies, Mummies, and Ghosts on the Cinematic Frontier*, Rowman & Littlefield, 2012.

Mittman, Asa Simon, and Peter J Dendle (eds), *The Ashgate Research Companion to Monsters and the Monstrous*, Ashgate, 2013.

Muir, John Kenneth, *Horror Films FAQ*, Applause, 2013.

Murguia, Salvador (ed), *The Encyclopedia of Japanese Horror Films*, Rowman & Littlefield, 2016.

Narine, Anil (ed), *Eco-Trauma Cinema*, Routledge, 2014.

Ndalianis, Angela, *The Horror Sensorium: Media and the Senses*, McFarland, 2012.

Nelson, Victoria, *Gothicka: Vampire Heroes, Human Gods, and the New Supernatural*, Harvard University Press, 2012.

Newman, Kim, *Nightmare Movies: Horror on Screen Since the 1960s*, 2nd edition, Bloomsbury, 2011.

Nowell, Richard (ed), *Merchants of Menace: The Business of Horror Cinema*, Bloomsbury Academic, 2014.

Och, Dana, and Kirsten Strayer (eds), *Transnational Horror Across Visual Media: Fragmented Bodies*, Routledge, 2013.

Odell, Colin, and Michelle Le Blanc, *Horror Films*, Kamera Books, 2008.

Packer, Sharon, and Jody Pennington (eds), *A History of Evil in Popular Culture*, 2 volumes, Praeger, 2014.

Peirse, Alison, and Daniel Martin (eds), *Korean Horror Cinema*, Edinburgh University Press, 2013.

Phillips, Lawrence, and Anne Witchard (eds), *London Gothic: Place, Space and the Gothic Imagination*, Continuum, 2012.

Picart, Caroline Joan S, and John Edgar Browning (eds), *Speaking of Monsters: A Teratological Anthology*, Palgrave Macmillan, 2012.

Pulliam, June Michele, and Anthony J Fonseca, *Encyclopedia of the Zombie: The Walking Dead in Popular Culture and Myth*, Greenwood Press, 2014.

Rayes, Xavier Aldana, *Body Gothic: Corporeal Transgression in Contemporary Literature and Horror Film*, University of Wales Press, 2014.

Reyes, Xavier Aldana, *Digital Horror: Haunted Technologies, Network Panic and the Found Footage Phenomenon*, IB Tauris, 2015.

Reyes, Xavier Aldana, *Horror Film and Affect: Towards a Corporeal Model of Viewership*, Routledge, 2016.

Richards, Andy, *Asian Horror*, Kamera Books, 2010.

Roche, David, *Making and Remaking Horror in the 1970s and 2000s: Why Don't They Do It Like They Used To?*, University Press of Mississippi, 2014.

Rose, James, *Beyond Hammer: British Horror Cinema Since 1970*, Auteur, 2009.

Russell, Jamie, *Book of the Dead: The Complete History of Zombie Cinema*, Titan Books, 2014.

Schneider, Steven Jay (ed), *100 European Horror Films*, British Film Institute, 2007.

Schneider, Steven Jay (ed), *101 Horror Films You Must See Before You Die*, Barron's, 2009.

Schneider, Steven Jay (ed), *Fear Without Frontiers: Horror Cinema Across the Globe*, FAB Press, 2003.

Schneider, Steven Jay, and Tony Williams (eds), *Horror International*, Wayne State University Press, 2005.

Shelley, Peter, *Australian Horror Films*, McFarland, 2012.

Short, Sue, *Misfit Sisters: Screen Horror as Female Rites of Passage*, Palgrave Macmillan, 2006.

Silver, Alain and James Ursini, *The Vampire Film from Nosferatu to True Blood*, Hal Leonard, 2011.

Simpson, M J, *Urban Terrors: New British Horror Cinema 1997–2008*, Midnight Marquee Press, 2013.

Subero, Gustavo, *Gender and Sexuality in Latin American Horror Cinema: Embodiments of Evil*, Palgrave Macmillan, 2016.

Towlson, Jon, *Subversive Horror Cinema: Countercultural Messages of Films from Frankenstein to the Present*, McFarland, 2014.

Vander Kaay, Christopher, and Kathleen Fernandez-Vander Kaay (eds), *The Anatomy of Fear: Conversations with Cult Horror and Science-Fiction Filmmakers*, NorLightsPress, 2014.

Vatnsdal, Caelum, *They Came from Within: A History of Canadian Horror Cinema*, revised and updated edition, Arbeiter Ring, 2014.

Waddell, Calum, *Minds of Fear: A Dialogue with 30 Modern Masters of Horror!*, Midnight Marquee Press, 2005.

Waldron, Dara, *Cinema and Evil: Moral Complexities and the 'Dangerous' Film*, Cambridge Scholars, 2013.

Walker, Johnny, *Contemporary British Horror Cinema: Industry, Genre and Society*, Edinburgh University Press, 2015.

Wallace, Amy, Del Howison, and Scott Bradley, *The Book of Lists: Horror*, Harper, 2008.

Watson, Devin, *Horror Screenwriting: The Nature of Fear*, Michael Wiese, 2009.

Wee, Valerie, *Japanese Horror Films and Their American Remakes: Translating Fear, Adapting Culture*, Routledge, 2013.

Weinstock, Jeffrey Andrew, *The Ashgate Encyclopedia of Literary and Cinematic Monsters*, Ashgate, 2014.

Weinstock, Jeffrey, *The Vampire Film: Undead Cinema*, Wallflower Press, 2012.

West, Alexandra, *Films of the New French Extremity: Visceral Horror and National Identity*, McFarland, 2016.

Wetmore, Kevin J, *Post-9/11 Horror in American Cinema*, Continuum, 2012.

Whitehead, Dan, *Tooth and Claw: A Field Guide to 'Nature Bites Back' Movies*, CreateSpace, 2012.

Whitman, Glen, and James Dow (eds), *Economics of the Undead: Zombies, Vampires, and the Dismal Science*, Rowman & Littlefield, 2014.

Williams, Tony, *Hearths of Darkness: The Family in the American Horror Film*, updated edition, University Press of Mississippi, 2014.

Willis, Stuart, *The New Flesh: 21st-Century Horror Films A-Z*, volume 1, CreateSpace, 2015.

Wilson, Laura, *Spectatorship, Embodiment and Physicality in the Contemporary Mutilation Film*, Palgrave Macmillan, 2015.

Videos

The 100 Greatest Scary Moments (2003) dir. Mark Murray and Helen Spencer
The American Nightmare (2000) dir. Adam Simon
Bloodsucking Cinema (2007) dir. Barry Gray
Going to Pieces: The Rise and Fall of the Slasher Film (2006) dir. Jeff McQueen
Nightmares in Red, White and Blue: The Evolution of the Modern American Horror Film (2009) dir. Andrew Monument
Scream and Scream Again: A History of the Slasher Film (2000) dir. Andrew Abbott and Russell Leven
Video Nasties: Moral Panic, Censorship & Videotape (2010) dir. Jake West
Why Horror? (2014) dir. Rob Lindsay and Nicolas Kleiman

Websites

Bloody Disgusting: http://bloody-disgusting.com/
The Dark Side: http://www.thedarksidemagazine.com/
Diabolique: http://diaboliquemagazine.com/
Dread Central: http://www.dreadcentral.com/
Fangoria: http://www.fangoria.com/
Rue Morgue: http://www.rue-morgue.com/#!
Shock Till You Drop: http://www.comingsoon.net/horror
Video Watchdog: http://www.videowatchdog.com/home/home.html

NOTES

Introduction

1 Roger Ebert, *'Wolf Creek'*, *RogerEbert.com*, 22 December 2005, http://www.rogerebert.com/reviews/wolf-creek-2005.

2 Eli Roth in Jon Hamblin, 'Eli Roth', *Horror: The Ultimate Celebration*, Future Publishing, 2015, p. 122.

3 *Ibid.*, p. 123.

4 Eli Roth, Director's Audiocommentary, *Hostel* Blu-ray DVD, Sony Pictures Home Entertainment, 2007.

5 Scott Derrickson, Writers' Audiocommentary, *Sinister* Blu-ray DVD, Summit Entertainment, 2013.

6 Robin Wood, 'An Introduction to the American Horror Film', *The American Nightmare: Essays on the Horror Film*, edited by Robin Wood and Richard Lippe, Toronto Festival of Festivals, 1979, p. 10.

7 Clive Barker in Stephen Jones, *Clive Barker's A–Z of Horror*, HarperPrism, 1997, p. 7.

8 David Robert Mitchell in Chris Alexander, 'Follow You Down', *Fangoria*, no. 341 (April 2015), p. 43.

9 James Watkins in Matt Risley, 'James Watkins Interview: *Eden Lake*', *On the Box*, 16 January 2009, http://blog.onthebox.com/2009/01/16/interview-horror-director-james-watkins-talks-about-eden-lake/.

10 Joss Whedon in Drew Goddard and Joss Whedon, *The Cabin in the Woods: The Official Visual Companion*, Titan Books, 2012, p. 173.

11 Neil LaBute, *In a Forest, Dark and Deep*, Overlook Press, 2013, p. 18.

12 Nina Auerbach, *Our Vampires, Ourselves*, University of Chicago Press, 1995, p. 145.

13 John Ajvide Lindqvist in Steven Peacock, *Swedish Crime Fiction: Novel, Film, Television*, Manchester University Press, 2014, p. 179.

14   Marcin Wrona in Sean Plummer, 'The Past Won't Stay Buried', *Rue Morgue*, no. 170 (September 2016), p. 28.

15   Brigid Cherry, *Horror*, Routledge, 2009, p. 210.

16   Larry Fessenden in *The Anatomy of Fear: Conversations with Cult Horror and Science Fiction Film Creators*, edited by Chris Vander Kaay and Kathleen Fernandez-Vander Kaay, NorLightsPress, 2014, p. 135.

17   Larry Fessenden, booklet insert, *The Larry Fessenden Collection* Blu-ray DVD, Shout Factory, 2015.

18   This book also discusses three films from the end of the last century – *The Blair Witch Project* (1999), *Ringu* (1998), and *The Sixth Sense* (1999) – because of their trend-setting influence on key aspects of twenty first century horror, namely found-footage films, techno-horror, and ghost movies, respectively.

Nightmares

19   Mary Harron in Andy Burns, 'Hip to Be Feared', *Rue Morgue*, no. 157 (July 2015), p. 20.

20   Mary Harron, Audiocommentary, *American Psycho* Blu-ray DVD, Lionsgate Films, 2007.

21   For discussion of another movie about a power-mad human monster, *Hollow Man* (2000), see Douglas Keesey, *Paul Verhoeven*, Taschen, 2005, pp. 166–76.

22   Dennis Widmyer in Christopher Jimenez, '*Shock* Interview: *Starry Eyes* Directors Dennis Widmyer & Kevin Kölsch', *Shock Till You Drop*, 14 November 2014, http://www.shocktillyoudrop.com/news/369925-shock-interview-starry-eyes-directors-dennis-widmyer-kevin-kolsch/.

23   Nicolas Winding Refn in Adam Woodward, 'Nic's Hot Line', *Little White Lies*, no. 65 (May–June 2016), p. 10.

24   Nicolas Winding Refn in Mekado Murphy, 'Nicolas Winding Refn Narrates a Scene from *The Neon Demon*', *New York Times*, 23 June 2016, http://www.nytimes.com/2016/06/24/movies/nicolas-winding-refn-narrates-a-scene-from-the-neon-demon.html.

25   Nicolas Winding Refn in Adam Woodward, 'Nic's Hot Line', *Little White Lies*, no. 65 (May–June 2016), p. 11.

26   Neil Marshall, '*The Descent*: Beneath the Scenes', *The Descent* Blu-ray DVD, Lionsgate Films, 2006.

27   Neil Marshall, Director and Cast Audiocommentary, *The Descent* Blu-ray DVD, Lionsgate Films, 2006.

28   Eli Roth, Audiocommentary, *The Green Inferno* Blu-ray DVD, Universal Studios Home Entertainment, 2016.

29   Eli Roth in Chris Tilly, 'Eli Roth on the Horrors of *The Green Inferno*', *IGN*, 1 March 2013, http://www.ign.com/articles/2013/03/01/eli-roth-on-the-horrors-of-the-green-inferno.

30 Eli Roth in Sean Plummer, 'Cannibal Ferocious', *Rue Morgue*, no. 148 (September 2014), p. 18.

31 Eli Roth in Chris Tilly, 'Eli Roth on the Horrors of *The Green Inferno*', *IGN*, 1 March 2013, http://www.ign.com/articles/2013/03/01/eli-roth-on-the-horrors-of-the-green-inferno.

32 Eli Roth in Steve Rose, 'Eli Roth: "I Miss Films Where You Think the Makers Were Insane"', *Guardian*, 11 February 2016, https://www.theguardian.com/film/2016/feb/11/eli-roth-the-green-inferno-miss-films-where-think-makers-were-insane.

33 Deborah Schurman-Kauflin, 'Autistic Kids Are Magnets for Ghosts: Those with Autism Often Are First to Recognize the Paranormal', *Psychology Today*, 30 October 2013, https://www.psychologytoday.com/blog/disturbed/201310/autistic-kids-are-magnets-ghosts.

34 *Heartless* (2009) is another film to explore the 'horror' of disability, in this case a 'monstrous' birthmark. For analysis, see my entry on Philip Ridley in *Lost Souls of Horror and the Gothic*, edited by Elizabeth McCarthy and Bernice M Murphy, McFarland, 2016.

35 William Brent Bell in Staci Layne Wilson, 'William Brent Bell Talks Creating *The Boy*', *Dread Central*, 10 May 2016, http://www.dreadcentral.com/news/165190/exclusive-william-brent-bell-talks-boy/.

36 Stacey Menear in Patti Greco, '*The Boy* Writer Stacey Menear Explains the Twist Ending and What Might Have Been', *Cosmopolitan*, 25 January 2016, http://www.cosmopolitan.com/entertainment/movies/q-and-a/a52604/the-boy-twist-ending-stacey-menear-interview/.

37 Leigh Whannell, 'Horror 101: The Exclusive Seminar', *Insidious* Blu-ray DVD, Sony Pictures Home Entertainment, 2011.

38 Scott Derrickson, Writers' Audiocommentary, *Sinister* Blu-ray DVD, Summit Entertainment, 2013.

39 Wentworth Miller in Christina Radish, 'SDCC 2010: Wentworth Miller Interview', *Collider*, 3 August 2010, http://collider.com/comic-con-wentworth-miller-interview-resident-evil-afterlife-3d-stoker-uncle-charlie/.

40 Wentworth Miller (aka Ted Foulke), *Stoker* screenplay, 18 January 2010, *HorrorLair*, http://www.horrorlair.com/scripts/Stoker-screenplay.pdf.

41 James Watkins in Constantine Nasr, 'The Making of Hammer's Gothic Ghost Story *The Woman in Black*', *Little Shoppe of Horrors*, no. 28 (February 2012), p. 68.

42 Daniel Radcliffe in Constantine Nasr and Tony Earnshaw, 'Daniel Radcliffe Talks about *The Woman in Black*', *Little Shoppe of Horrors*, no. 28 (February 2012), p. 81.

43 Daniel Radcliffe in Constantine Nasr, 'The Making of Hammer's Gothic Ghost Story *The Woman in Black*', *Little Shoppe of Horrors*, no. 28 (February 2012), p. 69.

44 James Watkins in Tony Earnshaw, *Fantastique: Interviews with Horror, Sci-Fi & Fantasy Filmmakers*, vol. 1, BearManor Media, 2016, p. 356.

45 James Watkins in Constantine Nasr, 'The Making of Hammer's Gothic Ghost Story *The Woman in Black*', *Little Shoppe of Horrors*, no. 28 (February 2012), p. 71.

46 Ann Pellegrini, '"Signaling through the Flames": Hell House Performance and Structures of Feeling', *American Quarterly*, vol. 59, no. 3 (September 2007), p. 912.

47 Guillermo del Toro in Dave Alexander, 'Del Toro's Dark House', *Rue Morgue*, no. 160 (October 2015), p. 52.

48 Ibid., p. 54.

49 Michael Dougherty in John Griffin, *Trick 'r Treat: Tales of Mayhem, Mystery & Mischief*, Insight Editions, 2007, p. 9.

50 Ibid., p. 56.

51 Michael Dougherty in Michael Mallory, *The Art of Krampus*, Insight Editions, 2015, p. 25.

52 Ibid., pp. 15–16.

53 Ibid., p. 9.

54 Victor Salva in Calum Waddell, *Minds of Fear: A Dialogue with 30 Modern Masters of Horror*, Midnight Marquee Press, 2005, p. 247.

55 Jennifer Kent in Michael Gingold, 'Dare You Look at *The Babadook*?', *Fangoria*, no. 338 (December 2014), p. 29.

56 Ibid., p. 30.

57 For more discussion of movie monsters and mothers, see Douglas Keesey, '*Super 8* (2011)', *Kamera.co.uk Film Salon*, 5 August 2011, http://www.kamera.co.uk/article.php/1206.

58 Lucile Hadzihalilovic in Dominic Preston, 'Lucile Hadzihalilovic Interview: "The Adult World Is Something Mysterious"', *Candid*, 5 May 2016, http://www.candidmagazine.com/lucile-hadzihalilovic-interview/.

59 Lucile Hadzihalilovic, 'Director's Note', *Evolution* Press Kit, 2015.

60 Ibid.

61 Juliet Snowden and Stiles White in Atara Arbesfeld and Ezriel Gelbfish, '*The Possession*, Drawing on Jewish Sources, Is Hollywood's Kabbalistic Version of *The Exorcist*', *Algemeiner*, 30 August 2012, http://www.algemeiner.com/2012/08/30/the-possession-drawing-on-jewish-sources-is-hollywoods-kabbalistic-version-of-the-exorcist-video/.

62 James Wan in Kellvin Chavez, 'Interview: Talking *The Conjuring* with Director James Wan', *Latino-Review Media*, 15 July 2013, http://lrmonline.com/news/2013/07/interview-talking-the-conjuring-director-james-wan.

63 Tim Robey, '*The Visit* Review: "The Most Gerontophobic Film Ever Made"', *Telegraph*, 9 September 2015, http://www.telegraph.co.uk/film/the-visit/review/.

64 Wallace Stevens, 'The Snow Man', *The Collected Poems of Wallace Stevens*, Alfred A Knopf, 1978, p. 10.

65 Diablo Cody in Jennifer Kwan, 'Cody Exorcises Demons from *Jennifer's Body*', *Reuters*, 14 September 2009.

66 The *vagina dentata* theme was further explored in *Teeth* (2007). For analysis of this film, see Douglas Keesey, *Contemporary Erotic Cinema*, Kamera Books, 2012, pp. 32–3.

67 The 2009 film *Splice* features another sexy female alien, this one created by science. For analysis, see ibid., pp. 59–60.

68 David Robert Mitchell in Michael Blyth, 'Tainted Love', *Sight & Sound*, vol. 25, no. 3 (March 2015).

69 David Robert Mitchell in Charlie Lyne, '*It Follows*: "Love and Sex Are Ways We Can Push Death Away"', *Guardian*, 21 February 2015, http://www.theguardian.com/film/2015/feb/21/it-follows-teen-horror-movie.

70 Guy Maddin, Audiocommentary, *Dracula: Pages from a Virgin's Diary* DVD, Zeitgeist Video, 2004.

71 Ibid.

72 Neil Jordan in Liisa Ladouceur, 'Blood Relations', *Rue Morgue*, no. 135 (July 2013), p. 41.

73 Neil Jordan in Declan McGrath, 'Life Among the Undead', *Cineaste*, vol. 38, no. 4 (Fall 2013), p. 12.

74 Jim Jarmusch in Nick Pinkerton, 'Jim Jarmusch: The Interview', *Sight & Sound*, vol. 24, no. 3 (March 2014), p. 54.

75 Ibid., p. 50.

76 For discussion of another female werewolf film, *Ginger Snaps* (2000), see Douglas Keesey, *Contemporary Erotic Cinema*, Kamera Books, 2012, pp. 30–2.

77 Amy Simmons, *Antichrist*, Auteur, 2015, p. 10.

78 Lars von Trier, Audiocommentary, *Antichrist* Blu-ray DVD, Criterion Collection, 2010.

79 Robert Eggers, Audiocommentary, *The Witch* Blu-ray DVD, Lionsgate Entertainment, 2016.

80 Danny Boyle, Audiocommentary, *28 Days Later* Blu-ray DVD, Twentieth Century Fox, 2007.

81 Bruce LaBruce, '*Otto*: An Introduction', *Incognitum Hactenus*, vol. 3 (September 2012), https://incognitumhactenus.com/otto-an-introduction/.

82 Bruce LaBruce in Manlio Converti, 'Interview with Director Bruce LaBruce', *Psychiatry Online Italia*, 4 November 2013, http://www.psychiatryonline.it/node/4635.

83 Bruce LaBruce in Catherine Knight, 'A Philosophy of Homosexuality – An Interview with Bruce LaBruce', *4:3*, 21 April 2015, http://fourthreefilm.com/2015/04/a-philosophy-of-homosexuality-an-interview-with-bruce-labruce/.

84 Bruce LaBruce in Ernest Hardy, 'Deep Zombie Throat', *L.A. Weekly*, 7 January 2010, http://www.laweekly.com/film/deep-zombie-throat-2163293.

85 Bruce LaBruce in Ariana Speyer, 'Up with Bruce LaBruce', *Interview*, 13 February 2009, http://www.interviewmagazine.com/film/otto-bruce-labruce#.

86 Bruce LaBruce, '*Otto*: An Introduction', *Incognitum Hactenus*, vol. 3 (September 2012), https://incognitumhactenus.com/otto-an-introduction/.

87 Bruce LaBruce in Sean Abley, *Out in the Dark: Interviews with Gay Horror Filmmakers, Actors and Authors*, Lethe Press, 2013, p. 50.

88 Bruce LaBruce in Richard Schemmerer, 'Interview with Film Maker Bruce LaBruce', *Pride Review*, 19 June 2012, http://thepridereview.blogspot.com/2012/06/interview-with-film-maker-bruce-labruce.html.

89 Bruce LaBruce in Gary Kramer, 'Interview: Bruce LaBruce', *Slant*, 19 September 2011, http://www.slantmagazine.com/features/article/interview-bruce-labruce/P2.

90 Marc Forster in Jamie Lincoln, 'Marc Forster: The Eye of the Swarm', *Interview*, 20 June 2013, http://www.interviewmagazine.com/film/marc-forster-world-war-z#_.

Nations

91 Bruce McDonald in Beth Accomando, '*Pontypool*: Interview with Bruce McDonald', *KPBS*, 23 June 2009, http://www.kpbs.org/news/2009/jun/23/pontypool/.

92 Gina Freitag and André Loiselle, 'Terror of the Soul: An Introduction', *The Canadian Horror Film*, University of Toronto Press, 2015, p. 6.

93 Ibid., p. 7.

94 Marina de Van, Audiocommentary, *In My Skin* DVD, Wellspring Media, 2004.

95 Ibid.

96 Charlotte Roche, *Wetlands*, translated by Tim Mohr, Grove Press, 2009, p. 193.

97 Charlotte Roche in Decca Aitkenhead, '"It Should Make You Blush"', *Guardian*, 16 January 2009, https://www.theguardian.com/books/2009/jan/17/interview-charlotte-roche-debut-novel-wetlands.

98 BA Harrison, 'I Guess Hollywood's Love Affair with India Is Officially Over', *IMDb Reviews*, 29 October 2011, http://www.imdb.com/title/tt1244093/reviews.

99 Gary Nafis, 'Snakes in Movies: *Hisss*', *California Herpes*, 23 April 2016, http://www.californiaherps.com/films/snakefilms/Hisss.html.

100 *Despite the Gods* DVD, Brink Vision, 2015.

101 Joon-ho Bong in '*The Host* – Bong Joon-Ho Q&A', *Time Out New York*, 7 November 2006, www.timeout.com/film/newyork/news/1514/the-host-bong-joon-ho-q-a.html.

102 Joon-ho Bong in Ji-youn Jung, *Bong Joon-ho*, Seoul Selection, 2008, p. 146.

103 Joon-ho Bong, Audiocommentary, *The Host* Blu-ray DVD, Magnolia Home Entertainment, 2007.

104 Tomas Alfredson in Josh Winning, 'Blood and Tears: *Let the Right One In*', *Horror: The Ultimate Celebration*, Future Publishing, 2015, p. 90.

105 James Watkins in Alan Jones, '*Eden Lake*: Paradise Bloodied', *Fangoria*, no. 279 (January 2009), p. 32.

106 Ibid., p. 35.

107 Ben Wheatley in Tony Earnshaw, *Fantastique: Interviews with Horror, Sci-Fi & Fantasy Filmmakers*, vol. 1, BearManor Media, 2016, p. 366.

108 Ryan Gosling in Adam Woodward, 'Ryan Gosling: "When I Was a Kid, We Lived with Elvis for a Year"', *Little White Lies*, 2015, http://lwlies.com/interviews/ryan-gosling-lost-river/.

Innovations

109 Steve Rothenberg in Phil Contrino, 'Marketing Horror in 3D: Exhibitors Will Have the Opportunity to Bring 3D Fans and Horror Fans Together with *My Bloody Valentine*', *Boxoffice*, January 2009, p. 15.

110 For discussion of all five *Final Destination* films (2000–11), including further consideration of their 3D aspects, see Douglas Keesey, 'Seeing Your Own End: Prefigurations of Death in the *Final Destination* Films', in *The Pleasures of the Spectacle: The London Film and Media Reader 3*, edited by Phillip Drummond, London Symposium, 2015, pp. 88–99.

111 Visual effects supervisor Robert Skotak in 'The Third Dimension', *The Hole 3D* Blu-ray DVD, Entertainment One, 2011.

112 Director Joe Dante in Jason Pollock, 'The *Chud* Interview: Joe Dante (*The Hole*)', *Chud*, 28 September 2012, http://www.chud.com/109874/tchud-interview-joe-dante-the-hole/.

113 Jee-woon Kim in Hyung-seok Kim, *Kim Jee-woon*, Seoul Selection, 2008, p. 118.

114 Roger Ebert, '*The Human Centipede*', *RogerEbert.com*, 5 May 2010, http://www.rogerebert.com/reviews/the-human-centipede-2010.

115 Roger Ebert, '*The Human Centipede 2*', *RogerEbert.com*, 7 October 2011, http://www.rogerebert.com/reviews/the-human-centipede-2-full-sequence-2011.

116 Tom Six, Audiocommentary, *The Human Centipede* Blu-ray DVD, IFC Films, 2010.

117 Ibid.

118 Tom Six in Rich Juzwiak, '"I Don't Like Human Beings": A Chat with *The Human Centipede*'s Tom Six', *Defamer*, 21 May 2015, http://defamer.gawker.com/i-dont-like-human-beings-a-chat-with-the-human-centi-1706049658.

119 Tom Six, Audiocommentary, *The Human Centipede 2* Blu-ray DVD, IFC Films, 2012.

120 The horror of sadistic enjoyment and masochistic suffering is also explored in Takashi Miike's *Ichi the Killer* (*Koroshiya 1*) (2001). For discussion of this film, see Douglas Keesey, *Neo-Noir: Contemporary Film Noir from Chinatown to The Dark Knight*, Kamera Books, 2010, pp. 143–5.

121 Jen Soska in 'American Mary: Interview with Filmmakers Jen and Sylvia Soska', in Horrorwood North, edited by James Burrell, Marrs Media, 2015, p. 125.

122 Brandon Cronenberg, Audiocommentary, Antiviral Blu-ray DVD, MPI Media Group, 2013.

123 Brandon Cronenberg in 'Antiviral: Interview with Writer/Director Brandon Cronenberg', in Horrorwood North, edited by James Burrell, Marrs Media, 2015, p. 123.

124 Brandon Cronenberg, Audiocommentary, Antiviral Blu-ray DVD, MPI Media Group, 2013.

125 This line is spoken by a Native American character who is shown as having more understanding of why nature is striking back. For further discussion of the 'national uncanny' – 'the return of what a country has repressed in order to establish its identity as master' – see Douglas Keesey, 'Weir(d) Australia: Picnic at Hanging Rock and The Last Wave', LIT: Literature Interpretation Theory, vol. 8, nos. 3–4 (1998), pp. 331–46.

126 Larry Fessenden in The Anatomy of Fear: Conversations with Cult Horror and Science Fiction Film Creators, edited by Chris Vander Kaay and Kathleen Fernandez-Vander Kaay, NorLightsPress, 2014, p. 136.

127 Larry Fessenden, Audiocommentary, The Last Winter Blu-ray DVD, Shout Factory, 2015.

128 Larry Fessenden in Neda Ulaby, '"Eco-Horror": Green Panic on the Silver Screen?', All Things Considered, National Public Radio, 14 June 2008, http://www.npr.org/templates/story/story.php?storyId=91485965.

129 Shane Carruth in Mark Allen, 'Shane Carruth Answers All Our Questions about Primer, Upstream Color and The Modern Ocean', The Awl, 4 April 2013, https://theawl.com/shane-carruth-answers-all-our-questions-about-primer-upstream-color-and-the-modern-ocean-b4deabb40de0#.4hkj7k4xx.

130 Ibid.

131 Shane Carruth in Eric Kohn, 'Shane Carruth Explains Why Upstream Color Isn't So Difficult to Understand and Talks about His Next Project', IndieWire, 3 April 2013, http://www.indiewire.com/2013/04/shane-carruth-explains-why-upstream-color-isnt-so-difficult-to-understand-and-talks-about-his-next-project-39752/.

132 Drew Goddard, Cloverfield Screenplay, 8 June 2007, p. 38.

133 Matt Reeves, Audiocommentary, Cloverfield Blu-ray DVD, Paramount Pictures, 2008.

134 Peter Strickland, Audiocommentary, Berberian Sound Studio DVD, MPI Media Group, 2013.

135 Ibid.

136 John Carpenter in Todd McCarthy, 'Trick and Treat', Film Comment, vol. 16, no. 1 (January–February 1980), p. 24.

137 Ibid., pp. 23–4.

138 Stephen King in Jeff Labrecque, 'Stephen King Sounds Off on New *Carrie* Remake', *Entertainment Weekly*, 20 May 2011, http://www.ew.com/article/2011/05/20/stephen-king-carrie-remake. For in-depth discussion of the original 1976 *Carrie*, see Douglas Keesey, *Brian De Palma's Split-Screen: A Life in Film*, University Press of Mississippi, 2015, pp. 92–105.

139 Kimberly Peirce in Romain Raynaldy, *Carrie* Updated to Troubled America', *Rappler*, 18 October 2013, http://www.rappler.com/entertainment/movies/41645-carrie-2013-remake-kimberly-peirce.

140 Kimberly Peirce, Audiocommentary, *Carrie* Blu-ray DVD, Metro-Goldwyn-Mayer, 2014.

141 Ibid.

142 Alexandre Aja, Audiocommentary, *High Tension* Blu-ray DVD, Lionsgate Films, 2010.

143 Paul Etheredge-Ouzts in 'Backlot Featurette', *Hellbent* DVD, TLA Releasing, 2006.

144 Joss Whedon in Drew Goddard and Joss Whedon, *The Cabin in the Woods: The Official Visual Companion*, Titan Books, 2012, p. 42.

145 Drew Goddard in ibid.

146 Jim Sonzero in Director's and Designer's Audiocommentary, *Pulse* DVD, Genius Products, 2007.

147 Gary Tunnicliffe in Director's and Designer's Audiocommentary, *Pulse* DVD, Genius Products, 2007.

148 Kiyoshi Kurasawa, 'The Making of *Pulse*: Behind-the-Scenes Footage', *Kairo* DVD, Magnolia Home Entertainment, 2006.

149 In another example of techno-horror, the 2002 film *demonlover* has a character literally drawn into the scene of a torture porn video. For discussion of this movie, see Douglas Keesey, *Neo-Noir: Contemporary Film Noir from Chinatown to The Dark Knight*, Kamera Books, 2010, pp. 145–7.

150 Stephenie Meyer, *Twilight*, Little, Brown, 2005, p. 23.

151 Eli Roth, Director's Audiocommentary, *Hostel* Blu-ray DVD, Sony Pictures Home Entertainment, 2007.

152 Ibid.

153 Marian Dora in 'Interview Marian Dora – Réalisateur de cinéma extrême', *Sadique Master*, 12 March 2014, http://www.sadique-master.com/interview-marian-dora-realisateur-de-cinema-extreme/.

154 Rhett Reese in Adrienne Gruben, 'Nut Up or Shut Up: Touring through *Zombieland* with Screenwriters Rhett Reese & Paul Wernick', *Examiner*, 1 October 2009, http://www.examiner.com/article/nut-up-or-shut-up-touring-through-zombieland-with-screenwriters-rhett-reese-paul-wernick.

155 Sam Riley in Cheryl Singleton, 'On Set: Love and Bloodshed in *Pride and Prejudice and Zombies*', *Fangoria*, 5 February 2016, http://www.fangoria.com/new/on-set-love-and-bloodshed-in-pride-and-prejudice-and-zombies/.

INDEX

Index

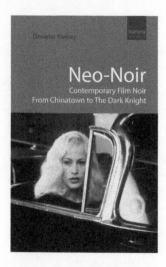

PB: 978-1-84243-311-9 **£16.99**
EB: 978-1-84243-412-3 **£9.99**

Neo-Noir

Contemporary Film Noir From *Chinatown* to *The Dark Knight*
DOUGLAS KEESEY

A world-weary detective, a seductive femme fatale, a mysterious murder, these elements of classic film noir live again in more recent hardboiled detective films from *Chinatown* to *Sin City*. But the themes and styles of noir have also spilled over into contemporary films about gangsters, cops and serial killers (***Reservoir Dogs***, ***The Departed***, ***Se7en***). New hybrid genres have been created, including psycho-noirs (***Memento***), techno-noirs (***The Matrix***) and superhero noirs (***The Dark Knight***).

Beginning with an introduction that shows how neo-noir has drawn upon contemporary social and historical events as well as the latest technological advances in filmmaking, this book discusses the neo-noir films that have made the biggest splash in the field ('landmarks'), the directors who have become cult figures of neo-noir, ('auteurs'), films from non-English speaking countries ('international') and neo-noirs that put a new spin on past noirs ('remakes').

kamerabooks.com/neonoir

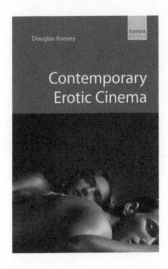

PB: 978-1-84243-363-8 **£12.99**
EB: 978-1-84243-646-2 **£9.99**

Contemporary Erotic Cinema

DOUGLAS KEESEY

Movies have constantly pushed at the boundaries of sexual representation, outraging censors, transgressing taboos and opening up formerly forbidden realms of sensual pleasure. Whether through an exploration of our dreamiest fantasies or our darkest desires, films have expanded our repertoire of erotic images and challenged who we are as sexual beings.

The first book to look at truly contemporary erotic cinema, this publication gives in-depth analyses of sex scenes from over 100 films, more than half of them released in the 21st century. Beginning with an overview of how depictions of sex on screen have changed over the last 40 years, the book is divided into three main parts, erotic genres, themes and acts. The films discussed include *9 Songs*, *American Pie*, *Bad Education*, *Black Swan*, *Brokeback Mountain*, *Intimacy*, *Last Tango in Paris*, *The Reader*, *The Wayward Cloud*, *Y Tu Mamà También* and many more.

kamerabooks.com/contemporaryeroticcinema

PB: 978-1-84344-910-2 **£16.99**
EB: 978-1-84344-911-9 **£12.99**

Italian Cinema
Arthouse to Exploitation
BARRY FORSHAW

From the unbridled sensuality of silent Italian films, to the neorealist classic *Bitter Rice*, to the astonishing imagination of Fellini and the more cerebral and fascinating movies of Antonioni, Italy has a filmic legacy unlike that of any other nation. And then there are the popular movies: the lively sword and sandal epics of the peplum era through to the inextricable mix of sexuality and violence in the gialli of such directors as Mario Bava and Dario Argento. All the glory of Italian cinema is celebrated here in comprehensive essays, along with every key film in an easy-to-use reference format.

This new and greatly expanded edition takes in major modern hits such as *The Great Beauty/La Grande Bellezza*. The new generation of Italian film and TV successes, important directors and movements of the past are are all given fresh and incisive evaluations.

PB: 978-1-84243-318-8 **£12.99**
EB: 978-1-84243-397-3 **£9.99**

Dario Argento

JAMES GRACEY

The stylistic and bloody excesses of the films of Dario Argento are instantly recognisable. Vivid, baroque and nightmarish, his films lock violent deaths in a twisted embrace with an almost sexual beauty. Narrative and logic are often lost in a constant bombardment of atmosphere, technical mastery and provocative imagery. It's a body of work which deals explicitly with death and violence, all the while revelling in perversely alluring stylistics and shot through with an unflinching intensity.

Setting the tone with earlier *gialli* films such as *The Animal Trilogy* and *Deep Red*, Argento has steadily pushed the boundaries; through his elaborately gothic fairytales *Suspiria* and *Inferno*, right up to his more recent contributions to TV's Masters of Horror compendium and the conclusion of his Three Mothers trilogy, *Mother of Tears: The Third Mother*. Along the way, his prowling camera work, pounding scores and stylistic bloodshed have only gained in intensity and opulence. This Kamera Book examines his entire output.

kamerabooks.com

PB: 978-1-84243-320-1 **£12.99**
EB: 978-1-84243-408-6 **£9.99**

Asian Horror

ANDY RICHARDS

Since Japanese horror sensations *The Ring* and *Audition* first terrified Western audiences at the turn of the millennium, there's been a growing appreciation of Asia as the hotbed of the world's best horror movies.

Over the last decade Japan, South Korea, Thailand and Hong Kong have all produced a steady stream of stylish supernatural thrillers and psychological chillers that have set new benchmarks for cinematic scares. Hollywood soon followed suit, producing high-profile remakes of films like *The Ring*, *Dark Water*, *The Grudge* and *The Eye*.

With scores of Asian horror titles now available to Western audiences, this Kamera Books edition helps the viewer navigate the eclectic mix of vengeful spooks, yakuza zombies, feuding warlocks and devilish dumplings on offer, discussing the grand themes of Asian horror cinema and the distinctive national histories that give the films their special resonance.

kamerabooks.com/asianhorror

PB: 978-1-84344-746-7 **£16.99**
EB: 978-1-84344-747-4 **£9.99**

Introduction to Film

A Director's Perspective

ALEX COX

Emerging filmmakers need to know the basics of their art form: the language of the camera, and lenses, the different crew roles, the formats, the aspect ratios. They also need to know some bare-bones theory: what an auteur is, what montage is, what genres are. Most importantly, all filmmakers require serious grounding in film. You cannot be a great artist if you aren't versed in great art. *Introduction to Film* covers all these aspects, from a director and filmmaker's perspective.

According to Cox, 'Academics have a very specific take on things, and a language of their own. That take and that language aren't mine. I'm a film director, writer, actor and producer. So my "intro to film" may be somewhat different from the standard introductory text. I am less focused on film theory, and more on a film's meaning, the intentions of the filmmaker, and how they got their film made.'

ABOUT US

In addition to Kamera Books, Oldcastle Books has a number of
other imprints, including No Exit Press, Creative Essentials, Pulp!
The Classics, Pocket Essentials and High Stakes Publishing
> oldcastlebooks.co.uk

For more information about Crime Books go to
> crimetime.co.uk

Check out the Kamera Film Salon for independent, arthouse and
world cinema **> kamera.co.uk**

For more information, media enquiries and review copies please
contact marketing **> marketing@oldcastlebooks.co.uk**